MAKING HEALTHY CHOICES FOR SENIOR LIVING

Welcome to an Exciting Reading Experience!

MAKING
HEALTHY CHOICES
FOR SENIOR LIVING

A Guide for an Enriched Retirement

KENNETH D. BARRINGER

Retired Pastor, College Teacher, and Clinical Psychologist

Choosing your lifestyle and core values are the most
important decisions for retirement. This book is a critical
guide for making those choices over your lifetime.

To order additional copies of this book, contact:
Xlibris
1-888-795-4274
www.Xlibris.com
Orders@Xlibris.com
636548

TABLE OF CONTENTS

MY ACKNOWLEDGMENTS AND GRATITUDE

The reader needs to know that this book is the product of much time and attention by many people. I am the sole writer, but I have been supported by many people who demonstrated real care and concern that I produce a fine, readable, and informative product. Let me list their names with my appreciation:

1. My wife, Joan, has been my constant and dependable support over the one-and-a-half years I have taken to write and publish this book, and I thank her for this assistance and valuable advice.

2. My book editor, Liz Bleau, has been invaluable over time to firm up the material, add and remove key items, and offer excellent ideas for organization of the key content and printed copy.

3. My publisher has been very helpful in giving me guidance about how the book can be put together in an attractive format and how it can be marketed so that I can reach a large saleable market.

4. The literarily hundreds of seniors I have counseled, taught in my classes, and worked with over the years of my own retirement, they have taught me much and helped me understand the behavior and mentality of the senior world

5. My good friend, Dr. Robert H. Trivus, has been so kind in writing the foreword and in giving me key suggestions for improving the book content.

6. Finally, I am happy for the support and encouragement from the members of my small study group at our local church in pursuing the writing and publication of this book. They wanted the message to get out, as I do, to the real senior world of today.

FOREWORD

MAKING HEALTHY CHOICES FOR SENIOR LIVING

BY ROBERT H. TRIVUS, MD, PHD
CLINICAL PSYCHIATRIST

Note: Dr. Trivus has been a distinguished faculty member of three major medical schools, including Harvard Medical School. He has also been a director for two locations of impatient services, among other prominent responsibilities. He is currently medical director for the South Shore Coalition for Mental Health and Aging. He sees patients daily who are seniors in crisis and need help and hope for recovery. It is his wise perspective and good clinical judgment that forms the basis of the following comments on this book.

"I am more than honored to have been asked to do the foreword on Dr. Barringer's new book on senior living. He is a remarkable and accomplished man, having personally achieved the goals he so eloquently desires to share with us in his book. He has successfully spanned many remarkable years in the ministry as a college professor and serving years as a clinical psychologist. Now in his retirement period, he continues volunteering and giving of himself to others even to this day."

"In retirement, Dr. Barringer went ahead to establish a coalition of volunteers and professionals named the South Shore Coalition on Mental Health and Aging. Its aim was to serve people from Tampa in the north to Sarasota in the south. All the while, he was doing this, he also found the time to help with treatment plans and to lead a group of women who needed support in the prison system.

Dr. Barringer is a tireless servant of God who still works with the Coalition of Mental Health and Aging in an advisory role and now with the National Alliance for the Mentally Ill. He has also won many accolades, including the Butterfly Award offered by the Coalition on Mental Health and Aging for outstanding service for seniors. The award committee used the symbol of the butterfly arising out of a cocoon for new life as a free spirit that is expressing his/her new life fully. The hope of the author is that his new book will help in the process of building a healthy, fulfilling long retirement lifestyle.

We honor and salute Dr. Barringer for his challenge to all of us to discover a more fulfilling and satisfying retirement. Readers everywhere will appreciate and salute the ideas in this book by a very competent writer. Readers all over will love the good illustrations and supplements that will challenge everyone to review their lifestyle and to make a new determination to make retirement the best years of their lives.

We honor and salute you, Dr. Kenneth Barringer, for the gift of this new creation.

PREFACE

DEVELOPING A PURPOSE AND PLAN FOR THIS BOOK

Writing this book was difficult because we seniors confront the twin challenges of facing many changes and losses in our lives today. It would honestly feel more comfortable if things would just stay the way they were before we retired. Of course, we adopt some of the new changes in our world, like computers, cell phones, expanded HD television, and our high-tech automobiles. But many of the newer realities of our world regarding health care, family relationships, financial pressures, and in the losses of loved ones threaten us to the core.

We see our adult children move frequently and faraway in search of new and better jobs. We witness our grandchildren living with partners without the benefit of marriage. People that we love and care about are getting sick and many are dying before our eyes. The world news seems constantly threatening and changing. Even the political instability in our own country bothers us as we read the newspapers or watch the news on television. Then we hear about the threat

of global warming, and we become even more anxious about our lives and future generations.

It has always appeared to me that when we live in a world where uncertainty and instability are a norm, we need to develop stability in our own personal affairs. Many seniors (ages 55 and over) I know have found their healthy lifestyle through setting realistic goals and by learning to live with the changes and losses they experience in their retirement. They have found also, through their struggles with life, about how to avoid becoming unglued. Most of them have faced the same issues we all deal with daily, but these successful seniors have discovered the coping skills and the resilience they need to survive. So there are keys to how to live a healthy senior life style, and these ideas are the core issues of this book. We can all benefit from understanding more about the values and the behavior of the healthiest among us. We can be happier by following the living examples of those who have succeeded best in managing their lives in the today's world.

Therefore, *the purpose of this book* is to discover how we seniors can make consistent and responsible choices about the way we live out our lives today. We will explore the mistakes we make in managing our retirement and the consequences of poor decisions. Real-life stories will be used to illustrate the costs of neglecting our needs or not managing our lives carefully. Probably, the key links in this book will be the basic principles of good decision making that govern all of us. A heavy emphasis will also be placed on ideas concerning better self-management tools that can provide us with greater personal health and happiness.

The heart of this book is a wake-up call for countless seniors across America who need to look in depth at their lifestyles in our changing world. It is my contention that a large number of retirees do not know where to look to learn about ways to live a more satisfying and productive life in retirement. They need to seek lessons on better heath, more emotional fulfillment, a richer spiritual life, a way to find new friends and better family connections, along with a sound financial plan and a clear purpose for their future. They are searching for a *wellness perspective* for their older years. This book attempts to respond to those needs by providing an extensive *checklist* for healthy senior living. By adopting those principles that fit your attitudes and values, you can be on your way to finding a fulfilling life in your senior years and a greater level of personal fulfillment.

THE PROCESS OF MAKING HEALTHY CHOICES: I want to emphasize the critical importance of positive decision making as a lifetime practice. It is becoming more aware that our days are filled with choices that determine the direction of our lives. Clearly, we need to be more thoughtful, responsible, and find directions we want to make for our happiness and well-being. I want to take you through this process to discern between healthy and unhealthy choices. In particular, I will share some critical guidelines that will be helpful for you in making the choices about your daily living experiences. I will highlight the importance of being conscious about how your life flows out of the decisions you make or fail to make and about how important are the life choices that we make every day.

To begin, be aware that we have to make scores of different choices every day just to function as a living human being. We choose when to wake up, what to wear, how to prepare for the day's activity, what to eat, who to see, how to behave, where to go, when to say yes or no, when to retire for the evening activity, what to do at home, and when to go to bed again. Every day is filled with choices, many of them thrust upon us. We may even be forced to face a health crisis with a family member or drive past a life-threatening highway accident. We simply cannot hide our head in the sand. We are involved in mankind, and we must choose how to respond.

Healthy choice making is an art involving several key steps that can be learned and valued. The key elements in this decision making are as follows: (1) being conscious that we need to respond to a question, an issue, a relationship, or even an event; (2) giving consideration about an intelligent response; (3) weighing our options about how we will respond; (4) considering the values that govern that decision; and (5) making the choice and then taking action to implement that choice and living with the result.

Unhealthy or defective decision-making involves a similar process, but it has several flaws in the execution of the decision that needs to be made. We may not weigh our options at all. We simply blunder along and do what feels good for the moment. Many seniors have no clear-cut values to guide them, so they do what they want for themselves or what pleases others. Sometimes they choose to follow the pleas of a friend or to get social approval or act for the thrill of a questionable activity. More often than not, they may procrastinate, run away, or give into an impulse. Their choice-making skills are immature and undeveloped.

The most dramatic illustration of this practice is the way seniors give into their lust for food in abundance and for tasty desserts, even when they are severely overweight. These same older adults engage in this practice clearly knowing that this decision is not good for their health. They give into their hunger for desserts and rarely weigh the consequences. Their decision to indulge is simply automatic. Therefore, we must realize that every choice has gains or losses, so the *act of choosing the habits and behavior of our lives* needs careful and thoughtful consideration. Weigh your lifestyle carefully because the pattern you choose always sets the direction of your future life. It can lead to a life of regrets or a life full of happiness.

Flawed or unhealthy choices involve several factors that we need to know about so we can avoid them in our daily activity. They are as follows: (1) emotional or impulsive buying, such as costly clothing, an expensive automobile, or even some attractive property; (2) careless health care decisions that might include choosing the wrong doctor, medication, surgery, or even a hospital where some questionable treatment is administered; (3) hasty or thoughtless decisions about dating or choosing a marriage relationship, which could prove to have serious and costly consequences that may take years to heal; (4) housing or relocation decisions that may prove to be unsatisfactory over time; and (5) deciding, as a relative of mine did upon retirement, to do little, seldom become involved, and just withdraw from active participation in the world at large and called this his retirement. Yes, even seniors who have lived long lives are too often still prone to make poor choices in managing their lives, and these decisions can have disastrous consequences.

My plea is that we each decide to exercise good discipline and better self-management over the way we live out our lives. For example, my wife and I have had a struggle over the care and upkeep of our property. I was raised in a rural farm community in Iowa where we were very carefree about our personal grooming, the upkeep of our clothing, and the maintenance of our living areas. My wife came from a different background in which her parents put a high value on personal appearance, the care and maintenance of personal property, and the careful upkeep of the living area of their home. She has insisted that we do the same in our marriage and home environment. We have struggled with this issue for years, but I am now moving closer to her value system. I see now the benefit of order, neatness, personal grooming, and an orderly and attractive living area. I am trying to look at the issue as a practice of better household management that will not only personally benefit us, but all those who come to visit our home. The conclusion is that we all need to learn to become better at working together in our decision-making roles, so we can change our perspective when new and better changes are needed. Being objective and open-minded about our choices in life helps makes this happen.

One final request is that we become more conscious about the process of daily decision-making and put a high value on *taking time* to think carefully about the choices we make in our life. Many college students, for example, fail to put a premium on the thoughtful, careful, and time-consuming efforts to make the right choice for a career. In a similar vein, it is not uncommon for seniors to fail to choose well where they want to live in retirement and how they will finance their retirement lifestyle. To illustrate, I have recommended that as part of pre-retirement planning, seniors should include a thoughtful list of what they need in a retirement location. They need to take time to make those choices, visit the perspective places, and interview not only the sales representatives, but the residents. Likewise, they need to develop a realistic annual budget for their retirement years. We followed this planning process, and it has served us very well. However, we have neighbors who have sold and left our retirement community after only a few months because they could not adjust to this new location, afford the new lifestyle, or could not live this far from their adult children and grandchildren. Poor planning became a costly venture.

Finally, I need to emphasize how good it feels to know your life is under control. In conversation with many successful seniors, they repeatedly said that they were healthier and happier when they learned to make positive choices. Those choices included the doctor they picked, the plan they used to buy their food, the church they attended, the home they purchased, the activities they enjoyed, and the place where they decided to volunteer their time. They felt real satisfaction about making good decisions concerning their life and the benefits that flow from those healthy choices day by day. It is a very fine feeling and an emotional and spiritual comfort that every senior needs to experience. But it does not come free! It is the product of an intentional commitment to strong ideas and values that lead you to this level of life satisfaction. It is learning how to make responsible life choices every day. Then we come to realize that the greatest benefits from healthy choice making are real happiness and contentment. This level of happiness is the product of a long series of positive choices we make day by day. It is the by-product of the healthy habit of good decision-making. This book is intended to help make that process an important pattern of your daily life.

Healthy decision-making creates an emotional and spiritual comfort that every senior needs to experience. But it does not come free! It is the product of an intentional commitment to strong ideas and values that are developed over time. It is really learning how to make responsible life choices every day, by trial and error. Then we come to realize that the greatest benefit from a lifetime of healthy choice making is the discovery of a life of greater satisfaction and one with rich benefits that improves the quality of our daily lives. This book intends to help make the process of good decision-making a pattern in your daily life. I hope to explain that it is an exciting and satisfying way to live. The best way to illustrate the value of healthy choice making is to refer to the rich value of building a life of healthy daily habits. By this, I mean you become aware of the value of positive routines that improve the quality of your daily life. This idea implies that you maintain healthy eating habits, restful sleeping practices, good social contacts, enjoyable work practices, uplifting recreational outlets, a strong value system, and good management of your living conditions and property. The goal is to be disciplined enough so you enjoy your whole day, each day, from the time you awaken until the time you fall asleep at night.

You become conscious of the importance of breaking bad habits like smoking, gorging on food, drinking alcohol to excess, spending foolishly, just wasting hours daily doing little or nothing, or letting stressful feelings accumulate. In addition, it is too easy to succumb to a mood disorder or a high level of worry that can disrupt your peace of mind and mental health. We need to become committed in our struggle to live a life of optimism, hope, and joy. In that better life, we can experience meaningful activity, warm personal relationships, and faith in God.

* Making responsible life choices, therefore, starts with the way we live every day. It can be as simple as choosing to be a responsible driver of our automobiles; being disciplined about how we spend, save, and invest money; or the way we keep in contact with extended family members. This key question

arises: Are the daily habits of your life making a positive impact on your retirement or are they handicapping your life and your future? Let's explore that question in depth now, together, as the book unfolds.

SPECIAL NOTE: There are extra topics, ideas, and suggestions directly related to each chapter in the *supplemental material* at the end of the chapter. They are relevant materials intended to expand your thinking about the chapter content. Hopefully, they offer fresh ideas that will bring you added perspective on each topic. Please view them as an expansion of the chapter topic and even pencil in answers when test materials are offered. Enjoy these add-ons and read them as additional resources to help you become a more capable decision-maker about your retirement lifestyle

Supplemental materials for the preface include the following: (1) Important Statistical Information about Seniors, (2) United States of Aging Survey: Aging Outlook Findings, (3) The Three Elements of Good Decision Making, and (4) Seniors who have Chosen Good Daily Habits for Living.

Supplement 1, Preface

IMPORTANT STATISTICAL
INFORMATION ABOUT SENIORS

1. The most common health problems of the elderly are high
    blood pressure, heart failure, asthma, diabetes, cancer,
    dementia, loss of bone and joint function, and the stress
    of coping with many of life's demands. The longer we live,
    the greater the chances are that we will develop a chronic
    illness or disease, such as arthritis, osteoporosis, heart
    disease, or cancer. Between 24 percent and 34 percent of
    adults between 50 and 64 already have at least one chronic
    medical condition.

2. One-quarter of today's older adults experience some
    mental disorder, including dementia. About 16 percent
    have a psychiatric disorder and about 10 percent have
    dementia, which is often tied to hearing loss and poor
    sleep habits. Depression can strike an older adult after he
    or she has suffered a hip fracture or heart attack or has
    been diagnosed with cancer. Often as a result of repeated
    and reoccurring illnesses, older adults are at increased
    risk of memory loss. In general, older adults with mental
    illnesses experience higher medical costs because they
    often trigger a co-existing physical problem.

3. A report by the Institute for Health by the University of
    Washington found that infectious diseases kill far fewer
    people globally today than they did just two decades
    ago. Diarrhea, tuberculosis, malaria, and measles have
    all dropped in the ranking of top causes of death. In
    a strange twist of progress, more people now die from
    obesity-related illnesses than from lack of food. The bad
    news is that millions of people still die from diseases

linked to *the choices they make*—like smoking, overeating, and under-exercising. Tobacco use alone claims six million lives a year. Preventing cancer, heart disease, and diabetes often means persuading people to change their behavior. That is not easy to do. The increase in lifestyle-related diseases means that while people are living longer, many of them are also living sicker and requiring more medical treatments over time, which drives up the cost for the nation (*Chicago Tribune* Editorial 2012).

4. The challenge for seniors today is to find a balance between the demands of modern life, the struggle to maintains strong family connections and enduring friendships, the need to keep themselves financially solvent, and the need to keep physically and mentally fit. The fact that so many succeed at that task is a tribute to the determination of senior adults to find a meaningful life even in the face of enormous challenges.

Supplement 2, Preface

NATIONAL COUNCIL ON AGING. U.S. OF AGING SURVEY: AGING OUTLOOK FINDINGS

1. Defining of Old Age

According to the survey, seniors nationally maintain a positive outlook on aging:

*   About 86 percent state they are very confident in their ability to maintain a high quality of life throughout their senior years.

* Both seniors and younger adults believe that "there's no such thing as getting old" because "age is a state of mind," while some see "being old" means becoming wiser.

* One in four seniors report that they have become more optimistic about getting older.

* Both seniors and middle-aged adults report that they rely on their family for support in their daily life.

* Nearly one in three low-income seniors cite "having a spiritual or religious connection" as most important to a high quality of life.

* One-fourth of seniors say "staying physically active" helps in maintaining a high quality of life during the older years.

* Nearly one-third of seniors think women have a higher quality of life in their senior years than men, and many seniors believe quality of life to be similar in urban, rural, and suburban settings, except more seniors believe suburban seniors have the highest quality of life.

2. Concerns and Satisfactions about Senior Living:

* When asked what worries those most about living a longer life, seniors are most likely to cite "not being able to take care of myself."

* Seniors report that "seeing children and grandchildren grow up" is what excites them most about living a longer life.

* When asked which aspects of their senior years are better now than for their parents' generation, seniors highlighted

access to technology, health care, and better physical health as the top choices.

This information about the aging survey represents four thousand telephone interviews, data from general population surveys, and general demographic statistics. For access to the full survey, visit *www.ncoa.org/UnitedStatesofAging*.

Supplement 3, Preface

THE THREE ESSENTIAL ELEMENTS OF GOOD DECISION-MAKING

1. To seek *wisdom* from God and those we respect and admire. It also comes to us from reading the Bible, from times of meditation and prayer. It can also be found by asking the counsel of others, seeking critical information, and learning from life experiences itself. Nevertheless, it is vital that we call on the wisdom we have accumulated to help us make real and responsible life choices. To act hastily, impulsively, or recklessly only complicates our lives, and we will live to regret it.

2. To seek *discernment* from the multiple choices available to us is a critical process we all need to follow. This step means that we consider our various options, weigh them carefully, and then slowly decide the best course of action to take. One method that works for me is to take a piece of paper and write out in a sentence or two the issue that needs to be decided. Below the big question, list the pros and cons of choosing one direction or another. Once you have done that, you will generally see that one direction seems clearer and better than the other. Take that course

of action, but evaluate the issue later to see if that was the right choice to make. Refine the process to let it work for you every time.

3. To seek *guidance* from God and the counsel of those you trust the most. We are fallible human beings who are limited in our ability to make responsible choices. Nevertheless, the way our world works today is that we are being pressed all of the time to make decisions we would rather avoid. So we cannot turn away from our responsibilities or the demands of others. We have to choose right because all of our available options have real consequences. Therefore, it is very essential we chose a wholesome pathway. To make the best course of action, keep in touch with the power of the Holy Spirit, seek spiritual discernment in prayer all of the time, and also search for the advice of those whose counsel you treasure. Be clear about your questions, and be certain about all of the answers that will come to you.

Conclusion: Read the morning papers and just count the number of articles you find about poor and irresponsible decision-making. You will be shocked, as I am, about the amount of harmful conduct and even illegal behavior often carried out by senior adults. It is critical if we want a healthy and happy life that we need to put a strong emphasis on making good choices day by day. So start now to decide that good, thoughtful decisions will become a core value for your life. The people we really do admire and respect are those who build their lives on a succession of positive choices, one after another. Take their modeling seriously and start *now* to make that a habit in your life. It is a real-life practice you will never regret. It is a lifestyle that can provide you with the kind of success and personal happiness you have sought for all of your lifetime. For Christians, it is very simply a pattern we are challenged to follow in order to be true disciples of Christ and active members of the family of God.

Supplement 4, Preface

SENIORS WHO HAVE CHOSEN GOOD DAILY HABITS FOR LIVING

It is important to look around you and observe the healthy habits that seniors employ every day. In fact, it is exciting to see how these practices enhance the quality of their lives. So I would like to encourage your own growth and provide some vivid examples of seniors in America who are happier because of the habits they now enjoy.

Maybe you have friends or neighbor whose lifestyle also inspires you all the time.

- Bob has been careful about his *eating habits*, and he not only eats nutritious meals at home, but he is also careful to be very selective when eating out. He is very aware of the dangers of overeating, gorging on deserts, selecting food that is fried with heavy crust on the meat served, and selecting items that are high in fat and calories. His slim figure gives strong evidence that he is a man in charge of the food he chooses to eat every day. He even gets sad that so many of his friends are overweight.

- Doris is a disciplined woman who has an *exercise routine* that helps enhance her health. She has a private pool in her Florida home she uses, along with exercise equipment. She takes pride in being very careful to set up a strenuous practice of doing exercises that not only stretches her muscles but also is good for her cardiovascular system. Other seniors choose group sports like tennis or golf, but the key seems to be consistent and determined to pick a sport that helps your body to develop its maximum potential for health for your age.

- Harry likes to play music with his base tuba at home, but his real enjoyment is a decision he made to join his local county band concert organization. He has found that choosing a *favorite hobby* enriches his life enormously. He likes the other instrumentalists in the band and the new music the director provides the members to learn. Their performances at special events in their community make him proud that he can contribute to the enjoyment and pleasures of people's lives. He takes pleasure in being a part of a talented body of musicians.

- Grace had a problem with self-esteem and with feeling worthy of the friendship other people offered her. It does seem odd that at her age, she still lacked a real feeling of confidence. She is happy, however, that she decided to join a *support group* that consists of many others older adults like herself. They have an excellent leader who has guided them carefully to address the issue. He gives them assignments that really challenge her to learn to love herself and to be bold in befriending others. She sees herself changing for the good, for her future.

- Charles has never been a religious person, but now that he has more time *to* think about faith issues, the nature of the Christian life is beginning to mean something to him. He is discovering that finding a *pathway to greater faith* is a quest that he is starting to enjoy. He has found himself, and he is at peace at last. He feels very good, as well, about the warm fellowship he has experienced with other Christians in his local church. They seem like a large extended family that really cares about each other. He has decided he wants to age and serve with this kind of rich company for the rest of his life.

SPECIAL NOTICE: Each chapter that follows will have a photo with caption of some seniors engaging in some activity. The purpose of the photo is to create a mood and highlight the theme of the information that follows. I hope you find it a valuable innovation you will enjoy.

"We want to learn about how to make better
choices for ourselves and our grandchildren"

CHAPTER 1

THE IMPORTANCE AND
THE PROCESS OF MAKING
HEALTHY CHOICES

Happiness is a choice and misery is always an option . . . If we go with the longing inside, we will choose happiness.

—Barry Neil Kaufman,
Happiness Is a Choice

Every day, we make countless choices. We are not always aware of the choices we have made by the time we even eat our breakfast. Much of this practice is a learned response to the demands of daily life. We have to sleep, dress, eat, use the toilet, clean up, talk to someone, and get on with our chores for the day. We all have our routines. New issues come up all of the time, such as unexpected bills, someone in the extended family facing a crisis, or the weather changes and we have to rethink our plans for the day. Sometimes, when we read the paper, listen to the news on television, or hear a disturbing report from friends, our world is affected. When we are confronted with conflicting values and issues, they require our response. Regularly, we are called to vote in a state or national election. Not only are there different people running for office, but often critical petitions are on the ballot that call for our support. So our lives are full of choices, some welcomed and some not so appealing. They are all key elements of our daily living experience.

What I am asking you to do now is to become more conscious of the choices you make about the management of your life and time. Stop to think about why you do certain things the way you do. I remember asking a friend why he always keeps a messy office, and his answer was predictable: "I guess that is always the way I do things." There was no justification, no real explanation, and no attempt to rethink the values of a well-organized office. You see, we simply slip into bad habits without thinking about the wisdom about what we choose to do.

Frequently, this human tendency to fall into harmful habits can cause disastrous consequences, such as when we as seniors overeat and under exercise. So it is time to look in depth at the choices we make in our lifestyle, so we can discover how to restructure ourselves and make better choice making a lifetime pattern and goal for us all. The rewards we will experience will probably exceed our fondest expectations.

Let me start this critical task by describing in detail the importance of being deliberate and thoughtful about the way we choose to live out our lives. The best way to explain this issue is to present the following **keys to positive choice making:**

- Positive choice making requires good intentions, weighing the many alternatives, seeking the advice needed, checking the best resources you can find, and taking time to make certain it is in accordance with your values and goals in life. You will feel better, therefore, when you follow the thoughtful steps outlined in this book toward the choices made in your life and relationships.

- Positive choice making usually means being more aware of the benefits our good decisions bring in long-term consequences for us and for others. Careless, hurried, or thoughtless choice making usually has disastrous consequences that can last a long time. It can impact our situation and even change the course of our lives. The careless mismanagement of your financial resources, for example, is a good illustration of the damage poor choice making can bring to your own home. The loss of large assets can damage your life and limit your options for living for years.

- Positive choice making is a practice we need to adopt as a routine habit. We need to become more objective about the patterns we adopt as our lifestyle, rather than fall into bad habits that harm us. Question practices that develop real problems for yourself, and stop those practices, even if they seem comfortable and often satisfying. My dental hygienist told me, for example, that people could improve their overall health significantly by simply flossing their teeth daily, but a majority of Americans still do not include that simple practice in their morning or evening bathroom rituals.

- Positive choice making is essential for a healthy and happy senior lifestyle. There are countless choices that need to be made, especially in our life during retirement. We can hope that our life will be a helpful model for our adult children and grandchildren. So a decision to not worry and obsess about every troublesome issue in our lives will not only benefit ourselves but also sets a high example for our extended family members to follow. They watch how we lead our lives, and they may find real inspiration in the way we deal with the stresses and strains of our daily life. When we help ourselves, we help them as well by the choices we make every day.

- Positive choice-making commitment can help us evaluate our lives and make us be more conscious about the way we manage all the facets of our daily activity. It can help us become more objective about the defects of our character, such as how we handle our personal property, what we do about caring for our personal appearance, and the manner or the way we manage our time. Psychologists are constantly reminding us that we need to be objective and even be critical about our habits, routines, relationships, and goals.

- Seniors need to fit into a well-managed, mature lifestyle that brings good health, happiness, and peace of mind. That is best achieved by healthy decision making every day. For Christians, it is the product of a life of prayer and of a willingness to act in accordance with a biblical view of life. We seek to practice what we preach and hold each other accountable for the way we live out our lives.

- Positive choice making reflects the good values you hold that guide your daily life. These are values like a belief in God, a commitment to be a loving and caring person, the expression of honesty and trustworthiness, the importance of being a moral person with a spiritual focus, a desire to be a good marriage partner, and being a responsible member of your extended family. You can even add the desire to get involved in serving others in your community in order to help build a better world.

- Finally, positive choice making means we learn to be consistent about follow-through after we make a choice to take concrete action toward our decision. Let me suggest these steps:

  1. Make the decision based on solid values

  2. Discipline yourself to implement it

  3. Move in the direction you planned

  4. Evaluate your plan and change it where needed

Let me now move on to provide real-life stories about positive decision-making in the senior world of retirement living. These are authentic examples of healthy responses to the challenges we all face regularly. They represent the best expressions I can find over what can happen when we are in control of our lives and when we manage ourselves in a mature way, with a value-centered focus. Here goes . . .

The Life of Mary, a Selfless Volunteer: This is a woman whose main passion and interest is in serving others as an expression of her strong Christian faith. She made a conscious choice when she retired to give her life to care for the helpless and the frail members of her local church. She organized a large group of volunteers who make regular visits to nursing homes, assisted living centers, and people confined to their own homes. When they visit, they bring news about the church and community, they offer encouragement and conversation, and they close with prayers. They can even convey messages to the family or communicate with a doctor about health concerns. The lonely, forgotten, and neglected praise her and her team all the time for their selfless service. Mary never takes the praise or boasts about it. She just goes on and on being a "servant of the Lord."

Ted Had Some Early Trouble with the Law: He was selling drugs illegally as a teenager. He was frequently truant at school, so the teachers never knew when he would show up for class. Ted came to a turning point, however, when his father died suddenly. It shook him to the core. He realized that his life was wasting away and that it was now up to him to take responsibility for how his life would play out from this point onward. So Ted changed and in radical ways. He gave up all drug dealing. He went back to school, graduated, and learned a trade. He worked in a furniture plant, first as a daily worker, then as a supervisor, and finally as a plant manager. Now in retirement, he can look back and be proud of the life he has led. His wife and adult children are pleased with him. His two sons feel that they want to live their lives as well-managed as their dad. He owes much of the credit for his turn-around to finding a church family that has been there and supported him over the many years of his life.

Bill and Mary Nearly Broke Up But Now They Are Happier Than Ever: Most people would agree that Bill and Mary seemed to be compatible and content in their working years. They seldom showed much affection for each other, but they were at least loyal and hard working. The miracle of change came into their lives when Bill was hurt at work and, as a result, became permanently disabled. They quickly realized that they had to restructure their schedule and responsibilities. More than that, they became aware that they could lose each other and the life they have had in their retirement. So they became lovers again and started to enjoy a new quality of relationship they had never known before. It became rich and beautiful for them and for all those who knew what they found in each other. They even realized Bill's disability was the blessing that brought them together. They are grateful for every day they are companions and partners in the struggle to find happiness, while coping with a limit on their physical activity together because of Bill's limited strength. Their marriage has taken on new meaning and happiness for them both. They feel blessed beyond words for what they have found together.

What is apparent now is that there are *key principles* that are evident in the lives that have been described. These are very important concepts about how we can exercise healthy choices in our lives. If we are going to take this challenge seriously, we need to understand these ideas and adopt them as an integral part of our lives. So read them carefully below and consider how they could be applied to your life and activity. In fact, you may want to identify where you may have failed to manifest the kind of life you have always wanted for yourself. Take a notepad and write these new principles in your own words and then write the application implied by each of the ideas shared, so they have real meaning in your own life. Here is the listing of keys to making healthy choices in life. It the best formula I can offer for living out your highest potential for your life every day.

1. *Take Responsibility for the Quality of Your Own Life:* We cannot simply blame others for the problems, obstacles, handicaps, and in our life. Life does not work that way. Few of us are free of difficulties. Seniors must learn to decide the way they want to live their older years. The satisfaction or dissatisfaction that comes your way is directly related to your willingness or unwillingness to take charge of your

life and its future. That means we have to make important decisions about the quality of our lives, and some may be popular, and others may be controversial. We cannot walk away from the ultimate reality that we need to plan and direct the course of our existence on earth, despite the potholes and the blocks we encounter along the way. Why wait for the end of life and then regret you failed to live well? Start the better living process now. Identify how you can better manage your own life so that it manifests the best or your time and talents.

Realistic Example: If we want to be a good parents and grandparents, we need to take real initiatives with those we love, to try to understand the issues of their daily lives. We cannot stand aside and criticize or remain indifferent when our family members are struggling with conflicts and choices. It is more important to make ourselves available for support and assistance. Let them know you are concerned and available for them in concrete ways every day. Demonstrate your love and offer assistance when they need it. Be available as a responsible family member.

2. *Patience and Persistence Can Help Us with Every Problem that Needs to Be Resolved:* Issues can arise so often that we lose patience in our problem-solving role. We jump ahead and frequently mess it up. This dilemma is most often evident in our auto driving experience, especially after we are tired and we have driven a long distance. What we need to do is to take more frequent breaks, so we let someone else drive. We can also get impatient with our doctor, with the clerk at the grocery store, or with the salesman at our door. Many older adults are rude to a neighbor or unkind at a party because of a perceived offense by someone else. They lose patience and pay a price in lost friendship or lose

good contact with a helping professional because of their anger. Calm down and be tactfully persistent, and you will win most of your battles. With patience, you will be recognized and rewarded for finishing a task that is well done

Realistic Example: Building a garden, like those of the master gardeners we know, requires much patience and persistence before you ever see the beautiful plants and flowers you have planted. These skilled workers conquer problems of impatience, and they work for long-term solid solutions. Take one step at a time and work on the goal of building a life others admire, like the gardens that you can love and enjoy. You will feel proud that you planned well. Others will admire the beauty of what you have done. Show that you have the ability to develop warm friendships, get involved in important volunteer roles, and make a contribution to building a better world.

3. *Learn How to be Resilient as You Face Change and Losses in Life:* We call this your "bouncing power" or your ability to adapt well to the unexpected and the unwanted changes in the world around you. One of the most challenging changes many seniors face is how to live in this new high-tech world. They are confronted with printed and visual aids advertising the newest computers, the values of notepads like an iPad, the best HD television provider, or the newest cell phone. A few of our friends have just refused to get involved, and they want nothing of this "new age." Those retirees who have mastered the art of using these new tools of communication and entertainment enjoy and endorse this new world.

But the pace of change bothers most senior citizens. They yearn for the stability and simplicity of a different time and place, even though they know it will never return again. That slowed-down and casual world is far gone, so a better alternative is not to get stuck in the past, but to be successfully resilient. Accept the new lifestyles of today and learn to live in this new world in peace and tranquility. Finding value in these new changes can help you live a better life. Fighting change only angers you and alienates others it leaves you out of valuable features that could add to the quality of your life experience.

Realistic Example: We have to learn to accept the loss of our parents and of dear friends. Go through a period of grief and let them go, so you can move on! It is very normal to be discouraged and to search for ways to memorialize your loved ones. Of course, we need to take the time to deal with the loss and then let them go, so we can move on. It is not healthy or realistic, however, to hang on to grief excessively and to put your life on hold forever. Most of our friends who have lost their married partners have gone through their grief and loss with courage, faith, and confidence. They have decided to take hold and restructure their life to find fulfillment even if they have to do it alone. They have found a new and different life for themselves, so each day is still meaningful and fulfilling. It is a healthy decision not to let grief and loss overwhelm you, but to recognize that there is still a way to live after a loss, and we have the right to claim it.

4. *Positive Thinking, Coupled with an Optimistic Attitude, Improves the Quality of Life:* In fact, there have been many human relationship studies to verify the value of a positive attitude. These reports have spawned a whole new emphasis in psychology. This new positive psychology movement, as it is called, is full of evidence about the importance of our thought world. We are actually happier

and healthier when we can confront our negative thoughts with positive ideas and alternatives. The danger many of us see among our senior friends is that they can easily slip into a cynical and pessimistic mood. Possibly, it is due to many disappointments in life or the struggles to rise above obstacles that have led them to become bitter and pessimistic. The reality is that this basic negative attitude is self-defeating and destructive. It drives people away, makes problem solving more difficult, and even harms health and recovery from health issues. Life is really more enjoyable and fulfilling when you can feel optimistic and hopeful. It is better to become excited about ordinary events in daily life: like the bursting of flowers, enjoying the rainbow after a rain, or the birth of a new baby. It is thrilling to see your favorite ball team win a game or your son or daughter get a promotion at work. So why not celebrate ordinary events and take on a happier attitude? It makes life more enjoyable, and it surely makes you a warmer and more loveable human being.

Realistic Example: People who are troubled and often withdrawn are caught up in a negative mind-set. Counselors will tell you that most of their senior clients worry a lot, are constantly mulling over problems, or are caught in a gloomy pessimism. Problems seem overwhelming to them because they frequently think that their problems are caused by someone else or by circumstances beyond their control. For successful therapy, a client usually needs to accept responsibility for the problems he or she may be creating. The troubled adult should recognize that these difficult issues have to be resolved, then commit to changing perspective, and start to become a positive problem solver. When you develop that positive mind-set, you can start addressing the issues while moving along on the road to recovery. There really is hope ahead for the hopeful.

5. *You Need to Forgive Yourself and Others and then Let the Past Stay in the Past:* So many senior adults are tied up with animosity over some preconceived event or relationship. They live with an expanding list of people they cannot tolerate or who have offended them deeply. They hang on to anger, hurt, regret, or bitter memories. The result of this negative attitude is internal turmoil and an absence of peace of mind. Sometimes, the focus is on self-hatred or a deep conviction that they have committed an unpardonable sin, and they will never be forgiven for any wrongdoing.

This viewpoint is neither necessary nor healthy. We must learn to accept our mistakes of judgment, learn from them, and then forgive ourselves. For the true Christian believer, it is also crucial to seek God's forgiveness as well. It requires a true change in perspective and often the advice of a friend, a counselor, or a spiritual adviser. Find that key person or therapist who can help you let go of your unforgiving attitudes and learn to forgive yourself and enjoy a better life ahead.

Realistic Example: One of the saddest experiences of many extended families is how many members are alienated from each other. Their family gatherings are often filled with quiet conversations about who will speak to whom and what will they say or do with each other. These events need not happen if the natural leaders in an extended family would take the initiative to bring in a trained therapist or ask a strong family member who could act as a facilitator to help them resolve their differences. Old animosities need to be aired and resolved. It can happen if key members have the will and determination to make it work. New dialogue can occur, and old wounds can heal if we really try. Better relationships can be formed once again. Why live out your life nursing old wounds when you can build new ties if you only take steps to build new understanding and better communication.

6. *Learn to Be More Grateful and Thankful for the Blessings of Your Life:* An attitude of gratitude is what brings joy and hope to us all. In America, we have so much to be thankful for because our country is full of good things. We still have our freedom to assemble and to vote, our freedom of speech, and the right to worship as we choose. We have material abundance beyond what exists in most countries in the world. We still have a great health care system, even as we struggle to improve it and expand its coverage. We have a wonderful national park program, great schools and libraries, and a good transportation system. People from countries everywhere are pleading to immigrate here for a better quality of life. They know they can find a promise of a better future living in America where we have freedom to fully express ourselves and to build a life of our own.

We are richly blessed as seniors in our country. In a survey of attitudes by *USA Today* (August 8, 2012), it was reported that "seniors are largely content, optimistic, and financially secure" in the United States. They have come out of an age when work was plentiful, life was simpler, and values were clearer. Their finances seem more stable, while services for senior citizens appear to be varied and plentiful for people in need. For all these things and for the richness of family life and our faith communities, we need to be very thankful, and we need to live in that spirit of gratitude every day.

Realistic Example: We have friends in retirement who meet their entire extended family every summer at a Christian family camp in Wisconsin. They are always looking forward to that weeklong experience because they celebrate their strong family bond at every gathering. How grateful they are for their ties together and for their Christian faith and for a country that allows their gathering to happen. It would be helpful if all of us could share in our family circle about the manifold blessings we enjoy. A real spirit of gratitude and joy needs to permeate our lives. We must continue to maintain that tone over time. It offers a powerful focus for living a life of happiness, even in troubled times.

7. *A Strong Faith, Backed by Strong Moral Values, Offers the Best Hope for a Happy Life:* It is amazing that the vast majority of Americans believe in a living and acting God, who is the creator and sustainer of our lives. Apparently, they see the courage and strength that a living, acting relationship with God can bring us all because the vast majority of Americans affirm that faith. In addition, recent reports confirm that people of faith are happier, healthier, recover faster from illness, and are less prone to emotional problems, and even live longer. My strong conviction is we need to enrich that faith better and continue to grow in our relationship with God by becoming an active part of a healthy faith community. It is difficult to sustain our faith all alone, or to grow spiritually by ourselves, or just with our partner in life. Vital churches are everywhere, and they would welcome your attendance and active participation.

Now just as important as being in a faith community is the adoption of a strong set of moral values, which represent the principles that guide your thoughts and actions. For example, honesty and integrity in every business transaction is a key value. When a business offers a product, the public expects that product to be exactly as advertised without deception. The executives of that manufactured product should be able to back the quality of their product. That is central to business ethics. Seniors want to buy quality merchandize that has a reliable reputation. In the same manner, when we perform a task, people should know they can depend that the work we do is the best of our ability. That is one more vivid way to live by moral values.

Realistic Example: Churches are usually full of more seniors than any other age group because we generally were raised in communities where the local church was the center of social, recreational, and religious activity. That is not as true today, as our adult children and grandchildren are drifting away from the local churches. Membership and attendance is down for all major denominations. Seniors everywhere report their family members are more secular and materialistic than ever before. We can see that change as a real challenge for communicating the values of our faith and moral convictions to a larger body of extended family members. Of course, our lives can serve as a model, but we do need to use every modern and moral means to talk about what spiritual issues are important to our lives. Our hope needs to be the example we set, along with the message we offer and communicate to others. We need to hope, as well, that the faith and moral values we hold will become a central part of our extended family's lives. That is the biggest legacy we can leave when life is over. We do need, as well, to intentionally witness to our own adult children and grandchildren, so they clearly know the depth of our faith and values. That sharing is one of the most precious gifts we can give them as we come to the end of our own physical life. They will treasure our message because it represents the authentic center of our own values.

8. *Avoid Procrastination and Confront Your Indecisions or Mistakes of Judgment*: It is often said that the hardest one to forgive is yourself. It is difficult to change and to work in areas of our life where we need radical improvement. Nevertheless, it is critical that we focus on self-improvement, or we pay a heavy price for neglect or avoidance. This book is a checklist of many areas of our lives that we may have failed to face or to resolve. Therefore, there is no time like the present to take the next step toward the decision that needs to be made. Do it now while you are reading these words, and you will never regret it. This book was written so that readers can find help in making some critical choices they have long delayed. So look hard at the changes you need to make in your life and resolve right now to stop the delay. The *new you* is just around the corner. Start now to let that better person inside emerge and make this new reality a permanent part of your retirement years.

Realistic Example: My favorite preacher and author, Bill Hybels, in his wonderful book, *Making Life Work*, tells how people can change their lives through a living faith in God. He writes about those who are committed to self-improvement on their own with no spiritual help. His contention is that they will soon make the same failed choices as they have done in the past. We need a motivator and that seems to occur when we seek God's will for our lives. Hybels tells of a man who "admitted that his own path, his own choices . . . have led him into a royal mess . . . the crash of his entire life." Bill, the preacher, tells him that we can fling open the doors of our heart and let God redirect our life and future. The point is that we all need to move forward to find real happiness in our aging years. That can happen when we take concrete steps to make realistic choices that will transform our lives and stop just dreaming about it. A strong personal faith can become the real motivator to make this new life a reality.

Before I close this chapter, ponder these words from *the success journal* written in 1986 under the title *This Day is What I Make It*: "The quality of my life today is up to me and no one else; I can make good use of it or I can waste it; since it will never come again, I will make the best of it; I will make this day one of: success rather that failure, joy rather than sorrow, love rather that hate, satisfaction rather than frustration, laughter rather than tears; The Choice is Always Mine."

****

Summary Comments:

My hope is that you have become aware of the importance of making healthy choices in every area of your life. Surely you can see that the consequences of making poor choices go on and on. You can also see that your healthy choices need to be based on solid values and on the seven principles described above. But they are just the start of a longer list of solid values that you need to let govern your life.

The central aim of making these thoughtful choices is to produce a healthy retirement lifestyle. My hope is that it will also provide the real-life experience of personal happiness and contentment we all seek so earnestly. Memories of my own life in the work world and in raising a family reflect that I was forever too task-oriented. There was always some daily job I had to do, some new level of achievement I wanted desperately in my professional role. Others around me— family, friends, and colleagues—were making demands that I had to meet. There seemed no time left just to enjoy life, love, and leisure. So may I plead with you, the reader, to *take that time to be happy now.* I have seen so many friends who looked forward to retirement and did not take time for the richness of life before they became seriously ill or died. So relish the "golden years" and enjoy every day to the fullest. Remember the message in Psalm 100: "Make a joyful noise to the Lord, serve the Lord with gladness."

Now let us examine the critical areas where healthy choices really matter. They are best grouped together in what is called the *wellness options.* They are a quick overview of the important areas of decision making in key areas of our daily life. My purpose in bringing this outline to you now is to help you visually demonstrate the critical area of healthy choice making in our senior years. Look at the shared ideas that follow and be prepared to incorporate them into your own life and future. Examine them carefully as they apply to your life situation. Recognize that together they offer the best opportunity for good decision-making and for a healthy retirement lifestyle today.

Hint: As you examine each of these areas of your life, make a list for yourself about what new choices you can make to enrich your retirement living. The quality of your life depends heavily on these critical decisions. Start the process now of evaluating your physical activity and health practices, your emotional well-being, social relationships, your faith issues, your financial affairs, your leisure-time pursuits, your end-of-life legal issues, and even your goals for the future. My aim is to help you create the best quality of life you can achieve in your golden years, but it does require that you take responsibility for good decision making to make that happen. So use this book as your guide and checklist for a richer life in the years ahead.

IDEAS ABOUT HOW TO ACHIEVE A HEALTHY LIFESTYLE

Physical Health Care	Emotional Health	Spiritual Well-being
-Pay more attention to proven preventive health care practices -Use good nutritional practices every day	-Build healthy self-esteem -Fight self-doubts, and fears -Express your talents	-Center your life with a living faith in God's care, sharing, and in helping others
-Maintain good health decisions and implement them now	-Cope well with crisis and changes -Be adaptable, resilient	-Be truly committed to moral values in choice making
-Practice balanced diet, limit calorie intake, set weight goals	-Maintain positive attitudes -Learn to be optimistic, hopeful	-Live your faith in your conduct and outlook -Share it often
-Do regular exercises -Keep healthy sleep habits -Calm down -Keep very active -Build body/mental muscle, energy -Take up an active sport or hobby	-Focus on possibility thinking -Be hopeful -Join a support group -Do stress management -Enjoy and share humor -Learn to be happy	-Give a helping hand to others. -Be a volunteer -Maintain strong values -Take leadership to bring positive changes -Take a stand for social justice, racial equality, -Witness to others

Social Health Issues	Intellectual Growth	Money/Material Management
-Establish strong family ties you value -Build relationships	-Commitment to lifelong learning -Keep a growth diary	-Seek help for financial planning, investments Keep an annual budget
-Build and treasure lasting friendships Develop social skills Volunteer your time -Take social initiatives -Help troubled neighbors and groups	-Be open to newer new ideas -Welcome positive change and ideas -Be adaptable -Read for pleasure, growth, insight	-Gifting to critical needs -Support worthy causes -Maintain good financial records Organize home office Take training in good financial management
-Enjoy creative leisure time -Enjoy hobbies, crafts, sports, music, fine arts, and travel -Help with social causes that you feel drawn to support	-Find a purpose for your daily life -Chart your direction for your future and family ties -Keep your mind active -Find ways to retain, build memory skill	-Practice a wise and careful supervision of your home, property, and stored records -Prepare all advance directive documents for your survivors

Note: It is also vital that each of us find a compelling purpose or direction in our senior years. That clear pathway can help us enjoy life more fully because we feel drawn to serve a larger cause than just staying home to care only for ourselves. Senior adults find great joy and fulfillment when they learn new skills, volunteer for special causes, engage in extensive travel, or even find new employment. Keep active and be a part of your community.

- All Issues above attempt to focus on a full wellness lifestyle for healthy living

- Wellness means we seek better health and well-being by being proactive as we focus on selecting practices that improve the quality of our daily lives

- We open our minds and hearts to habits and behavior that enhances our retirement lifestyle, so we can enrich ourselves and enjoy our golden years with new joy and enthusiasm

A Key Emphasis: This book is filled with fresh ideas and new ways you can enjoy your years out of the full-time-work world. Focus now on understanding how you can apply these better choices to your daily living as you read each chapter and the supplements that follow. Then enjoy the rich benefits of choosing a healthy life style as your senior years unfold. Share your new joy with your family and friends.

Read and enjoy the supplements that follow each chapter.

Supplemental materials: (1) Checklist for Health Choices, Better Behavior; (2) What Seniors Do to Harm Themselves; and (3) Important Convictions about Healthy Senior Living

Supplement 1, Chapter 1

CHECKLIST FOR HEALTHY CHOICES, BETTER BEHAVIOR

Risky Attitude and Behavior	*Healthy Attitudes and Behavior*
1. Continue to take illegal drugs	Give up on the drug scene
2. Remain angry and bitter	Practice acceptance and forgiveness
3. Drinks alcohol until he/she drops	Drinks moderately, if you drink at all
4. Lack of self-confidence	Build self-esteem, start to like yourself
5. Hold on to anger and resentment	You let it go and relate well with others
6. Have doubts about faith issues	Seek help for answers to doubts
7. Negative and pessimistic	Positive and optimistic
8. Self-centered is your normal pattern	Helping others gives meaning to your life
9. Worry constantly	Learn to be positive, eliminate worry
10. Does not adapt well to change	Embraces change, adapts well
11. People have to accept me just as I am	I want to make the best impression I can
12. Think all Christians are hypocrites	I will demonstrate the living of my faith
13. Afraid and fearful most of the time	Having faith calms my fears and doubts

14.	Hard to know what to believe at all	Define a core set of values and beliefs
15.	People can be so critical of what I do	Learn to love others makes my life joyful
16.	I tell lies just to survive	Living with honesty makes me feel good
17.	I hate many people	Learn to forgive and to accept others
18.	Review mistakes of the past	Learn from them but leave them behind
19.	I don't care about my health	Health preservation is important to me
20.	Setting goals is not my style	Setting goals helps me achieve more

ASSIGNMENT: WHAT KIND OF ATTITUDE AND BEHAVIOR BEST DESCRIBES YOU?

Supplement 2, Chapter 1

WHAT SENIORS CHOOSE TO DO TO HARM THEMSELVES AND OTHERS

A Catalog of Poor Choice Making in Senior Living

- Maintain a large weight gain that does serious harm to your health

- Poor management of hard-earned financial saving with poor spending habits

- Not weighing the value of volunteer roles that serve the needs of others

- Spending too much time in sedentary living with its loss to good health

- Failure to take sufficient initiative to develop close ties with extended family members and holds grudges that never goes away

- Paying insufficient time and attention to build a close bond with your marriage partner until you drift apart

- Turn away from an opportunity to develop a deep personal faith and community ties. Spends lots of time alone, developing bitter attitudes

- Choosing to drive an automobile far past the time in life when you should stop driving and ride with others

- Never developing a serious exercise program that helps keep your body in good health or developing muscle strength

- Hanging on to your anger and offense by close relatives and failing to resolve the conflicts of the past

- Hoarding physical treasures you love with little consideration to gift them to adult children or grandchildren

- Not developing your talents and likeness for new creative ventures that could bring joy and satisfaction to your life

- Rarely spending time to travel, try new entertainment, enjoy modern music or sports, or enjoying friends for social activity

- Maintaining poor dental care to the point you start losing teeth and need to get dentures or repair gums

- Doing yourself harm by denying hearing loss and not getting hearing aids when needed and not hearing the thoughts of others

- Older adults, especially men, fail to keep up their personal appearance by poor grooming and clean clothing

- Too little attention paid to lifelong learning and the challenge to keep the mind active and alert

- Developing cynical, critical, and pessimistic attitudes about the changing world where we live and relate to others

- Refusal to expand your world of friendships to replace those you lose by death or in a move to a new location

- Giving up on life and new ventures when your life partner dies or your marriage fails, so you withdraw from the world

- Having no new goals and causes you want to serve because you lost your passion to serve or to minister to others

- Putting little or no effort into being a good neighbor where you live or work daily. living a lonely life by yourself

- Failure to maintain your home and personal property in good order and upkeep

- Having no plans to draw up the proper legal papers for your family in case of your death

- Failure to prepare a living-trust document that defines your plans

- Not seeking help from a licensed counselor when personal problems overwhelm your life and cause you to dysfunction

- Failure to develop a strong social support system of close friends you can enjoy and appreciate by living too much alone

- Missing the opportunity to develop a very mature and meaningful personal faith and lifestyle by being very active in a faith community

- Showing a lack of compassion and taking no action to help a neighbor or friend in serious need of assistance

ARE THERE ITEMS YOU COULD ADD ABOUT YOUR OWN PERSONAL LIFESTYLE?

Supplement 3, Chapter 1

IMPORTANT CONVICTIONS ABOUT HEALTHY SENIOR LIVING

1. Retirement should be the very best time of your life, so enjoy it fully every day.

2. We need to experience more of the peace, joy, and happiness God intended for us to relish over our lifetime, but we need to do our part of make that happen in our lives.

3. We should do all the things, maintain the best attitude, and have faith that God will work with us to achieve this pleasant lifestyle over the course of our retirement years ahead.

4. We will be frustrated and anxious or even harm ourselves if we engage in a negative attitude and behavior that harm us and our future happiness.

5. We need to identify and target attitudes and behavior that hurt our enjoyment to life and take serious steps to change our ways of life, so we can be open to the joys of living every day.

6. Commit yourself to changing your perspective and your daily behavior when needed, so you can bring new happiness and peace of mind to your life and to those who touch your life.

7. Continue to learn and grow in the ways that lead to a richer, fuller life. Decide to remove any self-defeating attitudes and behavior you may maintain that only harm your life and impact on the life of others around you. Be a positive model or mentor to follow.

8. Continue to perfect your life as a personal goal and achievement. Never give up the task of setting a high standard to enjoy. Move along in your pursuit to living up to your best human potential in every area of your life.

9. Decide to leave a positive mark in the way you have managed your life, so the world will be a better place because of the legacy you have left behind.

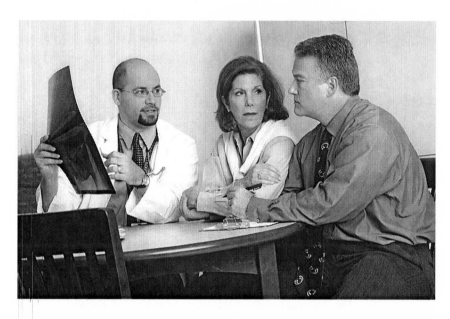

"There is rich satisfaction in having a medical consultant
to help guide us with health care decisions"

CHAPTER 2

KEYS TO ATTAINING MAXIMUM HEALTH FOR SENIOR LIVING

Healthy aging requires thoughtful, careful planning
and a commitment to a lifestyle. (In) individuals . . .
who are positive minded, proactive in their decision-
making and are well informed.

—Edward T. Creagan,
Editor, *Mayo Clinic on Healthy Aging*

No one wants poor health as we age. We all want the best physical health we can achieve. The key element to achieve that goal is to practice preventive health care, not to wait until a health problem arises. Therefore, the first task in maintaining your maximum health is to clearly understand the full scope of preventive health care. Let me explain:

Preventive health care means that you continue to be educated and fully informed about what it takes to maintain your maximum potential of health for your age and with your health history. This task may involve reading, consulting, and engaging in health-education programs that provide you current health information. Good health does not exist without intentional effort. It requires your concrete effort and action. Reading, attending health education seminars, seeking information from a good e-mail site (like www.lifelonghealth. com), and consulting with appropriate health care providers are a good way to start. Keep up-to-date and practice good health measures as a pattern for life, and you are on your way to a lifetime of better health and longevity. Do this too:

1. Keep in regular contact with the finest medical provider you can find so you are fully monitored with a regular annual health checkup as a routine practice. In addition, you can contact a medical specialist, as needed, if you have a special health issue that requires more detailed medical management. You can even take your written questions to your appointments. You are consistent about taking your annual flu shot and your appropriate pneumonia shot every seven to ten years. You pay attention to what you eat, so you consume nutritious food consistently and reduce the intake of "junk food." Maintain good sleep habits that give you the seven to eight hours of needed rest each night for good health. In addition, pay attention to fine dental care by brushing and flossing daily and seeing your dentist at least once a year for cleaning your teeth.

2. Take prescribed medication responsibly. Learn how to live with the side effects of the medication and keep the doctor informed about your responses to its use. Also, regularly remind him or her that you prefer the smallest dosage possible for good health and that you want to stop its use as soon as possible. If you take supplements, ask your doctor about the safety of their use, especially in combination with your prescriptive medication.

3. Assume responsibility for developing your best potential health by (1) engaging in exercises that are appropriate for your age and health condition; (2) keeping your weight under control so it is as close to an ideal goal as is possible; (3) paying attention to avoid excessive exposure to sunlight while using sunscreen, plus the use of UV-qualified protective sunglasses when needed; (4) refusing to use tobacco of any kind while avoiding any excessive use of alcoholic beverages; (5) being careful to stay away from situations where you could fall, be a victim of reckless driving, and expose yourself to infection or animal bits; and (6) refusing to work or engage in physical exertion beyond your capacity to endure it.

4. If you have some physical limitation or disability, take the precautions needed to maintain your well-being. It is reckless to push yourself beyond your limits and to endanger yourself by taking risks that are unnecessary. Find the right balance between being too cautious and being careless. It is also helpful to keep in touch with other disabled adults about how they cope successfully with their own limitations. Support groups are a good choice to help you share ideas and to offer emotional support in living with a disability.

5. Preventive health care involves an openness to adopt the best new innovations in health maintenance as they become available and affordable. For example, new digital hearing aids offer a wonderful and fresh world of hearing you may never have known before. Check them out, if needed, to see what they can do to expand your sound level and listening experience. On the other hand, be careful about quickly adopting every newly advertised product until it has been proven and endorsed. For example, the

new electronic wheelchairs can be appealing, but they are very costly and may not measure up to the claims made in their ads. Like most new medical aids, the real proof is in the way you improve your physical functioning and improve your quality of daily life.

6. We all need to become more aware that mental attitude and emotional well-being are a critical part of good health focus. You can be physically healthy, but you can lose that level of health easily by slipping into depression or giving into intense anxiety. If you have a personal problem that you cannot solve, put aside your reserve and seek out a recommended mental health provider. He or she can help you regain the right perspective and bring you back to feeling good again. Sometimes it is very helpful to locate a *support group* that is specific to your condition. An example would be a group that is associated with National Alliance for Mental Illness that helps family members cope with a family member who suffers from long-term mental illness. Without help, it is difficult to manage when a loved one has erratic mood fluctuations or even threatens his or her own life. Group support can offer ideas about better coping methods, as well as providing you with emotional support when you start to feel alone and helpless in caring for a troubled family member.

7. Brain health is also an essential part of healthy adult living. The aging brain is an issue that needs our special attention. Seniors begin to forget too easily. They have problems making decisions; they get confused while driving; and they lose much ability to organize and concentrate. The good news is that much can be done to stave off this loss and to retain brain function. Learn to focus on retaining good mental skills by doing everything possible

to challenge your brain's ability to function well. Here are a few ideas to adopt: learn a new language or a musical instrument; become very competent in the operation of your computer, camera, or other technological tool; and enhance your ability to remember names and events. Take pride in keeping a sharp mind for a better life and for good management of your retirement years.

8. Maintain maximum health by resolving issues that bother seniors too often: Getting a good night's sleep so you arise rested and energized for the day; being careful about food selections or when you frequently choose to eat food that is not good for you; or accepting helpful suggestions about breaking your habit of sedentary living. To illustrate, too many seniors often sit too much, seldom exercise their physical body, watch TV too long, maintain no hobby, and worry a lot about issues they cannot change. These are literally deadly practices in the senior world that have long-term consequences that harm life and health over time. Seek to develop habit patterns that enhance and not harm your health condition. One practice that healthy seniors adopt, for example, is to become active in a sport that keeps them moving, engaged, and gratified.

9. Recently, I attended a Florida conference on falls prevention. We were told that one of the most hazardous threats to the well-being of seniors is unintended falls. I discovered that seniors are more inclined to physically fall down stairways because of poor hearing, limited eyesight, or slowed reflex responses. Moreover, these falls can cause permanent injury and even reduce longevity. So it is critical that seniors take every caution to avoid falls as they move through the day and enter into vigorous activities. Refuse to engage in practices that have a high risk for falling.

Use a cane or walker if you need help to maintain your stability. Be especially careful about stairways, walkways, and ladder use.

10. Finally, *preventive health care* means we become more aware of the warning signs that occur to us all when a health symptom is emerging in our physical body. We have friends who have neglected, to their regret, real red flags with their daily health care. They have dismissed a reoccurring pain as unimportant or minimized a deepened depression. They failed to report constant bleeding, a serious sleep disorder, a persistent shortage of breath, a pain in the chest, or a recent fall to their doctor. They simply waited too long to report these problems. Sometimes, they lacked the information they needed to recognize when a symptom is telling them to go for help right away. So become better informed and become more sensitive about when to seek help.

Remember to make good health care decisions. It is critical that you make responsible choices when a health problem does arise and needs treatment. As you age, it is inevitable that you will need to pay more attention to emerging health care issues that impact the quality of your life. Helpful guidelines to consider in seeking the best treatment available are listed below:

1. Search carefully for the best medical services you can find. Many seniors get into the habit of finding a clinic that is close and accessible, rather than one that may be more effective and specializes in their area of special need. Search diligently for the best quality of services and the best medical service available. Some items to include in your search should include the following: cost of services,

recommendations by objective sources, successes in relating well to senior residents, hospital privileges, good health insurance contract coverage, and recommendations by your family doctor. For example, we have a young dermatologist in our area who is the subject of much chatting between friends. Their comments are all full of praise and approval of his work. He is also highly rated by the medical community. In addition, he relates well to senior patients, and he has the reputation for offering the best services available. He also has been well recognized by community leaders and many referral sources. He is a good example of an appealing physician.

2. Learn all you can about the health problem you have to address. If it is a new diagnosis of diabetes, for example, you need to become knowledgeable about this health issue. You need to find the best specialist in the area that treats that condition and consult with your own doctor about making a referral. Once you have an appointment, go prepared with questions and a willingness to follow through on treatment recommendations. Be on the lookout for over the quality of over the counter medication or poor supervision of your prescriptive medical. It is important that you and your physician become a fine-tuned team. If you do not see real progress in your treatment plan or you need to question why your treatment is not working well, changing your doctor sometimes becomes a necessity.

3. Take responsibility for the success of your treatment. It is not uncommon for seniors to become emotionally dependent and mentally confused about their health care network. They worry about health care insurance coverage. They feel doctors are often not communicating with each other, or with them, and about their latest developments.

Often, questions about their ongoing treatment program are not answered well. So taking firm control over the medical care offered to you is an important reminder every senior citizen needs to heed. In some instances, it may be necessary to seek a *second opinion* from another medical team because you are not happy with the doctor treating you now. Take initiative to get your questions answered and your needs fully met.

4. Learn to read and understand your health care rights. They are usually printed and readily available at all hospital locations and private clinics. These rights include the following: a right to have access to your own medical records, to receive prompt and reasonable response to questions; your right to know the rules that apply to your own conduct; whether Medicare and Medicaid covers your expenses; a right to express your grievances or concerns about the medical competency of your doctor; and a right to know the reasons behind and the expectations for recovery of a treatment program planned for your physical symptoms. Remember, it is important for you as a patient to exercise these rights so you will not feel abused or neglected by your medical team. Follow through and exercise your right when necessary. Demand to be heard and understood!

5. Seek the best proper professional assistance for your recovery from surgery. Visiting nurses, for example, can treat you at your own home if your physician agrees. If rehabilitation is needed, it is critical that you are referred or you find the best specialist. Sometimes, long-term recovery may involve joining a support group, such as a group for cancer survivors, or it may involve taking training in the use of a motorized wheelchair. Do whatever needs to be done to

make your recovery smooth and successful. Become an informed patient and follow instructions carefully.

6. My suggestion is that you seek and find continued support from a medical social worker, physician assistants, parish nurse, hospital chaplain, or pastor or priest, geriatric care manager, or whoever is available to assist with long-term adjustment and acceptance of a major change in your health condition. It is often difficult to do this alone. It may be advisable to see a staff psychologist to deal with your feeling of physical loss. Focus, as well, on your need to change your level of activity and lifestyle. We need to understand how to adapt and accept these losses

Use good nutrition and calorie limitation. Few of us know enough about proper nutrition. It is helpful, therefore, to learn a few fundamentals. With that information, we can be more careful about our daily food consumption. Most texts in the field will cover the following topics and suggestions for achieving better eating habits:

1. The goal of better eating practices is to provide proper nutrition and the right calorie intake so we not only maintain good health but also keep our body weight under control. By avoiding being overweight, we reduce our risk of high blood pressure, diabetes, painful joints, arthritis, and disruptive sleep. We do need to realize that our pattern of food consumption has real long-term consequences for the health of our bodies, as does the activity level we maintain and the way we cope with the stress of daily life. I am frankly alarmed over the diabetes crisis in America and the number of seniors who are victims of their own neglect because of their addiction to high-calorie food and sweets.

2. In order to keep our weight under control, we need to set a maximum calorie intake for each day, which each of us can maintain by being more aware about what we eat and the volume we consume. We can help ourselves, as well, by reading the labels on the food we purchase and deliberately avoid high-calorie items. Successful seniors have learned to eat little or no desserts. They insist on small portions when ordering food at a local restaurant or share one meal when they eat out. These successful seniors also cut their calories by limiting their snacking during the day and by being very selective about the kind of nutritious food they eat and enjoy.

3. It is helpful to know the calorie and fat content of major food groups and to reduce the consumption of certain foods that have high-calorie content. We can also learn to cook food differently so that we use low-calorie dressings, olive oil for cooking instead of lard or butter, and even be careful about the calories in the liquids we consume. Fruit juices are usually better for us than soda. Coffee or tea is acceptable if we refuse to add a lot of cream and sugar to our cup. In addition, try to avoid a regular snacking habit between meals. Here is where the pounds can be added with little effort at all.

4. It is encouraging to see a healthy trend emerge today in restaurants and even in fast-food establishments. They now offer low-calorie food and list the total calories for many of the food products they serve. Some food outlets even make available small-size servings of certain food items, especially for the senior patron. We know that seniors love to eat when they gather to socialize. Some better-disciplined retirees eat lightly and pick their food choices carefully and then often skip desserts. We need to be more

conscious of the value of lowered calorie consumption. Research indicates over and over that we can all live on less food and be quality conscious of the food we do eat. This habit can help us to be healthy and active. It might even help stave off a health problem that requires a prescribed diet and medical intervention.

5. It can be an interesting exercise to learn creative ways to do low-calorie and low-carbohydrate cooking at home. Start with healthy snack foods of fruit, carrot sticks, whole grain crackers, or string cheese. Learn to broil food rather than frying. Use multi-grain bread rather than white flour bread. Use honey and cinnamon, spices and herbs to add flavor to food as basic supplemental food items. Reduce sugar-centered foods whenever possible and remember that lean meats, chicken, and fish can be enjoyed and eaten in smaller portions after being cooked in low-calorie buttery spread. Lots of fresh fruit and lettuce salads provide an attractive table setting and are healthy supplements to main meals. The bottom line is that we all need to have a plant-based diet with a high intake of fruits and vegetables along with the use of water-based beverages, like iced tea and coffee, with a minimum of artificial sweeteners.

6. Let me add some general suggestions about maintaining a healthy diet. When shopping for food, prepare a careful list of the best food products and stay close to that listing. Impulsive buying of fatty food is a common weakness for all of us. Become better informed about the nutritious values of key foods you enjoy, so you can be selective about the right bread, fruits, vegetables, meats, and liquids that are good choices for your diet. Become better informed about creative ways to prepare your meal servings, not only for better nutrition, but for attractive serving of the

food prepared at your table. Finally, develop a pattern of real self-control over not only the quality of food you consume but also the volume you consume. Limit your total calorie intake each day. Learn to become proud and pleased with your overall eating pattern. Set the goal of reaching your ideal weight so you can be pleased with your appearance and the new energy you can now enjoy.

7. Doctors and nurses in conventional medicine are skeptical about the practice of taking supplements with our food each day. Nevertheless, a large number consume them for their own personal health because they do see their value. For example, taking antioxidants as a protection against the free radicals in our body makes sense. Including selected vitamins as prevention against the absence of certain vitamins in our diet can be a healthy practice. There is more of a consensus on the value of fish oil supplement to help us reduce the risk of coronary heart disease and for brain and eye health as well. Many nutritionists also see the benefit of taking calcium plus D3 as a way to strengthen our bones and to ward off osteoporosis. Whatever you decide about supplements for health preservation, be certain you let your family doctor know what you are taking and always respect and heed his or her input. Their use should always be compatible with your prescriptive medications.

8. Let me now add a series of suggestions for making better food choices and eating habits for good health care. These relate to your maintenance of a healthy diet plan. Please consider these ideas for your use of good nutrition:

   • Consider the use of the MEDITERRANEAN DIET as your regular plan for daily food consumption. This is a naturally healthy food pattern that includes more mono unsaturated fatty acids, fruit, vegetables, whole grains, legumes, and fish while limiting red meat and refined sugar. It encourages the consumption of fat in olive oil, nuts, and the value of the responsible use of red wine in moderation. In a Mayo Clinic study, this diet was shown to reduce the risk of heart disease, cancer, Parkinson's, and several other major illnesses. It is the only diet recommended by a majority of many health organizations. (Place a search on your computer for the Mediterranean Diet to discover more information about the nature and values of this popular diet).

- When shopping for food, prepare a list of the best food products you can purchase and stay close to that listing. Plan ahead for good nutrition and direct your attention to the best selections you can find. Take pride in the way you think ahead about what is best for the health of your household.

- Use lots of green vegetables, unsweetened juices, fruits, chicken, rice, or fish. Avoid a heavy dependence on fatty meats and pork for your main meal. We always need to be aware of the danger of consuming excessive carbohydrates or meat products. Read helpful articles about food selections to avoid and those to enjoy. Specialize in learning more about low-fat foods that are tasty, and find foods that are low in fat with high fiber content.

- Use plenty of liquids but avoid heavy dependence on alcoholic beverages. Use low-calorie milk and natural juices for breakfast. One danger to avoid is dehydration from consuming too few liquids. Avoid liquid intake after the evening meal, however, so you can stop the nighttime trip to the toilet. It is also helpful to cut the use of diet drinks, soda pop, and that all-too-frequent nighttime alcohol-laced nightcap. A simple decision not to order a sugar-laced drink at a restaurant could be a healthy choice for life. It is an example of how the small food choices can have long-term consequences for good or could cause real harm to our physical well-being.

- Become better informed about the nutrition values of key food items and liquids. Learn to be a discriminating shopper, especially when you order food from a fast-food outlet. Be especially selective and limit your use of certain deserts or ice cream because of their high-calorie content, but be willing to reward yourself with some limited sweets to give flavor to your meal.

- It is helpful as well to learn more about good cooking practices. You can benefit enormously by cooking in low-calorie liquids or using the microwave rather than grease-based fried foods. Barbecue cooking on an open fire can add variety to meat or fish and some vegetables. Slow cookers are an added way of preparing food, and they can add flavor and variety to your family meal. Always be conscious, however, about the calorie content of the total meal you deliver to the table. In addition, urge everyone to avoid second helpings to cut the bulk consumed. It is a good way to keep your weight under control. Certain foods can become addictive, so cutting the volume consumed is a helpful habit.

- In addition, it is always beneficial to serve food with flair. Decorate your table, use cloth and napkins, add a flower or center piece, and begin eating after your prayer of thanksgiving. Mealtime needs to be a period, at least once a day, for good conversation and warm fellowship. Invite guests over to share your meal and enjoy their friendship and conversation. Put an emphasis on changing your menu often so you add variety to your food choices. Some seniors even plan a week in advance so they have a thoughtfully prepared menu to serve at home.

9. A final suggestion concerning your health care practices is to keep close tabs on your overall physical well-being. Place a strong value on maintaining annual physical exams and blood screenings. It is amazing how much a doctor can learn from tests, from pap tests, mammograms, and from testicular and anal examinations. A blood test, for example, can reveal that your calcium level is low, your sugar level is too high, or that you are deficient in key vitamins.

Some doctors may even recommend that their patients visit the hospital nutritionist so they can look at their eating pattern and recommend appropriate changes that may be needed. Either way, it is critical that all of us look at the choices we make concerning the food products we consume, so that we do our best to develop healthy eating habits all of our lives. The biggest concern is that we need to stop overconsumption of food products because seniors everywhere are gaining too much weight, which can become a real threat to their health and longevity.

10. Do develop a routine of regular exercise and a ritual of good sleeping habits. We read about examples of senior citizens who have practiced amazing discipline over their physical body. The senior games are an outstanding illustration of the achievements of senior residents who have accomplished a great deal in excelling at a sport. Separated into age groups, these seniors compete in open games in a variety of sport activities in local communities all over America.

Then there are also organizations in many senior communities that highlight the value of kayaking, wind sailing, surfing, and even fly fishing etc. Other communities lift up local softball competition, pickle ball competition, volleyball matches, and intense golf tournaments. Seniors have caught on to the idea that daily physical activity is a strong and important value for good health and happiness In addition, we need to emphasize the value in better sleep habits for healthy living. Let us look at some guidelines that will help us keep well and safe in what we do for our leisure time and in our health practices.

- Any good coach will tell you that you should not try to exceed your capacity to engage in any healthy sport. We need to understand our physical limits and to honor that. It is important to pick variety of experiences and to enjoy the fellowship with others. In our senior community, we have an optional activity for just about every interest: golf, volley ball, softball, tennis and pickle ball, table tennis, lawn bowling, long-distant biking, hiking, and all water sports, to name just a few. The importance people place on these activities helps keeps our community alive and an exciting place to live. It is a common practice for younger seniors to start out with very active sport competition, and as they age, they move toward less vigorous and demanding activity. This is a wise trend, and it protects them from physical injuries and the stress of a too-demanding sport. So as you age, change the physical activity and exertion to reflect your declining physical capacity. Keep active, but be aware of your limitations.

- What is apparent to most leaders in sport medicine is that a regular exercise program has a direct and positive effect on sleep habits. It enhances our need for deep, restful, and refreshing sleep. When the heart and lungs are stretched and exerted, the body responds by needing a deeper and refreshing period of rest. Take pride, as well, in developing a regular habit of restful sleep at night, with a short nap in the middle of the day. Put a strong emphasis on avoiding eating heavily or taking a lot of liquids just before sleep time. Pick a good bed, establish a regular sleep pattern, and avoid getting too stimulated just before sleep by a disturbing movie or a difficult personal decision. Learn how to quiet your mind and thoughts, so you can let your body rest well. Take pride in developing healthy sleep habits.

Our sport trainers remind us, as well, that we must strain and strengthen our muscular system. It is not enough to play ball. It is better to bowl or lift weights or even engage in a muscle-strengthening program at home with special equipment for personal use, such as dumb bells, jumping rope, or a back-strengthening rubber rope. We need strong muscles to engage in most of these sport events. It is recommended that we find a staff person at a fitness center to help us design an exercise program for our particular needs and health condition. Follow that plan by keeping a record of your exercise practices. Then maintain that routine to keep in good physical fitness so you can benefit from the surging energy and feelings of well-being that flow from good physical conditioning.

*   The healthiest seniors around us have a regular exercise program suited to their physical ability and schedule. They like variety in the sports they choose to enjoy. They may do power walking, play pickle ball, visit the exercise center, and join an exercise class, or even go social dancing. It would be healthy for most of us to engage in some water sport like swimming or pool walking, sailing, or even biking. The key is to become disciplined about a habit pattern of regular exercise, even if it is not always convenient or enjoyable. Do it for your health and well-being. The benefits are so critical that taking time to *work out* needs to be a part of your thrice-weekly schedule of activity for both men and women. In inclement weather, you could benefit from home exercise equipment with a planned routine that strengthens your heart, lungs, and muscle system.

*   All healthy seniors want a routine of restful sleep at nighttime despite some physical or emotional limitations. Unfortunately, a significant number of older adults have disturbed sleep, often due to body pain related to a health problem, the stress of daily living, or the side effects of medications. Sometimes, just living a sedentary life or having to cope with a disability is sufficient cause for sleep disturbance. Whatever the reason, it is imperative that seniors try to resolve their concern over sleep disruption and find a solution that lets them enjoy restful sleep.

Some of the best solutions relate to better management of our prescriptive medications. Each patient needs to be forceful with their doctor to find medications that do not cause disturbed sleep. Finding a good mattress, the right room temperature, the best time to go to bed and awaken, along with the avoidance of food and liquids a few hours before bedtime can be good practice. Clearing your mind of worry, fear, and doubt and preparing your mental attitude for a restful night's sleep can be critical to your success. In the end, if all these approaches fail, you may have to seek professional help by going to a reputable sleep disorder clinic in your area. Realize now that this is a time in life when you need to maintain restful sleep for good health. A time of meditation, prayer, and devotional reading before bedtime can be a helpful routine as well.

Some Final Words about Maintaining Physical Health Care: Seniors need to take charge of their own health care. Choose to do whatever is necessary to maximize your best potential for a finely functioning body for your age and health history. That means that you need to accept some fundamental responsibilities that require your constant attention and action. Here is a list for your consideration:

1. Maintain good health records that you have read and understand. There are several sources for keeping your records in an electronic storage bank for easy access that you may want to use. Start by going to a government service named healthIt.gov or a private company called: webmdhealthrecord.com or for veterans: myhealthevet. com. These sites believe we all benefit from better information about our health care and recovery from illness. Moreover, if we see a specialist, we can request those records be added to the private records we keep in our home office file. Stop relying on your memory or your scattered notes. Keep good, organized records. Keep your

records current by recording every medical visit right after the visit and follow the recommendations listed.

2. Become familiar with the health care system. Find what medical specialties are available for critical health needs; where you can find the best doctor in that system who addresses your issue; and the best health insurance coverage you can find. You need to understand, as well, the referral process and the hospital staff roles so you can adapt well if you need hospitalization. Keep a file of the finest medical specialist in your area. Ask around for a recommendation from friends and key professionals so you will know where to go when you need assistance. For major medical crisis, go to nationally recognized medical firms (i.e., Mayo Clinic, John Hopkins, the Cleveland Clinic, etc.) that specialize in giving second options about diagnosis and treatment that your local doctor finds difficult to diagnosis and treat successfully.

3. You should become informed about your health reimbursement policies and the limits for your care. Talk to your health insurance representative about your questions. Look for the best policy that fits your special interests and needs. Carefully check medical billing statements and how well your insurance company paid for its share. Be sure you advocate for yourself if you feel you have been overcharged and wrongly billed. In addition, check your bills for prescriptive medication for accuracy and for proper coverage by your health insurance or Medicare reimbursement. Make certain, as well, your doctor uses as many generic medications as possible to keep the cost of medication under control.

4. Never be reluctant to get two estimates for any medical service you need. That includes examining the cost structure for hospitalization as well as hiring a medical specialist. It is possible to ask about costs in before using a medical center and specialist. For example, outpatient or freestanding medical clinics often perform even major surgery, and their costs are significantly less than a local hospital. Hospitalization usually costs more, so raise the issue about where good surgery can be offered at the least cost possible. Question the cost of hospital care and the choice of inpatient care with your doctor before you decide on a hospital.

5. If you have a long period of recovery from surgery or need a structured course of rehabilitation, make certain you plan well. Talk to the chief of surgery or the director of that recovery program. Ask key questions and develop a plan for recovery. People usually do better if they know what they need to do and what precautions to take. Find ways, as well, to keep your mind active and maintain social contacts and family connections. Try to normalize your life as much as you can. Try to find tasks you can complete and enjoy while you are engaged in rehabilitation or recovery.

6. One area in planning for senior health care that is neglected is planning for long-term care. If you do no preparation, it is likely it will be forced on you in a crisis situation. Unfortunately, long-term insurance is too expensive for even the middle-class today. Some life insurance policies have a rider you can select for long-term coverage, while some long-term policies cover just a small portion or a specialized part of your risk. Nevertheless, develop some contingency plans that will allow you to hire a home-based

caregiver or for someone close to you to care for your needs. This move seems preferable today over nursing home care or even assisted living. We all appear to want the familiar surroundings of our own home and neighborhood. But if that is not possible, draw a plan for serious care giving services in a setting with a staff you can trust. For more information, check with CareFamily.com or CareLink. com. A sudden health crisis can change everything, but it needs to be managed well or the uncertainty of the new issues can add more tension.

7.   Now let me close by endorsing the use of *hospice care* for all end-of-life issues. It is not only a wonderful organization, but its staff and services for the dying patient have been outstanding. Most physicians now routinely refer senior adults to its care for the last six months of life. In many cases, *hospice* staff can even service families who want to receive care at home, instead of a hospice center. It is so helpful because the staff and chaplains have been trained to attend to the dying patient and the grieving family involved. Many adults who need care and comfort when faced with death and dying issues also call upon their local church or synagogue to send parishioners to provide the kind of love and compassionate care they need at that time. Whatever you do, give love and support to the dying adult in the final days of life. You may need the same kind of care and attention someday yourself.

Real-Life Stories about Fitness And Food:

Before I close this chapter, I want to share a brief summary of two seniors who made outstanding choices about how they managed their lives. Let me start with the life of Charles Atlas, the famous bodybuilder who became a legend for physical fitness in his life. He started out as a skinny, scrawny boy in New York, being bullied by his peers. Nevertheless, he made a choice to change his life and to build his body. He joined the YMCA and began numerous exercise routines until he found the combination that worked for him. He became so proficient at bodybuilding that he turned it into a career to teach others what he had learned for himself. He founded a fitness company that begin to market and sell fitness products. His bodybuilding ads started to appear everywhere until America caught the fitness fever. Finally, he was highlighted in the national media and lifted up as an example for excellent bodybuilding. He even posed frequently with his muscles at full strength. He inspired a whole generation of younger men to keep themselves in good physical shape. His company still exists today and continues to emphasize the importance of bodybuilding for all ages. Seniors can learn much from his example of self-discipline and determination. Make physical fitness a lifetime goal that never ends for you.

A second senior I want to highlight is Julia Child, the world-famous chef who taught more about the selection, preparation, processing, and serving of food than anyone has ever done. Her career started in World War II when she enlisted in the OSS as a secret intelligent service agent for our government. She achieved an outstanding record there before she discovered that food preparation was her real love. After the war, she studied to be a chef with the best food connoisseurs in Paris. She then began to teach cooking throughout Europe before she settled in Cambridge, Massachusetts.

Her passion was then focused on helping America become more food conscious. She wrote a news column, started to do radio, and then turned to live television to get her message out. She ended her career publishing twenty books on various aspects of healthy food use and preparation. Her image of preparing food with delicacy is buried deep in the memory of countless seniors across our country. In a fitting close, she was even giving advice to others when she died just before her ninety-second birthday. She was honored and remembered so well that her pots and pans and memorabilia now occupy a space in the Smithsonian National Museum of American History in Washington, D.C.

The simple lesson from these two lives is straightforward and clear: make thoughtful and helpful choices about the way you live your life and cook your food. The rewards are real and lasting when you do, even if you do not become famous or popular as these two talented figures have done. Learn from them about the values they taught, even if you never achieve their fame and fortune. Remember there is great value in fine- tuning your physical body and making an emphasis on eating sensibly with a flair for elegance and beauty.

Supplemental Materials: (1) Keys to Maintaining Our Physical Health Care: Core Concepts, (2) Developing Fitness Program that Works for You, and (3) Tips for a Longer Life (4) Make Your Home Safe; Prepare to Handle Emergencies.

Supplement 1, Chapter 2

KEYS TO MANTAINING OUR PHYSICAL HEALTH CARE: CORE CONCEPTS

Physical health is one of our most valuable assets. To lose it and to become even partially disabled limits our life, energy, and enthusiasm for living. Make physical well-being a major goal in your daily routine. Become well informed about good health practices in senior living and engage in these practices all your life. Make adjustments in the activities you choose, of course, as you age, and you cannot engage in the active sports you did when you were younger.

To retain our health requires a plan and a program that we implement every day. To just let circumstances and aging eat away at our health is reckless and self-destructive on our part. A do-nothing philosophy does not work. Be very proactive when it comes to maintaining good health practices. Carefully pick a pattern of exercise that is appropriate for your age and health.

The best approach is preventive maintenance. It works and it lasts, but it requires thoughtful planning and consistent efforts to keep it working. One approach that works is to put in writing your promise to maintain specific guidelines for health maintenance. Share these goals with others and seek their help to keep your good health habits. Check with key resources for ideas about keeping yourself in good physical condition. Talk to the healthiest seniors about what works best for them. Try new ideas to see if they work for you.

We see the impact of physical health on our emotional, social, and recreational life. Poor health can devastate all three. Read about the damage neglect and ignorance can bring to your physical health. Read about and talk to seniors who are suffering health loss to discover what you can do to avoid the handicap they often created for themselves.

When we do have a health decline, we must work at maintaining our maximum flexibility and mobility. Keep moving and keep involved. To withdraw from contact, from involvement, and from making a contribution to others is to limit and restrict our whole lifestyle. Maintain as active a lifestyle as you can so you do not retreat from social involvement. Keep moving and keep your interest alive in the activities of your community. Be selective, but continue to attend as many social activities as you can so you do not retreat from life.

Take advantage of the best of modern medicine. I often recommend the approach of the Mayo Clinic, which specializes in offering *second opinions* about a large number of medical problems that seem unsolvable. Their entire staff of specialists also talks to each other to reach a final diagnosis and treatment plan. Seek help from the best medical team you can find. Once you have a diagnosis and treatment plan, be conscientious to follow that plan. Modern medicine works best when the doctors and the patient work in careful cooperation and communication to bring about healing.

Find a good health insurance company that will supplement Medicare or Medicaid. Compare rates and policies from at least two companies before you sign up for that supplement. Investigate, ask lots of questions until you are satisfied you have found a plan that best fits your needs.

Keep in mind that good dental care can be a critical issue in maintaining good health. A poor mouth of infected gums can lead to other health problems. It can also be very costly to fix the neglect of good dental hygiene. An annual checkup is a good standard to follow so that you can find any change in your gums, teeth, and mouth cavity. Prevention is always better than seeking a cure.

Seek mental health care when there is a need for help with your emotional life and relationships. It has a direct impact on your physical well-being. It is difficult to be physically healthy when depression, high-living anxiety, and worry control your life. Get over any reluctance you may have about sharing your deep emotional thoughts and feelings with a professional counselor. There is a lot of real evidence that good counseling can make a positive impact on your life.

Take prescriptive and non-prescriptive drugs with care and caution. Urge your doctor to constantly evaluate if you can reduce or stop some medication. Ask your provider to advise you on your use of off-the-counter supplements. Be disciplined about taking the right dosage at the right time every day. Look at what you are taking with complete concentration, so you avoid making mistakes by taking the wrong medication.

Physical health is one of our most valuable assets. To lose it and to become even partially disabled limits our life, energy, and enthusiasm for living. Talk to seniors who have lost an eye or a limb, and they will tell you how living with a disability weighs on your quality of life every day. Do whatever is necessary to maintain the best health you can achieve for your age and genetic history.

Retaining our health requires a plan and a program that we implement every day. To just let circumstances and aging eat away at our health is reckless and self-destructive. A do-nothing philosophy does not work. The healthiest seniors work at maintaining their good health. They are conscious that this task is one of their most valuable assets. So refine your skills and get motivated by engaging in the best health habits you can maintain. Add years to your life by keeping at the task of practicing good health care day after day, year after year

The best approach is preventive maintenance. It works and it lasts, but it requires thoughtful planning and consistent efforts to keep it working. Attend educational programs that focus on health problems, and you will be fortified with helpful information that helps to keep you well. Subscribe to health-focused magazines and find the best Internet sites that offer helpful ideas about good health practices.

Our physical health greatly impacts our emotional, social, and recreational life. Poor health can devastate all three. Older adults who have poor health can tell you about how it impacts their quality of their life. Sometimes participation in a health-focused support group can be a life saver. It is helpful to hear about how other seniors have dealt successfully with a health issue that troubles you and needs to be addressed.

When we do have a health decline, we must work at maintaining our maximum flexibility and mobility. Keep moving and keep involved. To withdraw from contact, from involvement, and from making a contribution to others is to limit and restrict our whole lifestyle.

Take advantage of the best of modern medicine when you have health issues that need to be addressed. I often recommend the medical team approach, in which several specialists work together to determine your diagnosis and treatment plan. Sometimes you may need to look out of your local area when major surgery or a very serious health issue emerges. Do careful investigation to find the best medical service available. Your family doctor may help you in your search.

Become aware of how to prevent falls. Unintended falls are one of the most common health problems in the senior world. They are usually due to slowed reaction time, failed eye sight, lack of concentration, and sheer neglect. So become more self-conscious about the danger of falls and give more attention to fall prevention. One way to heed this warning is to avoid getting on ladders, lifting heavy weights, or to trying to jump large distances. Using common sense goes a long way to avoid falls.

Take prescriptive and non-prescriptive drugs with care and caution. Urge your doctor to constantly evaluate when you can reduce or stop some medication. Ask your provider to advise you on your use of off-the-counter supplements so they can complement your prescriptive medications properly.

Maintain good medical dental and behavioral records that can become an accurate account of your overall health picture. In addition, it is good information for your medical providers in the future. Sometimes it is critical that your health care provider knows your past health history in detail when he or she is deciding what your proper treatment should be.

Supplement 2, Chapter 2

DISCOVERING A FITNESS PROGRAM THAT WORKS FOR YOU AT YOUR AGE

Concepts: Everyone needs a fitness program designed for their particular needs. The program should also change as we age. Seniors know when a program is too strenuous. Cost for lessons or equipment is another consideration. So where do we start? Most retirement communities or senior centers have a consultant available to help you plan a program that is available, affordable, and fits your needs. All that's left is for you to develop the strong motivation to exercise intensely and regularly.

1. Make certain the program emphasizes aerobics or any activity that pushes your heart and lungs, legs, arms, and muscles to their limit. That goal may include running on

a treadmill, playing tennis or golf, or swimming. Some instructors often suggest you keep a chart listing your specific goals for each encounter and date your activity.

2. Another worthy goal is muscle strengthening. That assumes that aging weakens and reduces the size of our muscular system. It is critical, therefore, that we engage in activity that strengthens muscles through lifting, pulling, stretching, and using our muscle to the maximum. For example, I have found that doing lower back stretching in bed in the morning before I get out of bed helps reduces or eliminates pain and lower-back muscle loss.

3. It is an essential goal to develop ease of movement and real flexibility. So seniors do back bends or use a rope or heavy rubber wand to stretch their muscles in a home exercise program. In fact, there is a large variety of exercise aids for home use available at most sport equipment stores. The advantage here is that you have exercise at times convenient for you, and you do not have to be under the supervision of someone else all the time. Be sure, however, that you have clear goals and a concrete plan in place that works for you and challenges you.

4. A final goal for exercise is to persist by exercising discipline over your exercise habits. It is so easy to pass it by, make an excuse why it is not now convenient, or let other's needs take precedent. I find most sport coaches suggest a balance between a personal program and involvement in a group sports activity. In most communities, there is a large variety of options available to you, plus even instruction in the use of this new sport. So take initiative and engage in a sport that fits your interest and skill level. Most exercise physiologists suggest a minimum of three times a week

with a group, and the other days, you can develop your own program for private exercise activity.

Supplement 3, Chapter 2

TIPS FOR A LONGER LIFE IN OUR SENIOR LIVING EXPERIENCE

Note: Harvard Medical School publishes very helpful health reports that offer constructive advice for a healthier life (see *healthbeat@mail.health.harvard.edu*). These publications are inexpensive and easily obtained through their website. Following is a partial quote from their publication *Living Better, Living Longer,* and other various sources.

1. Control and firmly stop any bad habits that may contribute to declining health or a health crisis, such as smoking, using chewing tobacco, overuse of alcohol, compulsive eating, consuming a high level of sugar or high cholesterol foods, or becoming addicted to sedentary living.

2. An abundance of research supports the idea that we will have fewer health problems, we move around with more agility, and we will sleep better if we achieve maintain our ideal weight level as we age. Obesity hurts our total health picture.

3. We can enjoy life more fully if we learn how to laugh and take life with a lighter touch. One of our handicaps as seniors is that we have seen so many changes, losses, and real crisis in our lives that we can end up being too sober and serious minded. You will enjoy life more if you see the beauty around us, the goodness in people, appreciate the joy in daily living, and celebrate the blessings of God.

4. Those who seem to rejoice in the holidays are the seniors with strong, healthy family connections. They relish the time with their grandchildren or time catching up on the news about their adult children. They enjoy immensely having a spirited visit, good food, and family activity when everyone participates in the activities.

5. Seniors who have a good marriage enjoy that warm companionship. We have noticed, however, that many single seniors also learn to bond together with other singles so they can have close friendships. Many healthy seniors, as well, find a wonderful outlet in offering their volunteer time for worthy causes. The key seems to be in building love for others and acceptance for yourself as you age

6. Healthy seniors end up finding that they need a strong set of values to guide them and a faith community to support them. That combination is a winner every time. There is no better alternative than being in a group of caring, understanding, and enjoyable people. My experience is that you are likely to find them in great abundance at a local church.

7. Find some cause, hobby, or work role that can become your passion. Seniors who become fully engaged in a worthy project find purpose and meaning in that effort. That keeps them motivated, and they learn to love the effort they put into this goal. We need something that captures our full attention and our total commitment.

Supplement 4, Chapter 2

MAKE YOUR HOME SAFE; PREPARE TO HANDLE EMERGENCIES

- For emergencies call 911 or for phone numbers call 211

- Keep phone numbers on refrigerator for ambulance, doctor, police, fire department, and nearest helpful neighbors

- Prepare a kit of emergency medical supplies for urgent care. Have these kits available in your home and automobile

- Take training in first-aid treatment to give knowledgeable assistance for injured parties

- Keep fire extinguishers stored near stoves or baroque equipment

- Install smoke alarms at key locations in the home and garage and keep their batteries charged

FOR A SAFE HOME ENVIRONMENT AND TO PREVENT FALLS, DO THESE THINGS:

- Remove scatter rugs and all objects that could cause falls

- Plan for non-skid floor cover and the surface of all stairways

- Use hand-rails where necessary and especially on all stairways

- Keep night lights on during the evening in strategic locations in the house

- Always use rubber matting in showers, and in slippery areas outside the home

- Pets should be under control and taught to avoid electrical equipment and food storage

- Discard outdated medications and supplements plus old unusable medical supplies

- A good habit is to turn off all electrical equipment (including computers) before bedtime

- Develop your own listing that applies to your location and make a copy for every family member

"We enjoy our retirement years. It is good to feel comfortable about our lives and activity."

CHAPTER 3

DEVELOPING OUR EMOTIONAL HEALTH AND HAPPINESS

"I can foresee a day when education will routinely include human competencies . . . such as self-awareness, self-control, and empathy and the arts of listening, resolving conflicts, and cooperation."

—Daniel Coleman,
Emotional Intelligence

Let's start our exploration into emotional maturity with a clear definition of emotional health. It is the ability to accept and love yourself; the skill to relate well to others; and the ability to successfully meet the strong demands of life. Emotionally healthy adults are usually able to (1) adapt well to the location where they live, are socially active, and enjoy the company of others; (2) are generally free from high-level worry, anxiety, depression, and fear; (3) adapt well to the changes and the challenges of daily living and even manage the unexpected crisis that comes to all of us; (4) make the necessary value choices so their life is in a wholesome balance; and finally,

(5) have a clear set of goals that include good health care, a positive work ethic, and wholesome family ties. They find real meaning and purpose in living well every day of their lives.

You may wonder if there actually are people so well adjusted, and I will tell you that they are all around us. They may not make the newspaper, be highlighted by local community leaders, or even be a central personality in their neighborhood. They are real, and they live out meaningful lives. Most of us can name someone like that in our past that was loved and appreciated by everyone. I have several people in my memory bank that were mature, likable, loving, and caring adults. Some of them have been mentors or role models because of their fine human qualities. You can probably name a teacher, a minister, a community leader, a compassionate doctor, or a neighbor that will come to your mind right away. Focus on them as you read on about how we can attain real emotional health.

The best way to begin my commentary on attaining emotional well-being is to center on the key factors that usually help us grow into mature human beings. These forces are real and helpful in molding our lives. (When they are absent, they have a negative impact on our emotional well-being). So value these keys to emotional well-being and treasure them. They are part of the essential elements in the life of senior adults who live stable and emotional mature lives today: Here is where we see the evidences of mature adults living out their wholesome lives:

They are Healthy and Loving Marriage Partners Who Nurture Each Other and Provide Support for Their Extended Family: It is indeed a wonderful gift to live in a loving marriage where you give your best to building the quality of your lives together.

We should not take that for granted because there are a large number of widowed or divorced seniors today who must live alone. Sometimes the death of a senior partner comes all too early, and the loss is difficult to manage over time. Therefore, while we still do have each other, emotionally mature seniors enjoy their companionship and treasure the time they have for rich fellowship and social activity. In addition, married seniors enjoy watching their adult children mature, and they also enjoy the rich achievement of their grandchildren. It is a valuable treasure to grow older together when your marriage is strong and loving, and you create wonderful memories together.

In addition, good partners enjoy hosting family gatherings over the holidays, being responsible for remembering birthdays, and being present when each grandchild is born. It is such a joy to watch the young families grow and develop into a closely knit social unit. To be there to support those growing-up years is one of the pleasures of a healthy marriage. Many couples mark their time together by the milestones in their family unit: the first days of school, birthdays, graduations, college years, a new marriage, and the arrival of their new grandchild. These are wonderful times in a good marriage and the product of a happy extended family life together.

1. *They Appreciate Warm and Supportive Friends who Were Present in the Crucial Years of Their Growth and Development:* Most of us who were benefactors of this childhood gift can remember clearly how important these close colleagues were as we moved through the growing-up years. They were there for the fun and games of childhood, the dating years of youth, and the young adult years of college and first jobs. These treasured souls enjoyed us and listened to us, even chided us when we

were wrong. They gave us the gift of exciting memories at sports events, the dances, the movies, and the parties that made up our youthful years. What we all most treasure is the way they loved us, affirmed us, and even bragged about being our best friend. These were the wonder years. They were precious times indeed.

2. *They Are Grateful for a Good Education, a Supportive School Environment, and Products of that Culture:* Most of us can remember our first years of schooling: the play yard, the games we enjoyed after school, the contests we tried and sometimes won, new discoveries in science classes, or the debates we had in civics classes. Many of us were able to achieve some moments of fame when on a football team, in a school choir, or playing an instrument in the local band. For those who went to college and completed a degree in their chosen field, there was added joy from that achievement. Now as a senior adult, it is a pleasure to recall and appreciate the wonderful contribution a good education made to your long life. Those skills have lasted, and the insights they gave you about different fields of knowledge continue to enrich your life over and over again, even today.

3. *They Enjoy the Ability to Weather Losses and Handle Family Crisis Together:* Most of us do not remain unscathed as we move into the senior years. More than not, we have memories in our family history of someone dying tragically, of a lengthy illness of a favored relative, or of the mental breakdown of an uncle or aunt, or even the unfortunate death of a parent when you were still young and needed their guidance Handling these crisis experiences requires a lot of faith and the loving embrace of a strong family tie. Somehow, over time, you find the trust in God, the

inner strength and determination to carry on. When that occurs and we manage our losses or crisis moments, we do become stronger and wiser than before. That victory not only tightly knits our family together, it also helps us to appreciate more the values of our family connection. We learn to adapt better than before the event and to appreciate the benefits we have enjoyed because of our strong family bond and the presence of supportive friends who never fail us or let us down.

4. *They Have Benefited by Observing and Living with Adults who Made Good Choices over the Way They Managed Their Lives:* Nothing influences us more than a good example of healthy living. Many of us have been the benefactors of having healthy minded adults who lived good productive lives. It does not take me long to remember an outstanding schoolteacher, an inspired community leader, a loving parishioner in our local church, or even a co-worker in our years of employment who were models of high achievement. The fact that these people do exist means that they have learned how to be emotionally healthy. That path is open for us to live that way as well. We may want to look into the factors that made them that way, but we do value the examples they have set for each of us. Sometimes our own career choices or even marriage patterns are modeled after these people who have shown us the way to live a healthy lifestyle. Look around you and observe these outstanding examples of positive living experiences. They are there for you today to serve as an example in your own lives today.

5. *Finally, These Healthy Adults Are Surviving because They have Developed the Drive and Determination to Overcome Great Odds against Them:* It is not uncommon anymore

to read stories in the newspaper or see on television about how some ordinary person has overcome a huge handicap. It could be a man who runs in the Olympics with two artificial limbs. It may be a woman who is the first female to climb Mount Everest. You might read how a paralyzed adult on a wheelchair wins the annual race at a wheelchair competition. Think, also, of the thousands of single parents who must work and raise children despite having little financial resources. What about the countless caregivers who have spent a great share of their lifetime caring and ministering to a mentally handicapped partner or child? These people are the heroes of our American life, with all due credit to our honored servicemen and women. They have demonstrated in dramatic ways that we can overcome the limitations that come into our lives. These people of character have shown us that we can make the best of bad situations and still survive. They have taught us to believe that we can overcome obstacles in life and still find a quality of living that is very satisfying and resourceful. We can even become stronger emotionally because of the obstacles we have faced and have overcome.

Now we turn to a fundamental cornerstone of emotional well-being. Here, we explore the *Keys to Building our Self-Worth and Contentment* in a world where we are dealing with *change and challenges every day*! As a clinical psychologist, I have seen the question of finding self-confidence raised all the time in and out of my counseling sessions and while on the lecture stage. So here is what I have learned and taught others to adopt for themselves:

1. *Learn to Like Yourself. Build Your Self-Esteem.* It is not uncommon even in the senior community to witness adults who have poor self-worth. You can spot them by

their downward looks, shifting legs, restless bodies, and low voices. It is a sad sight to see a husband or wife work hard at covering up the shyness of their marriage partner. It is embarrassing to try to listen to someone who has few words and is talking in mumbles or a low sound. Most of us can spot the struggling adult who whispers, who stutters, who is always apologizing, or who even stands behind her or his partner in a social gathering. The problem of poor self-worth is everywhere, and it needs to be addressed and resolved.

The best way to tackle the issue is to acknowledge it and become determined that it will be resolved. Start to believe you are a worthy child of God who has value and abilities you can share with the world. Begin by practicing with the support of others, and embark on new initiatives to show others your real worth and ability. Gather your courage and practice being more verbal and sociable. Give yourself credit for making small gains. Build upon your successes, and you will grow. You must start to believe that you can change and be the person you want to be. Start to work at this change today.

2. *Build a Network of Supportive Family Members and Friends:* One of the most consistent needs we all share is our desire for people to love and care about us. We simply function better and life takes on greater meaning when we are surrounded by others who show continued interest in our lives. As seniors, we love being a happy parent of adult children and a great-grandparent to grandchildren. One of our other pleasures in life is to eat out and enjoy the company of other retirees. Or it is so refreshing to have a senior neighbor call and invite us to a movie or a ball game. When illness strikes, it is very comforting to

have a dear friend accompany us to the doctor or visit us regularly at the hospital when we have surgery. We can enjoy celebrating birthdays with companions or enjoying those special moments when dear friends celebrate a half century of marriage together. In addition, it is so good to spend the holidays with family members where we can enjoy a special mealtime and have fun on the beach or in the pool together. Just to feel they are proud of your role and place in the family or a friendship circle makes life more fulfilling with every pleasurable contact.

3. *It Is Critical that We Resolve Our Anger, the Lost Relationships, the Bitterness of the Past:* We need to move on with our lives and not be hamstrung by the many unresolved issues of our early life. As a therapist to seniors, I became acutely aware how many of my clients were troubled by thoughts of earlier conflicts with others that plagued their lives. Some became so alienated with a close relative they never spoke to each other for years. Many were living with guilt over a statement, an action, or a failed contact with a close friend that was never resolved. It was a common occurrence to talk to a client who was still angry after years of no contact with a distant business associate over a work-related clash that went badly.

You need to know that to allow negative thinking to dominate our mind can limit the joy and happiness of our daily activity. It is very necessary that we come to that critical juncture when we decide to rid ourselves of these burdens of our past. Decide to let these lingering feelings go and agree to move on to a brighter and better future. The essential decision is to choose to stop ruminating about the past; to let it go in your mind and heart; to offer forgiveness for yourself and others, even if it is not requested. We need to move on to enjoy the present and the future, unimpeded by the bitter memories of the past we have held on to far too long.

4. *Learn to Cope Well with the Stress, Worry, and Demands of Life:* All of us have tension and worry over issues that we need to resolve. Right now, we are dealing with friends where the wife is the caregiver for a very sick husband. Her constant health problems keep them running to the doctor all the time, with its strain on their time and budget. They are handling this unwanted issue in their lives with remarkable determination and a positive attitude, but the strain on their life and marriage is noticeable. They have learned to manage the tension of his enlarging health complaints by not dwelling on his symptoms, by finding diversity in their schedule, and by seeking the best medical help they can find. They also communicate well and have learned to be open about their feelings and their support for each other. We can handle the demands of life, but we need to find a strategy that works in each situation for effective living. They have found a formula for handling the stress of life, and we must find one for ourselves, as well, especially if a health crisis arises.

5. *We Need to Be Involved in Meaningful Employment or Satisfying Volunteer Roles to Keep Ourselves Active and Alive:* Our health and happiness levels are often tied directly to the fulfilling activity of paid employment or a volunteer role that uses our abilities and talents in the service of others. It is very satisfying to find a job that you enjoy and where you use your God-given skills. Many seniors are working longer today because they enjoy being employed. Hopefully, they have found employment, which challenges their abilities and gives those contacts that are fulfilling, as

well as being financially rewarding. Others have discovered the excitement and joy of helping as volunteers in an area of service they understand and have skills that can meet a real need. Either way, it is satisfying to feel useful and to find that we are making a contribution in a satisfying job or in helping someone in need.

Our retirement community, where I live and enjoy my own retirement, is known for its large number of volunteers who step up for every task imaginable. We have seniors who serve on our security patrol, the hospital staff, central management positions, with our emergency squad, and even in many teaching positions at our church college or library. They all benefit from the contacts they make daily, and our community is always enriched by their presence. So those older adults who choose to do nothing for others, but to stay home alone, or do only for themselves, are missing out on a critical opportunity in their lives. They have not learned that real enrichment comes when you are fully engaged in the work of earning a well-deserved income or being engaged in improving the lives of others by being a volunteer to meet real human need in your own community.

6. *It Is Very Meaningful to Have a Plan for the Creative Use of Our Leisure Time:* We are more fulfilled when we use our time and talent in the pursuit of healthy activities that we thoroughly enjoy. Most retirement communities have a heavy emphasis on providing many leisure-time options and activities. Most communities across the country have community centers where many crafts and creative activities are available. Busy and engaged older adults are rarely bored and are usually excited about their experiences and accomplishments. We noticed that the

excitement of involvement also exists when attending the senior games, such as golf, tennis, lawn bowling, biking, and most water sports. The lesson is clearly there: finding your place in the leisure world brings real fulfillment. The plea is obvious as well: avoid isolating yourself and living away from others. Get involved in an activity that challenges your mind, brings you great pleasure, and brings you joy in the contact with others. Keep interested and involved because it makes for a richer lifestyle.

7. *One Final Suggestion I Would Offer Is to Write Your Ideas about Your Growth Areas in a Treasured Notebook or Journal or Keep Them Stored on an Internet Account.* Create a proposed deadline for completion of the plans and then set new ones as needed. Sometimes sharing these ideas gives you encouragement and new thoughts. You might also welcome an occasion when friends and family are together and enlist their suggestions on the direction of your life. They might add ideas that never occurred to you when you planned your own future.

****

Now it is important to *highlight the kind of regular activity needed to keep you functioning at your best level of emotional health and well-being.* These attitudes and routines are necessary if you are to avoid the damage of personal neglect and high-level stress due to the demands of life in your world.

1. Develop the habit of positive or possibility thinking. Dr. Robert Schuller has written a wonderful book on the topic called *If It's Going to be Up To Me.* He maintains that we need to discover and respond well to "needs that must be filled . . . challenges that inspire us to act . . . problems

waiting to be solved . . . and pain that cries out for help." In other words, there is a host of things we can do if we envision a way to live a more fulfilling life. That is also the message that is highlighted in the recent emphasis on optimistic thinking in the new field of positive psychology. The key idea here is to maintain a positive outlook in your thinking and planning for a healthy lifestyle. We need to learn to practice mindfulness—the practice of living in the moment—and experience and feel a full range of good thoughts and emotions each day in our lives.

Seeing the value of being optimistic and hopeful is also part of this picture. It involves developing a spirit of gratitude for the blessings we share in our nation and in our communities at large. One other important emphasis is the recognition of our own personal strengths and positive qualities. Acknowledging them and building on these attributes can give us new confidence and satisfaction. Finally, savoring the good and beautiful in our world can also add to our joy and happiness. Not enough of us take time to just stop and notice the small and large factors that make our life very fulfilling. It can be as simple as enjoying the beauty of a sunrise or cloudbank in the sky. To make a habit of being positive and optimistic gives life much more joy and meaning. Positive thinking can make it happen, but it needs to be cultivated so that it becomes natural part of your life and experiences.

2. Another important reminder comes from the clues we have learned about stress management. Almost every day, we can depend on experiencing some stressful event or experience. It could come in the form of a telephone call, a near accident while driving, or even the visit of a family member. It is, nonetheless, very disheartening and

tension building. How we react to these ordinary events are a real challenge to us all. What we need to learn is self-control, the ability to not overreact to negative news, the skill to stay calm, along with the ability to make careful and responsible decisions. We need to rely on good judgment, the wisdom to weigh options, and to seek the advice of expert opinions. There are too few adults who are successful in coping with stress. It does not come easily, but handling the high pressures well in today's world is critical for our survival. So read and learn the skills and become proficient in coping with the pressures of today, and you will be a happier person and a valued member of your family circle. They will turn to you when things fall apart because you have discovered how to be the rock they can lean on when crisis comes and you know how to thrive.

3. Rid yourself of all the bad habits that many seniors bring with them into retirement. We need help to get rid of negative behavior that hurts us. Seniors must face the reality that these habits are hard to break, but necessary for health and well-being. You may need to consult your doctor about the issue or even seek a counselor to help you learn the means to break patterns that have held you in their grip for far too long.

4. Develop a healthy routine for each day that creates a level of rich satisfaction with your life and circumstance. It can bring structure to your life and give you comfort as we anticipate, then complete each task. Having meal times about the same time and location, doing routine household duties, completing work assignments, and maintaining a regular time for relaxation provides needed structure to our life. Part of that plan, however, needs to include a

vacation break so you get away from the demands of daily life. Most seniors visit relatives, travel to some appealing place for fun and recreation, or just take off to get engaged in a learning venture or retreat experience. This break in schedule brings new experiences, new joys and contacts, and a fresh look at the world around you.

It is worthwhile if we can find pride and pleasure in the tasks we undertake each day. On the other hand, it is also a positive practice to change our routine from time to time to add zest to life. Do daily jobs with an entirely different schedule. We have found value, also, in changing our home environment, such as moving your furniture location, putting up different drapes, or adding a fresh coat of paint on the walls. It gives new pleasure and new perspective to your daily tasks. Pleasant changes can bring new enjoyment. Find a pattern that fits your lifestyle and keep it going so you vary your routine and refresh the location where you live.

5. Brain health is an essential part of healthy adult. The aging brain, however, is an issue that needs our special attention. Unfortunately, a significant size of older adult succumbs to serious impairment in their brain function. They begin to forget, have problems making decisions, get confused while driving, and lose the ability to concentrate and organize. All of these losses make it difficult for the senior adult to function alone at all.

The good news is that there are reliable ways to hold on to our mental functioning and memory skills as we age. We can consciously remember names, places, and events by becoming more committed to retain our memory. Engaging in mental exercises and routines can stimulate our mental skills. A healthy lifestyle provides the positive benefit of being able to retain healthy mental functioning as well. Finally, reduce stress and anxiety, develop warm social contacts, and engage in stimulating community events to help us all keep more alert and content.

Sadly, most assisted living locations have what they call a "memory unit." It usually consists of numerous residents of a retirement community who has succumbed to dementia, usually of the Alzheimer's type. They will spend the rest of their lives in this locked facility with only a minimal amount of activity and shared interests. This is the end of the line for very worthy seniors who have simply "lost their mind." Take action now to not end in that same kind of confinement and limited living. Do everything you can to keep your mind healthy, active, alive, and a positive source for a fulfilled retirement.

6. Maintain pleasurable social contact that keeps you alert and satisfied with the friendships you enjoy. But learn to initiate these relationships on a regular basis, rather than waiting for others to always reach out to you for contact. Lively conversation and connections with others keep us alert and socially satisfied. It is part of the spice of life. Seniors also love the contacts with their extended family by phone or through a computer connection, such as the use of Skype or Facebook, which allow the users to maintain a live face-to-face connection or personal identity with each other at great distances. However you choose to do it, keep communication flowing with friends and family. If you do, they will be there for you when you need interest and support.

7. Engage in volunteer roles that make a significant emotional impact on the lives of others. You choose what is comfortable for your time and interest by picking an area of real need you can satisfy, like volunteering to help with the homeless, with the Red Cross, or your local church, etc. My favorite activity that is so appropriate for seniors is *intentional mentoring*. That means that I choose to offer my interest and time to help and befriend a much younger person(s) with sincere friendship. It is really surprising how many young adults are out there with no positive family connection or memory of a healthy family experience in their growing-up years. They need an older adult to take an interest in their lives and future. It may mean taking them to the ball game, sharing a birthday, helping to write a job resume, or giving them help with furnishing an apartment. Do what is the need of the moment, but become the loving person they need. You could help save a life and make a contribution to another person that will be life lasting. To find those needy people, call on a local social service agency, talk to a local clergyman, or just wait for the right opportunity to connect with someone your family finds. Either way, enjoy the helping experience. It can rejuvenate your life and give you rich satisfaction.

8. Plan recreational and leisure outings that bring joy to your daily activity. Picnics, a trip to the movies, going to a theme park, visiting the zoo, or even taking a long hike can bring the opportunity for enjoyable times together. Refuse to let work and responsibility become your only tasks in life. So take time to plan a month of social events in advance and work to keep your family calendar up-to-date. Most seniors in our community eat out often not to consume fine food, but primarily to socialize and to share their life with others

9. Work at the task of lifelong learning so we never stop growing as seniors. No matter how much formal education we have completed, we never run out of the need for new growth and understanding. There are always opportunities in every community to enrich yourself. Some seniors like to specialize with a focus on a single task like photography. Others like to take formal classes at a college. Many seniors like to learn new skills that involve crafts or handyman roles. In our circle of friends, they choose to take Bible study or participate in a Sunday-morning adult class at church. The Road Scholar Program (www.roadscholar. org) out of Boston offers opportunities around the world for seniors who want to study, learn, and discover new natural wonders in nearly every state in the United States or in most nations around the world where you prefer to travel.

10. Maintain open communication at all times between you who are marriage partners and for you who may be alone. Seek to create a wide circle of close friends. That means you need to practice telling others how you feel, what you need, and how you want to be treated. This process involves honesty and tactful conversations with others that may get tense or even blow into a major confrontation. Nevertheless, it is usually worth the encounter, so you can all be clear and understand the needs and convictions of one another.

Think for a moment about what the elements of real friendship are. It usually involves being honest, open, loving, patient, and maintaining a strong desire to be together. Be honest and open with everyone you meet. Try to handle the conflicts that come in all relationships with skill and consideration. Exercise positive thoughts and good feelings for everyone involved. Build a network of associations that benefits everyone. If married, develop the skill to be a good partner who is loving, sensitive, dependable, comfortable, and exciting.

11. Practice finding optimistic people. Clinical evidence supports the value of surrounding yourself with wholesome personalities. For instance, you can have a better day being with those who are positive and optimistic and are not overwhelmed with pessimism. You can learn to be a healthier person with a sense of hope and enthusiasm. Nevertheless, when we associate with those who maintain a constant tenor of bitterness and cynicism, it impacts our mood. They seem to view every situation with a bleak perspective. It is even hard to be with them because their dark attitude can become contagious. So I suggest you avoid those people and look forward to meeting and enjoying older adults who have a wholesome perspective. They are uplifting and inspiring to be with. You may choose to be with the beaten and forlorn if you want to help them deal with their struggles. If that is your life's mission, then do it well and choose carefully how you help them find a new and hopeful perspective on the world around them. You may even guide them slowly to seek professional help with a therapist.

12. Keep active and busy with your daily schedule. A senior friend of mine believes, as I do, that part of good health is to keep moving and to get out of the house every day, to engage in some meaningful activity. Seniors are in danger of falling into the trap of sedentary living, or sitting, resting, or relaxing to the exclusion of everything else. This lack of physical and social activity is not only hard on your health, but it becomes a damper on your spirit. Most

physicians will tell you that physical movement is critical for better blood pressure, good toilet habits, restful sleep patterns, and good muscular retention. The best advice I have heard from exercise physiologists is to find a healthy balance between rest, activity, and leisure pursuits.

13. Take time for meditation, relaxed reading, or listening to music, praying, or just enjoying a hobby that is fulfilling and restful. We need this time apart from the rush and responsibilities of the day. It is one of the great benefits of retirement. You might call it your time apart, to get in touch with yourself, and to focus on self-fulfillment. I have an Apple iPad I use for my quiet time. I can find the latest news, a biblical resource, a book to read, music to hear, and even computer games if I choose. My pleasure is to read the Bible or to share a devotional time together with my married partner, usually just before bedtime. Whatever is your real interest for leisure, pursue it with a passion and enjoy it to the fullest. It can bring freshness and enthusiasm into your life.

14. Finally, it is important that I close with suggestions about how we can avoid a decline in our emotional health and becoming one of the four Americans impacted by some mental disorder. Let me offer these key ideas: (1) Maintain positive thinking and acting as a basic attitude toward your daily tasks. Mental disorder starts to creep in with negative or distorted thinking. Bizarre behavior follows, and you are on the road toward mental illness and decline. (2) Do not fail to get professional help from a mental health professional if you are feeling out of control, extremely depressed, or highly anxious. Seniors are especially resistant to admitting the need for counseling because of our commitment to being self-sufficient at all times, but

that attitude is always self-defeating. (3) Stay physically and socially active. Avoid social withdrawal and self-pity. Few seniors who follow this formula get discouraged and easily offended. Learn to simply enjoy the experience of living life to the fullest and feast on the day. One last idea is to (4) learn skills that assist you to retain your memory and reasoning ability. We need to feel valued and useful to ourselves and others, so keeping as mentally alert as we can is critical to that goal. There are many new tools for brain health (parade.com/brain games) that we can find and use so there should be no hesitation from adopting the practice of keeping yourself mentally alert and responsive to the world all around us today. Brain health is a critical goal for senior living, and we should pursue it with a passion that never eases. Ways that work well are to keep reading, enroll in adult education courses, and join a discussion group to keep your mind challenged and alert.

Closing Comments about Our Emotional Well-being: It is critical that we look in-depth at the way we are living out our retirement years. Finding an emotional maturity, maintaining our mental health, and living with positive thinking are key elements in that process. This chapter has attempted to highlight this emphasis, but it is only a futile exercise if it does not change your thinking and your behavior. My hope is that somewhere I touched a chord or a light was turned on by something you read in this section. So be thoroughly honest with yourself and look at not just how you can maintain your physical health, but how you can become emotionally whole and happy with yourself and others. You can do all the things your doctor prescribes for retaining a healthy body and still miss the important ingredient of feeling right about your lifestyle. So make your emotional health, a happy you, a part of the whole process of making responsible life choices, now and into your fine future.

My most important advice to seniors who hunger for help in coping with the challenges in their daily life is to learn to cultivate *resilience*. That is the skill of being able to adapt well to the changes and the challenges of aging. We never know when a health problem might emerge, a friend may die, or some financial crisis might hit us. The people who are resilient are those who survive and *move on*. They have learned to bounce back, to not be overrun by crisis. One way to do that is to become more flexible and avoid rigidity. I have met so many seniors who are tight, controlled, and have a narrow mind-set. Their view is that there is only one set way to do tasks or to cope with issues. When that perspective does not work, they are lost and confused. It often happens when they lose a spouse. They are overwhelmed and discouraged, and they may remain that way for some time. On the other hand, the resilient senior who loses a partner has the capacity to move on fairly quickly and succeed in being alone. So it is a critical part of good emotional health to develop this ability. You will never suffer or feel incapable if you discover how to thrive by becoming more adaptable and flexible as you move along in your aging years.

Now a Real-Life Story of a Strong, Resilient Senior:

In the wonderful book by Wolin and Wolin, *The Resilient Self*, they tell about the quality of resilience in various people in troubled situations. They share how injured survivors "heal an injured self." They give case after case of people with strong adaptive skills surmounting amazing conflict and troubled situations. They found bitter or controlling family relationships a source of most of the intense conflicts experienced by the people they interviewed. What was interesting to find was how creative the victims of abuse were. They used several methods to deal with their troubled relationships, and among those were to leave a setting that was a quagmire, to go for counseling, to stop dwelling on the past, to use humor, to write poetry, to start to recognize their strengths, to learn creative alternatives, to gain new insight, to take strong initiatives, to discover fine values, and to find real love where it can be given.

They said that the real skill we all need to develop is "the capacity to rise above adversity by developing skills" that turn into lasting strengths that help us cope with the difficulties life brings to us all. Their book is a long record of how a variety of real people faced this dilemma and found creative ways to resolve the issues they had to face head on. That is certainly a lesson we all need to learn.

One of the issues we see developing all of the time in a senior community is the death of a loving marriage partner. In fact, we have a support group in our local church on adjustment to losses, and recently, our community opened what is called Grief Cafes to help people meet and to share their losses. The one common denominator is the reality that many life partners must now live alone. What we have found is the most emotionally and spiritually mature weather best. They seem to take it in stride and move on with their lives. Certainly, they have their days when the loss is overwhelming, but in general they are capable of adjusting to change. So it is a tribute to their inner strength that they can cope and manage their future when it becomes necessary to take that initiative. That quality could be also called resilience. It appears to be in good supply in those who have learned to be emotionally mature.

Supplemental Materials: (1) Keys to Emotional Health, (2) Positive and Negative Emotions, (3) Attitude, (4) Thought Diary Suggestions, and (5) Emotional Wellness.

Supplement 1, Chapter 3

KEYS TO DEVELOPING GOOD EMOTIONAL HEALTH

- Describing the best qualities for mental and emotional health

- Developing a feeling about a sense of contentment in life

- A zest for living and the ability to laugh and have fun in life

- The ability to deal with stress and bounce back from adversity

- A sense of meaning and purpose, in both activities and relationships

- The flexibility to learn new things and adapt to change around us

- A balance between work and play, rest and activity, etc.

- The skill to build and maintain fulfilling relationships, friendships

- Exhibiting self-confidence and high self-esteem with people

- Maintaining healthy extended family connections

- A commitment to moral and spiritual values which keeps you strong

1. What Seniors Do to Harm Their Own Emotional Health and Stability

- They are either too controlling or they neglect their extended family.

- They often fail to keep growing and learning about managing life.

- They neglect their mental skills and often fail to challenge their mind.

- They allow themselves to be overweight and under exercised.

- They let issues of the past haunt them and fail to resolve these concerns.

- They get into heavy drinking, abuse of prescriptive drugs.

- They do not respond well to their care-giving role and do self-harm.

- They do not realize the importance to finding a deep passion or interest.

- They are too often filled with boredom, indifference, and hopelessness.

2. How We Can Respond Better to the Stress of Life, Change, and Crisis

- Realize we need to develop our ability to be flexible and resilient

- Find and maintain a strong friendship circle and support system

- Develop a healthy optimism, a positive attitude, and a cheerful outlook

- Find a strong faith that sustains, guides, and challenges you every day

- Keep growing, learning, and discovering new joys in your daily living

- Read and learn new techniques and new approaches to solve old issues

- Create a strong network of supportive friends and family members

- Develop your self-confidence and self-worth so you feel strong self-esteem

- Learn patience, confidence, and hope that troublesome issues will be resolved

Supplement 2, Chapter 3

POSITIVE AND NEGATIVE
EMOTIONS IN SENIOR LIVING

List of Our Positive Emotions—List of Our Negative Emotions

1.	Self-confidence, self-love	Self-hate, feelings of incompetence
2.	Loving concern for others	Hate for others, rejects help
3.	Gladness and joy in living	Sadness and lack of joy in life
4.	Creativity, being innovative	Dullness and indifference to ideas
5.	Love of learning with others	Lack of interest in new directions
6.	Open-mindedness about change	Closed-mindedness about change
7.	Positive attitudes, optimistic	Negative attitudes, being hostile
8.	Shows strong courage	Cowardliness and fearfulness
9.	Curiosity about new discoveries	No interest in new discoveries
10.	Perseverance, determination	Real desire to give up easily
11.	Zest and enthusiasm	Passivity and indifference
12.	Expresses kindness to others	Avoidance to offer help for others
13.	Fairness in dealing with other	Lying and cheating is a norm
14.	Enjoying teamwork for tasks	Each person just takes care of no. 1

15.	Forgiveness of self and others	Holding a grudge, resentful
16.	Being cautious and prudent	Impulsive and defensive
17.	Being self-disciplined	Lack of discipline, being sloppy
18.	Gratitude and appreciation	No appreciation or thankfulness
19.	Ongoing hope and expectation	Pessimism and bitterness
20.	Humor and enjoying laughter	Always serious and very gloomy
21.	Feelings of awe being nature	Taking natural beauty for granted
22.	Wisdom and discernment	Shallow thinking and indifference
23.	Good decision-making skills	Acting without good judgment
24.	Being a true friend to others	Living alone, distrusting others
25.	Having a strong faith in God	Full of doubt, agnostic

Supplement 3, Chapter 3

ATTITUDE
by Charles Swindoll

The longer I live, the more I realize the impact of attitude on life. Attitude, to me, is more important than facts. It is more important than the past, than education, than money, than circumstances, than failures, than successes, than what other people think or say or do. It is more important than appearance, giftedness or skill. It will make or break a company, a church, a home. The remarkable thing is we have a choice every day regarding the attitude we will embrace all that day. We cannot change our past . . . We cannot change the fact that people will act in a certain way. We cannot change the inevitable. The only thing we can do is to play on the one string we have, and that is attitude.

—Charles Swindoll

Supplement 4, Chapter 3

THOUGHT DIARY: A Tool for Self-Improvement

Our thoughts determine our moods and our behavior. Therefore, mood and thought monitoring is important for all of us to do for our emotional health and well-being.

In these four stages, using a wire bound notepad or a three-ringed folder with lined pages, write your thoughts as follows:

Step One: Be clear about what you want to focus on or the problem you want to resolve.

You may want to simply describe the issue in detail and divide the subject into three components: your thoughts, your feelings, and your behavior.

Step Two: Describe the difficulty the problem is giving you in your life and the lives of others. Explain who or what is described as obstructing your personal happiness and your desire for a fulfilled life. Decide how your attitude and conduct is impacting others around you. What steps do you need to take to resolve the issue?

Step Three: List the attitudes and behavior you need to change about yourself. Realize that the greatest danger to personal growth is to project the blame on to someone else. Take personal responsibility for what you need to do to change yourself and the situation. Decide what steps you will make to resolve the issue in terms of new attitudes and conduct on your part.

Step Four: Describe the steps you will take to make the necessary changes in attitudes, beliefs, and new behavior. Realize you are defining the new self that you hope will emerge from your own growth in relationships. Set some time frames for what you will do to start with new attitudes and behavior. Record how others react to this new you and then define how you go forward into the new person you want to emerge.

Keep your *thought diary* and record what is happening with your new efforts at taking positive initiative to make changes in your life. Share your diary with some very important person in your life and celebrate together the positive changes you are now experiencing in your life and relationships. Keep on growing and responding in a new and wonderful way.

Celebrate the new *you* that emerges. If it worked this time, continue the process of personal and spiritual development all of the rest of your life. You will be pleased, and those who love you will truly enjoy the new person that they see emerging from this conscious act of self-improvement.

Supplement 5, Chapter 3

EMOTIONAL WELLNESS: A Resource Review

Exploring the Best Qualities of Emotional Wellness:

1. Being well adjusted to your environment and location

2. Reasonable worry free; enjoys life daily

3. Can handle the tensions and crisis of daily living

4. Generally he or she is free of fear, anxiety, distrust, and depression

5. Adheres to vital convictions and can make value choices

6. Maintains a core of strong values, supportive friends, and family

7. Adapts well to change and challenges in life

8. Feels a deep sense of positive self-worth and skill

9. Sees the importance of finding and maintaining the goal of living a life of holistic health in body, mind, and spirit.

What Prevents the Development of Emotional Health and Wellness?

1. The Environment: The bad history of experiences with people, the family, school, or on the job, which creates tensions and depression.

2. Physical Causes: Body chemistry may play a part of our dysfunction, such as brain injuries, aging issues, accident and falls, etc.

3. Heredity: There is a clear relationship between heredity and some forms of mental and physical illness.

4. Crisis Events: The major changes that come to life: the death of close friends or family, a job loss, marriage failure, or financial crisis can trigger emotional upheavals and distress.

5. Overwhelming Stress: Circumstances that cause heavy frustration, enormous pressure, excessive demands, and moral conflict can lead to emotional instability.

How Do We Maintain Emotional Health and Wellness?

1. Talk it out with someone you trust.

2. Get away to reflect, meditate, and pray.

3. Take one step at a time.

4. Decide on a responsible course of action.

5. Do something for someone else.

6. Work out your old fears and resentment.

7. Start to feel really good about yourself.

8. Keep yourself physically fit with a fitness plan.

9. Find a meaningful purpose and direction for your life.

10. Locate and join a faith-based community for support.

"There is great comfort and strength that come to
us as we worship and learn to serve the Lord"

CHAPTER 4

BUILDING A SPIRITUAL LIFE FOR A CHANGING WORLD

Researchers have shown that those who internalize
biblical teachings . . . have high levels of satisfaction
in life, a sense of well-being, and overall happiness.

—Walt Larimore,
10 Essentials of Happy, Healthy People

Let me begin this commentary on the value of spiritual
commitment and growth for senior living by first declaring
my Christian bias. I am a lifelong Christian and have trained
and been ordained as United Methodist minister. My faith
is key to my life, perhaps more so now that I am in my
senior years. But when I speak of the faithful, I am not just
referring to my Christian brothers and sisters, but to those
of you who are non-Christians but who have a faith focus in
their lives—Jewish, Muslim, Unitarian, etc. For those who
do not have a religion or a faith, perhaps this chapter will
help you to discover a spiritual path that calls out to you.
It is not unusual for people who have lacked faith or are
disconnected from their childhood religion to connect or
reconnect with one in their senior years. Vern Bengtson,

professor of gerontology and sociology at the University of Southern California, says, "Many of them don't know it yet, but growing old, regardless of what generation you belong to, brings on dramatic changes that can propel people to seek new meaning in religious services." Although studies on the baby boomers have not yet been conducted, Bengston believes they will react as earlier generations of retirees and return to a religious commitment.

Let me begin by commenting on the status of the Christian church today in America. What is happening is not welcome news, but a challenge and an opportunity. The church in America is in numerical decline! Yes, all the major denominations are suffering from membership losses. Fewer people are worshiping on Sunday morning. More people declare themselves as unaffiliated with any major denomination. There appears to be a rise of secularism. Atheists are becoming more aggressive in seeking recognition of their views and causes. More emphasis is being made in the political arena on freedom from regulations and on individual rights rather than the value of working together for the good of the whole. It seems that we are becoming a nation of self-seeking individuals who are focused more on personal fulfillment and on material gain, less on the values of love, faith, and community.

In the light of these trends, I maintain there has never been a time when we needed a stronger spiritual life more than today. In fact, there is equal evidence that Americans still have a strong faith in God and have a spiritual hunger and need for the power of an active faith, although they are not as related to the institutional church as we were in our earlier generation. They realize the great value of a spiritual life, and yet, they are seeking to meet that need in non-conventional ways. The mega church movement or large non-affiliated local churches are developing rapidly across our country to fill the gap. The use of meditation as a resource for comfort, ease of mind, guidance, and building confidence is expanding rapidly. The chaplaincy program in the Armed Forces is alive and well and serving our servicemen and women all over the world. The hunger for Christian reading materials is strong in and out of the local church community. The Bible is still the most popularly published book across our county and across the world at large. Christian schools and colleges have record enrollments. People pray all the time because they feel helpless and confused, so they turn to the guidance of God through prayer. The focus on teaching moral and spiritual values in our colleges and universities is still a strong emphasis.

So let me begin now by describing in some detail what a strong spiritual focus can do for each of us to support and strengthen our daily lives. My assumption is that we need to understand the values of focusing on a spiritual center in our lives if we are going to enjoy a fruitful and fulfilling life. Look now to the following comments and discover how a strong faith and spiritual connection to God can enrich each of us in our daily activity, if we only choose to make this emphasis a central part of our world:

1. To focus on our spiritual life means we concentrate on seeking to know and do the will of God. This reality is best expressed by being in a worship setting with other seekers and by enjoying the warmth and love of a faith community. For Christians, this is why Jesus established the Christian church as a place of focus for believers to gather, to share the scriptures, and to hear the biblical message preached and taught to people of faith. We are enjoined, however, to not only come to worship God, to

be instructed in how to live out our Christian faith, but we are commissioned to share that faith with the world around us. We also are to act out on what we believe and to live daily by the moral values that are taught in our local churches. Other religions share similar principles, such as Jewish congregations, who gather to study the Torah, to pray, and to do good works in the world and live moral lives.

In Judaism, the emphasis is on the sovereignty of God and his power over His people. For Jews, their emphasis is heavily on the traditions of their faith, the biblical history of their people, and the loyalty of their members to keep their holy holidays and their core beliefs in a holy and righteous God. They are still looking for a prophet to lead them to the promised land they long to find. For other world religions, like Mohammedanism or Judaism, their core beliefs and practices bind their communities of faith together. They seek diligently to honor their religious traditions and to find the comfort of a strong faith. These different faith communities also maintain that their core members richly benefit from enriched faith-centered lives.

2. There are many reports in the media about the inherent values of a faith-based life. People who have a strong faith and seek to live out their beliefs have a healthier life; they ward off physical health problems more successfully; they live longer; and they are more motivated to serve the needs of others. My contention is that they are also happier individuals, and they are more satisfied with their daily choices. In addition, they are better able to cope with the changes and the losses in life that come to us all far too often. These benefits are true because the major emphasis on all world religions is on faith, love, service to others,

and living out a moral life. People of faith are enjoined to act as ministering angels for those in need. It is so good to witness that reality in books, videos, movies, and in dramatic stories in the daily newspapers and the public media. It is the evidence we need that a vital faith works for the good of the individual, and it strengthens the life of an active community.

3. If we are people of faith, our faith needs to challenge us to become aware of the rich value of living a life with sound spiritual values. So honesty, integrity, trustworthiness, kindness, dependability, and loving concern for others in need are more than just words. They take on real meaning in the activity of the believer's daily relationships. That is why it is not uncommon to hear stories in the newspaper about the great support people of faith offer others in critical situations. People of faith are enjoined to act as ministering angels for the many people in need all around them. It is so good to witness that reality in books, videos, movies, and in dramatic stories in the daily newspapers and the public media. It is the evidence we need that a vital faith works for the good of the individual, and it strengthens the life of an active community.

4. Men and women of faith are also divinely guided to take certain courses of action. For the Christian believer, it is the action of the Holy Spirit or the activity of God giving them ideas and a sense of direction they need to take in making important decisions in their lives. They feel guided in their thoughts and actions. We all have choices to make concerning the direction we choose to take in our personal circumstances. For believers, there is this great and rich source of divine help when a troubled decision needs to be made or a relationship needs to be resolved. It

usually comes as a result of prayer, meditation, or reading scriptural passages, but it can come in a worship service or in the office of a spiritual adviser or home of a beloved friend. Nevertheless, God does not leave us alone. He is there to help us along life's way if we learn to listen to his still, small voice in our hearts and minds. He does guide us if we are just patient and trusting.

5. We need to become more aware of how our country has been the benefactor of the compassion of great men and women of faith. They have founded colleges and universities, great hospitals and health care clinics, social service agencies, research projects, and even homes for disabled senior citizens. Much of the vast social system of service to others that is part of the fabric of our American life is due to the leadership of religious leaders who saw a need to help and who responded to that need. America is richer and better off by far because of the faith communities' loving concern for the lost and troubled among us. They responded to meet the needs of a growing nation and offered a valiant service for the future of our country, sometimes at great cost to themselves

6. It is important to remember that we are better marriage partners, more sensitive parents or grandparents, better friends, and better neighbors because we are people of faith. It is my firm conviction that we can measure the quality of people's lives by the amount of faith they affirm. The authentic faithful among us go about every day doing the good work and serving their god with faithful obedience. They are the quiet believers who simply live out their faith in the ordinary activity of daily living: being kind to others, forgiving the offender, guiding the lost souls

around us to find a faith, and taking action when evil forces start to take hold. They are the true believers.

- Now that we have established the values of a faith-based life, it is equally important that we review in-depth about how we can develop that lifestyle for ourselves in our senior years. In fact, as people age and move into retirement, they do seem more open and receptive to a message about spiritual growth. They are more conscious of their aging and that death is nearer than ever before. They are more responsive to the message of the religious leaders about preparing for an eternal life. Here are some key ideas about how to keep faith alive in your life:

1. Make a strong and firm commitment to the articles of faith your church or synagogue highlights as its core beliefs. Study them and live by the core values that guide your fellowship. For it is critical that we become active in our faith community and offer ourselves as volunteers in some area of service, in addition to making a sizable gift of financial support for the work of the local church or synagogue's program of service to others. The bottom line is that there is great value for us if we make our faith community's primary message the center of our daily lives.

2. Learn to become more disciplined in living by your faith in all your decisions and relationships. That means you establish patterns of obedience in which you learn more about your faith, establish habits that help you grow, and seize opportunities to witness your faith to others. You attend adult classes and special seminars or retreats to help you grow spiritually. Illustrations of these healthy patterns include starting a Bible reading program, engaging in daily

devotions with a devotional guide, keeping a personal journal about your spiritual growth, reading spiritual books and literature, subscribing to a religious magazine or enjoying a spirit-centered website, or joining a support group or adult class for personal growth. All of these things can help you grow in your faith, rather than to leave yourself stagnant and uninformed. Lack of involvement gets you nowhere. So get yourself actively involved in a faith-based community.

3. Discover the value of actively volunteering with your faith community. Many seniors feel more useful when they give their time and talent to a cause. Just recently, we had a strong need for help with a ministry for children and youth in our senior church community. Our pastor felt we should be a senior-focused local church with a ministry to the whole family. So we are now reaching out to the communities of young families living just outside of our senior residential area. We are thrilled that so many seniors have stepped up and are now active volunteers to help provide Christian education and activity for young people near the age of their own grandchildren. The seniors are involved and feel useful and needed in an exciting new ministry.

4. Start seeking answers for many of the faith issues that may have troubled you for years. Certainly, for senior adults, the issue of how to spiritually prepare for death and dying is critically important. The whole question about spiritual healing needs to be explored as well, so you know what, how, and when to pray for family or friends in need for healing after a major health crisis or how can we grow spiritually or understand the Bible with more clarity and how it applies to our daily lives. Usually, a church in your

community will have a support group or study group that explores faith issues, so join one to develop a good understanding about important moral issues that still trouble your life. Be assured that finding real answers to important faith-centered questions is a very beneficial task for everyone. Do not neglect this vital decision in your own faith journey.

5. Finally, we do need to realize how a faith-focused life can change you and bring out the best of your human potential. People of deep faith have always been my mentors over the years. They have shown me by their words and deeds how to live out my life. People with strong religious values have been leaders in our country and have contributed to the greatness that is the best expression of the American dream. People within the faith community have shown great compassion for causes in the community that need to be addressed, like services for the homeless and troubled members of our inner cities. Very frequently people with a strong trust in God often share how they have addressed a troubled relationship, a financial issue, a bad marriage, or even a health breakdown by turning to their faith for support and strength. More than not, they have shared that their personal trusting relationship in God has made the critical difference in finding the solution to these issues. They recognize that a faith-centered focus has often been a life-saver.

Let me close these comments on building our spiritual lives by telling you that there is countless evidence in real-life stories about the helpful working of a vital faith. I would like to point out just three popular printed resources where Christian stories appear in print. I will list the reference and then quote a small section from each one to illustrate the value of engaging in quality reading as a vital resource and encouragement to help us all develop a rich Christian faith for today's troubled world.

1. *Guideposts* magazine (Box 5814, Harlan, Iowa, 51593) offers a series of very wonderful true stories of living faith in people in every walk of life. I like the section on "What Prayer Can Do" and the other special feature on "Mysterious Ways: More Than Coincidence." A recent issue featured Robin Roberts, an anchor for *Good Morning America*, who tells about how her mother has been her real inspiration over her entire life. Her story is about how her mother, who is eighty-eight, came through the Great Depression and the Civil Rights Era and still survived. She shared that her mother, Lucimarian Roberts, has even written and published her own life story in the book, *My Story, My Song*. Robin concludes her article with this wonderful quote: "Mom's right. We sing the melody to our life's song, but the people who touch us provide the harmony. And understanding it all, guiding us and supporting us, is the rhythm of our faith."

2. *The Upper Room* devotional guide (Palm Coast Data, PO Box 430235, Palm Coast, Florida 32143) is a popular daily devotional guide that has been published around the world for many years, in thirty-seven languages. The July–August 2012 issue tells about a weeklong spiritual retreat each year called Soul Feast in the mountains of North Carolina, sponsored by the guide. The publisher told about her family friend, Mabel Harris Webb, age ninety-three, who attended the retreat. She said about Mabel, "Anyone who has met Mabel can't help but notice she is lit from within by Christ's love. Every time I'm with her I leave wanting the joy she seems to so effortlessly

exude." She says she practices the disciplines of prayer, meditation, and service daily. She is still seeking, however, other ideas about how to find tangible ways to strengthen her faith. For Mable, every moment is an opportunity to praise God, and she does it in all of her daily contact, even when she talks on the phone. People share that they see her as a living example of a true Christian life.

3. *Our Daily Bread* is another example of a very popular daily devotional guide (RBC Ministries, PO Box 2222, Grand Rapids, Michigan 49501). What is so unique about this publication is that it is not only free, but it has three sections for every day of the year: a wonderful true story, a scriptural reference, and a section called "Insight," which highlights the lesson taught. In a recent issue entitled "Tear Down that Wall," the author talks about tearing down the wall between East and West Germany some fifty years ago. The wall was torn down, and now the two German divisions are one. He suggested that we need to take down our own wall of indecision that prevents us from accepting God's gift of a life in Christ. He even referred to the scripture of Ephesians 2:14–18. In the "Insight" section, the writer said that Jesus Christ has shattered the dividing wall between Jew and Gentile and has promised that all of us can be one people of a living faith.

Before I close this chapter, let me add this item: Listing some of the best qualities that appear to be the product of a faith-focused life. My contention is that not only does a life centered in a vivid faith in God help us cope with life more effectively, but it helps us become warm and caring human beings in the process. These appealing evidences are the products of a life focused on serving God with our whole heart, mind, and daily conduct. We could ask ourselves if we exhibit these qualities in our own lives, and if not, why not now, and if not now, when do we make it happen in our own lives? So let me examine these personal qualities that challenge you, the reader, to measure your own life by what you believe and how you live out your faith in your daily life:

1. Being a loving, caring, and compassionate man or woman in all our relationships is evidence of a spiritual life. Many images flood my mind when I mention this quality of warm concern for others: the nurse who spends extra hours watching over an ill or dying patient when no family chooses to visit; the man who jumps into the cold ocean water to save another man floundering for help; or the family who invites a homeless man to dine with them on a cold December night. You can add your own memories of people of faith who have gone beyond the call of duty to show loving concern for a stranger in need. Illustrations of self-giving lives are everywhere. Therefore, put your faith in daily service for others.

2. Being a pray warrior who daily offers prayers for the needs of people within the church family, for people who are sick and suffering in the community, and for a world in conflict and turmoil. You could argue that this is just unnecessarily wasted time, but I contend this is an essential ministry of the Christian believer. We need to practice intercessory prayer as part of our Christian discipline. Learn, as well, to celebrate as your prayers are answered and healing occurs. It is a discipline that we all need to practice as a part of our daily routine. It is a natural outlet in the caring ministry of Jesus Christ.

3. Being a person who supports his or her church or synagogue with your gifts, talents, and service demonstrates what you

believe. You could ask yourself why be just an observer when you can get fully in helping your faith community come alive. What the local church or synagogue really needs is for you to fully immerse yourself in its outreach to the world. Willing volunteers are needed to use their special talents and to offer a financial contribution. People who invest themselves that way have been the lifeblood of vital Christian churches and synagogues. They are the spiritual army that makes vital services happen. My experience also is that as we give, we also receive. We are blessed, in turn, as we share our life and resources to meet the needs of the church and the many mission programs it supports in our country and around the world. We can rejoice over the fact that we a part of a vital ministry to mankind.

4. Being a positive spiritual witness who is happy, optimistic, hopeful, and kind can be a powerful advertisement for the benefits of a faith-filled life. I see these people all the time in our local church, but the people outside the fellowship of the church community may not find them readily. They are there in the world doing what God wants them to do with their daily lives. It means that they call on a sick neighbor, visit a hospital patient, care for a house when the homeowner is away, or offer a needed ride to the doctor without fanfare. These are the worker bees that provide quietly the little duties that are necessary to keep a neighborhood alive and well. This is where people of faith show their true colors of concern for the welfare of their community. This is an expression of kindness for others, and it is one of the best qualities of our faith-based outreach to the world.

5. Being a person that does not let anger, hostility, prejudice, cruelty, or bitterness take over a life is a strong evidence of a true Christian life. The true believer deals with those negative qualities and conquers any tendency to be motivated by negative feelings. Of course, people of faith are not perfect human beings. They have flaws like everyone else, but they are conscious of their own weaknesses, and they earnestly seek to overcome them. It is a commendable quality of the faith community members that they are open to seeking to move on to human perfection, even though they never may attain it. We know we need to continue to grow and develop our lives, and with God's help, we can live better lives with the support of our faith and community.

6. Being a person that takes your faith with you in the workplace or in a volunteer role can make a difference. These are men and women who live out their moral convictions in delicate situations where moral issues are being tested. Business leaders are facing moral questions almost every day. They desire to be leaders who have strong moral values that can guide our business communities in their times of testing. Even in our volunteer roles, there are questions of right and wrong that have to be answered. Being a Christian in the world today is tough and demanding, but the best of our moral witnesses do not shrink when they are put to the test. They stand for real principles in a day when moral relativism is a common practice. Their desire is to be a strong force that seeks to build more concern for good values and maintains a consistent desire to help people in need. For example, the simple principle that honesty is the best policy is not just an old acumen beta daily value that is honored in the lives of those who hold to strong Christian principles.

7. Being a person who is full of gratitude for his or her life and for the blessings that life has brought in your older years is in the mind of every true believer. Being a grateful person means that you have not taken the wonderful life we lead in America for granted. All you have to do is to travel to several countries across the world (as we have done) and make a comparison. Go to the impoverished nations of Africa especially, and look at their lifestyle. You will find that housing, food, transportation, employment, health care, and leisure-time pursuits are grossly different (or lacking) in the African continent. In addition, one of the most appealing advantages of living in our country is the freedom to live up to your best potential and to achieve your fondest dreams. Be thankful for the many privileges we have here and offer prayers of thanksgiving for the continued blessings we experience every day in the United States of America. If you live in other democratic nations, be grateful, as well, for the freedoms and privileges you share with others. It is still a rare nation that gives real freedom and economic opportunity for its average citizen to enjoy so they can achieve his/her best human potential.

Finally, my hope is that you are a person who believes that God answers prayers, helps to guide us in our daily choices, and even shows his love so well we need never feel alone. My strong belief is that God created the world; He loves us so much He gave his only begotten Son to redeem mankind; and that He continues to minister to us day by day. That kind of God does *not* leave us helpless in our critical need for help in making choices, in finding the right direction for our life, and in deciding between right and wrong. So develop that close relationship with God, especially as we see Him in Jesus Christ, and keep close to Him through prayer, meditation, writing, nature walking, worship service, service to others, and even in fasting. He will help you especially in your biggest task: making responsible life choices in a time of moral confusion and political uncertainty. You can have a very good and fulfilled life, even a happy and contented one, but it requires that you find the right pathway to that great end goal. The first and best step is to find your center in a vital personal faith in a loving and caring God, as we see Him best revealed in Jesus Christ. The rest of your life will unfold better with that good beginning.

Summary Comments on Maintaining a Vital, Living Faith: Maintaining a vital spiritual life involves daily choices. As a therapist with years in the counseling room, I can state categorically that we cannot do well as human beings in managing our lives alone. We are weak and lonely in our pursuit of happiness. We need the vital contribution that a living, realistic faith can bring us, along with the supportive help of a faith-centered community. If we try to handle life's challenge with our own sheer will and determination, it simply does not work. We need a strong spiritual life to help us live out our lives, so make this emphasis a critical part of a wholesome, healthy lifestyle.

Participate in some spiritually centered growth group or Bible study. Use daily devotions as a regular daily exercise. Talk about your faith and witness to your faith with others. Attend your local church or synagogue and become an active volunteer in the life of that rich community. So I plead with you to include a faith focus in your daily life. Be truly committed to deepen your devotional life and in living as a real witness in your contact with others. It is really worth the effort. The benefits of a faith-filled life continue throughout your lifetime.

Here is Evidence in a Real-Life Story:

Billy Graham says in his latest book, *Nearing Home*, that the "greatest legacy you can pass on to your children and grandchildren is not your money or the other material things you have accumulated in life . . . it is the legacy of your character and your faith." In giving that statement serious thought, let me suggest you consider your own legacy and that of your parents or grandparents.

My parents were simple Iowa small-business owners and farm managers. My father had only an elementary education, while my own mother had two years of college, but both of them succeeded admirably in their marriage and careers. They raised three boys in a small town and attended the local Methodist church faithfully. Their values were straightforward: Love and serve God; be honest in business and relationships; love our country and be proud of our heritage as a nation and your connection with your extended family. The impressions they left me as the eldest son were as follows: (1) Your faith is central to life, and they reinforced that by worshiping in church every Sunday. (2) Give your time and talents to the work of the Lord, so my father served as the head of the Building Committee of the new church building, while my mother busied herself serving actively and taking leadership in the local women's society. (3) Maintain a strong family connection by keeping close contact with our extended family members during many of the national holidays. It is a heritage that served me well, and I treasure the memories of a stable family life, especially as I married and raised my own children.

What is the legacy you can remember about your family? Were the spiritual values real and vivid? If those roots were rich and meaningful, have you modeled them for your own adult children and grandchildren? If your memories were not pleasant and commendable, you need to consider how you will choose to model a better lifestyle for your loved ones today. Either way, consider what legacy you want to leave behind when you pass away. Lay plans to leave a mark they will never forget, at least in the area of a life well lived, and a faith in God. Sometimes family reunions can be a choice opportunity to build memories of family ties and share the values and life experiences that have meant a great deal to each of us. My wife and I have many friends who gather together from across the country with their many relatives for special occasions, such as a fiftieth wedding anniversary. They always seem to have a special time when precious memories of the past are shared and best wishes are always passed around. It is always a period when younger children or teen-agers can be introduced to the history of that family unit. They learn to appreciate the values and experiences very particular family members treasure most.

What is happening in these gatherings is that these young children and youth are learning to appreciate and understand the lifestyles of their extended family. They are beginning to value their extended family and to feel accepted and incorporated into the larger family circle. It is an essential process to keep the network of family connections alive and well. So if you do not maintain a family-togetherness time, you might want to take responsibility to bring them together for a family reunion. It can build ties and offer rich experiences that will be remembered by many over their lifetimes. Here is where family worship, group prayers, and sharing of your faith can also be scheduled and enjoyed by the whole family unit, and it can enrich the lives of all who participate.

Supplemental Materials: (1) Data on the Values of Maintaining a Spiritual Life, (2) Article on a Faith-Filled Life, (3) Seek to Prevent Elder Abuse and Emotional Neglect (Facing a Serious Moral Issue), and (4) Help in Making Right Choices.

Supplement 1, Chapter 4

DATA ON THE VALUES OF MAINTAINING A SPIRITUAL LIFE

A strong faith has always been given a positive report by those who do polling. So here is the good news about the value of being a spiritual person over your lifetime: People with a religious commitment usually have fewer symptoms of a mental or physical disorder. They tend to have reduced risks to various diseases, including cancer or even coronary heart disease. For those who attend weekly religious services, they have a one-third less death rate than those who attended less often. The researcher found that women with strong religious beliefs recover faster after hip replacement than those who had a less of a real religious commitment.

The investigation as to why a strong faith seems to improve overall health revealed that certain factors were present: (1) People who attend weekly worship services find that they are a part of a supportive community with shared values and with an emphasis on loving relationships. (2) People who participate in religious organizations are encouraged to engage in healthy practices that produce better health, such as regular exercise, eating better food, and avoiding cigarettes and the heavy use of alcohol; in teens, they are less likely to use illicit drugs than their contemporaries. (3) People with positive values and beliefs tend to be those with a strong willingness to grow. They are more satisfied with their lives, so they have less anxiety, depression, and mental illness. (4) People who have a strong faith practice prayer and meditation, which are valuable forms of personal health care. It helps them relax and to deal more effectively with troublesome issues.

It seems important to conclude from the comments of hospital chaplains that people of faith do have a more successful recovery from illness when they have a strong religious faith and trust in God. If they have a church connection, the recovery is enhanced also because people from the faith community come to the hospital to offer love and support for those who are suffering. Having a strong faith is also a strong factor in the successful recovery from surgery and hospitalization.

Reference: Consumer Report on Health, June 1998, pp. 7–8

Supplement 2, Chapter 4

KEY BELIEFS IN A FAITH-FILLED LIFE

There is great value in believing in and living a faith-filled life. The way we do that well is to hold on to some fundamental beliefs that guide our daily choices. Here are some vivid beliefs that will help you live out that faith-filled life:

1. We live in the presence of God, our Creator and Sustainer, every day of our lives. We meet him in our daily prayer and communion with the Holy Spirit.

2. We are totally dependent upon His love and care for us as we seek His wisdom and guidance for the living out of our lives.

3. Belief in the community of faith, the fellowship of Christian believers, who gather for worship and who express their faith in action by ministering to the needs of the world.

4. Belief in the value and understanding of the Holy Scriptures as the primary source for the true understanding of the nature and will of God in our unfolding lives.

5. Belief that our lives should be examples of Christian character so we can set a standard of faith and conduct for others to follow: A strong belief in being the intentional disciples of Jesus Christ.

6. Belief that we are to love our neighbors as ourselves and to pray for our enemies without ceasing. Belief that we need to engage in charitable acts of good will to help relieve the pain and the suffering of those around us in need.

7. Belief in a Christian marriage relationship of one man and one woman who are committed to living out their lives of faith in a strong family relationship of love and devotion.

8. Belief in the opportunity of Christian parents to raise their children in the love and obedience to a living God. Belief in the value of nurturing our children so they grow up with a strong faith and a moral life.

9. Belief in the value of setting goals for our future and in achieving those goals that challenge us and are goals that enhance our skills and contribute to the welfare of mankind.

10. Belief in renouncing evil thoughts and deeds that destroy good will and undermine the lives of others.

Supplement 3, Chapter 4
(Here We Are Facing a Serious Moral Issue)

SEEK TO PREVENT ELDER ABUSE
AND EMOTIONAL NEGLECT

One of the issues too-seldom discussed in senior communities is the amount of personal and emotional neglect that exists in many forms. It could be the abuse and rejection of a married partner. It may happen in a whole neighborhood when a family is shunned or avoided because of their race, religion, or lifestyle. Sometimes, it impacts on the life of a disabled adult who has difficulty with mobility or care of a home or property. In the most blatant form of abuse, an older senile adult can be neglected and physically harmed by extended family members who may feel embarrassed by the presence of this adult or burdened by the support this dependent adult requires.

Elder abuse means the infliction of physical, emotional, or psychological harm to the older adult. It can take the form of avoidance, social criticism, physical injury, or restraint. It is seldom ever justified and almost always harmful to the affected party. Abuse can also be expressed by social isolation, financial exploitation, sexual abuse, and physical neglect. Whatever form it assumes, it is elder abuse, and it needs to stop and not reoccur. There are better ways to cope with conflict or tension in relationships.

Abuse most frequently occurs when family or friends move in together. The close proximity of contact can accelerate tense personal relationships. Even caregivers can be abusive if they are drug users or are offended by the behavior of some older seniors. Sometimes the stress of the moment, emotional instability of the attending party, or bizarre behavior of the older adult can cause an explosion of hostile feelings and emotion.

To prevent elder abuse, take these important steps: (1) recognize the rights of disabled seniors to be treated with respect and kindness, despite their own conduct; (2) help secure the best medical and psychological care available for the affected party; (3) offer respite care by arranging for someone else to manage the frail adult for an appropriate period to give the family a break and help relieve tension; and (4) social contact and activity can help reduce conflict and frustration of the dependent senior under supervision. Of course, counseling for the whole family where elder abuse has occurred would be the recommended procedure to follow. Prayers for wisdom and guidance are also always helpful as well.

Supplement 4, Chapter 4

HELP IN MAKING RIGHT CHOICES IN LIFE

Psalms 119:105, "Your word is a lamp to my feet, and a light to my path." God's Word is the Christian's guide for making Godly, successful choices in life. Before you make your decisions, compare your desires to what the scriptures say and ask yourself the following questions:

1. Would you be able to ask God to bless it? Would your decision be something that you can take before God with a good conscience and ask Him to bless it? Or is it something that you know the Lord would not be enthused about?

2. Could you thank Him for it? Would your decision be something that you can openly express gratefulness and thankfulness to God? Or would it be something that would seem inappropriate to thank him for?

3. Would it be to God's Glory? Would your decision be something that can bring glory and honor to the Lord ask yourself how the Lord would be lifted up or be blessed by your plans.

4. Would it be of the world? Would your decision be an indulgence in worldly, carnal appetites, or lusts?

5. Would it be a stumbling block to others? How would your decision affect the lives of your brethren in Christ? Even if you don't feel it's wrong, could it offend or harm the sensitive faith of those who don't share your convictions?

6. Would it be a weight or hindrance? Would your decision be something that would drag down your Christian life or influence you toward disobedience to God?

7. Would it please God or man? Whom do you hope to please by your decision? Will it bring pleasure to God, or will it only appease self or man?

8. How would the devil react? Would your decision or actions be considered a victory or a defeat by the devil's forces? Would hell celebrate your choice as a fulfillment of Satan's desires, or would the enemy be angry and disturbed by your decision?

9. What would the consequences be? What kind of long-term ramifications would you have to face for your decision? Remember, God will forgive sin and poor judgment, but you may have to live with the results of your decision for the rest of your life.

10. Would it edify you? Would your decision or actions bring you closer to God or pull you father away?

11. Will it edify the Lord, or will it weaken your confidence or the Lord's strength in your life?

Section Reference: An article by Dr. Dale A. Robbins

"Finding and enjoying friendship is one of the greatest pleasures of retirement living."

CHAPTER 5

ACQUIRING GOOD SOCIAL SKILLS AND PLANNING LEISURE ACTIVITY

> While Americans value independence and autonomy
> across their lives, they also value a sense of belonging,
> friendship, and being known . . . Decades of social
> science scholarship examines the positive effect of
> social ties across the life (cycle).
>
> —Meika Loe,
> *Aging Our Way.*

One issue that is often neglected in discussions about senior living is the sheer failure many seniors exhibit with their social life. More men than women come to a new senior community and fail to reach out aggressively to find and retain new friends. In fact, it is a critical problem in our retirement center when seniors come to retire in Florida or Arizona. They usually need to start all over with building their friendship base and professional contacts after they arrive here. This task seems so overwhelming for many new retirees; they simply give up and move back to their old hometown or withdraw into self-pity or social isolation.

It is also not uncommon for new widows in retirement to comment that their core of coupled friends no longer call or seek them out. They do not fully realize that our society is a couple-oriented world, and it functions that way for all of the time. No offense is intended when couples do not relate often with single seniors when a social occasion is planned. Single seniors simply have a new status, and they need to recognize that and fit into this different social world. There are single groups everywhere that welcome single adults into their membership, but you need to be adaptable to make that happen. Frequently, older seniors retreat into self-pity and remorse when they lose a spouse. They need to understand how important peer support is for them so they can meet their needs for social contact and support. They will find real value if they decide to reach out to find new social outlets for singles. It is part of the changing reality of senior living.

Social acceptance and the friendship of others are critical for a healthy and a happy life. It is becoming more common in our digital age when we shelter ourselves at our computer or move often to a different job, that sheer loneliness takes over. We are becoming a nation of strangers who are frequently out of touch with each other's lives. Reports from several keen observers note that there is more social isolation, single living housing, and depressed adults who have fewer valued contacts with others. They lack, as well, friends and trusted colleagues in the work world or community where they live. Even seniors who have lost a spouse, never married, or are divorced, understand how hard it is to start to build a body of new single friends. Often the burden of loneliness takes over.

Another time when social loss and isolation occurs is when an older adult becomes disabled. They readily discover that their physical limitations curtail their ability to attend many social occasions. As a result, too many of these adults, with limited mobility, simple retreat into their homes and maintain only a few contacts with the world they knew before their setback. Caregivers need to offer more assistance for the dependent adult and to devote more time to nursing care. Many people with limited physical ability, however, *have* learned to reach out to others in amazing ways. They do phone frequently and have engaged in lengthy phone connections; they can use the Internet for news and information, and then keep up-to-date with their companions by e-mail or Facebook; and some make physical contact with mobile devices and with the use of vans equipped with wheelchair access. Many courageous seniors with disabilities have refused to be isolated because they want to be fully involved with others. There are a number of ways many seniors fail to build a social network and its loss in their lives can have a great impact: The brief listing below is illustrative of some of the sad social deficiencies that are evident in the lives of many seniors. They have failed to succeed to find healthy social outlets for themselves, and the results of that loss is clearly evident in the two summary columns that follow:

Personal Acts of Social Immaturity	*The Damage to Their Lifestyle*
Intense and persistent shyness	Few people know who they are
Hostile and belligerent behavior	People get hurt and stay away
Suspicious attitude, distrust	No trust and confidence in others
Shifting eyes and restless body	Others feel very uncomfortable
Embarrassed being overweight	Friends observe their discomfort

Self-centered focus on himself	He does not get to know anyone
Radical social critic of leadership	Seldom does anyone agree
Appears bored and indifferent	Drives others away
Desire to dominate and control	People don't want to be controlled
Insecure and weak personality	Others are not drawn for friendship

You can see by the listing above that it is critical we develop our social skills and make positive social interaction a part of a healthy lifestyle. We are seldom satisfied if we are drawn into regular contact with anyone who has the characteristics in the first column above. You can see, therefore, that it is very important that seniors continue to develop into warm, loving, and sociable human beings who are attractive and easily accepted by others. If they have any social deficiency, that issue needs to be addressed and resolved. Here is a place where being in a support group, going to a licensed counselor, or visiting with a local clergy person would be very appropriate. You need to evolve into the kind of person that cultivates a warm and rewarding social acceptance with family and friends. It is an essential part of our makeup as senior adults, and we need to continue to develop that part of ourselves. We must pay attention to adding the social skills we are missing to our lives because we need that quality of personality for a happy life in our church family, our friendship circle, and in our community relationships.

Now let me move to describe in detail some of the best ways we can learn to express our social needs for a healthy contact with others in our senior world today. These are positive suggestions and illustrations about how we can make good choices that will enhance our social lives and build ties with others that can last a lifetime:

1. *Develop family ties that enrich your daily living experiences and last to the end of your life:* It is important to put time and effort to keep family ties alive and well. Now is the time to face and overcome old animosities that have lingered far too long. This is the time to cultivate a loving marriage relationship and learn to celebrate milestones together. Here is the time and opportunity to support your adult children and grandchildren with frequent contact. We can do that through letters, e-mail contact, the use of regular phone calls, and even finding ways to use Skype or Facebook for establishing a video contact where each person sees and interacts with the one who called. Helping with financial support, offering goods, used clothing, or household furniture or appliances are other tangible ways your struggling families can receive assistance. Whatever avenue you choose, it can bring rich rewards in building closer ties with your loved ones. So now is the time to take those initiatives. Do what needs to be done now to build the connections that last a lifetime . . . and do it soon!

2. *Strengthen strong friendships among peers and in your neighborhood:* Here is where you can show real love and enjoyment of dear, lasting friends. Keep in touch, show interest in their lives, offer support, and help when needed, and enjoy joint activities together. I have observed some beautiful friendships throughout my life. They are a wonder to behold. I witnessed friends loaning their home when they were away to other friends in need of temporary housing. I have seen friends calling on other friends in the hospital for days when serious surgery was performed, and recovery took time. It gives me chills to recall how one

couple drove across country to visit and enjoy a vacation time with other friends. It is so inspiring to find what some friends will do when one of them becomes incapacitated. Their friends and neighbors offer a helping hand by doing their chores and caring for their property while the party involved recovers and copes with a new handicap. Good friends can be the hands of God, and they can be His instruments in times of joy and in times of need.

3. *Discover the special quality of friendship, a spiritual tie, which is available in our faith communities:* We are active in our local United Methodist Church. We find that it is a wonderful body of caring, loving people. They show interest in our personal activities and our evolving goals. They really want to know about our struggles in life, and they are willing and ready to pray for us or be there as helping companions.

Just recently, we saw this great compassion in action when our church organized a congregational care ministry of over forty senior volunteers. Its role was defined as a focus on our dependent and disabled senior residents. The task was to visit and support the large number of disabled, demented, and elderly adults residing in the assisted living and nursing home centers of our retirement community. The volunteers call on dependent adults regularly and attend to their physical, emotional, and spiritual needs. There is no charge for this ministry because it is a true act of compassion by our church family for its handicapped members. Many of those volunteers tell us they are blessed by offering their time and presence for others. Everyone benefits, and it is a shining example of a church at its best.

4. *One of the finest qualities of American life is the creative way we respond to special needs:* We live in a retirement community, like so many others, that has support groups, interest groups, skill groups, and educational seminars set up to meet every need. In our support groups, we deal with loneliness, depression, and the hunger for friendship. In our interest groups, we help single adults find companionship and dating partners. In our skill groups, we teach seniors how to dance, exercise, swim, play ball, or learn to enjoy games. In our educational seminars, we have focused on concrete ways to deal with health concerns, build friendship ties, and find ways to service one another when a crisis comes. So no important issue in our social setting with senior adults is neglected. We are always trying to find new ideas to help people connect and deal effectively with the social needs they have now. That is the genius of our democracy when it's working at its best. So find your place in some activity and enjoy the experience of building ties with others who also enjoy what you do. Develop connections that provide the opportunity for finding new friendships that can last a lifetime.

5. *Make the decision that we all need a few close friends and several casual acquaintances:* There is plenty of solid evidence in social science literature that strong friendship ties are critical to good health. Consequently, we need to intentionally develop close ties to a few good and enjoyable friends over our lifetime. That process is not as easy as it may seem because seniors often report that very close companionship often eludes them. Either many older adults are too particular or those they seek out are too demanding. Sometimes, they are uncomfortable with being completely open and honest about their needs and

their lives. Whatever the reason, it is harder than it appears to locate close, lasting friendships for many senior adults.

Nevertheless, the keys to good companionship are readily available: find likable prospects, seek social occasions to meet them casually, invite them to new and special events, share openly and honestly about yourself, and be comfortable with the contact. I often suggest that you encourage your new friends to tell as much as they want to share and always promise confidentiality. Learn to listen carefully and enjoy the process. Hopefully, they will do the same with you, and then you both are off to a great start. Enjoy more sharing and common activities you both enjoy. Once you click and are fully at ease with one another, you have the basis for a tie that should last for years to come. You will discover it is a treasure and a value you will enjoy as you see the years ahead unfold before you. It will be a rich pleasure as you share different events and activity together. Therefore, always be alert to finding these new friendships that are available for you at numerous occasions. Strike up a contact, and begin the process of building new ties and realize when you have just made another new friend.

6. *Recognize your need to let go of your ties to family members and friends of the past who are no longer meaning ful or supportive:* Just as you want to find and develop new friends, you need to draw closure with those who have no more meaning for neither of you. Relationships are often tenuous and not all are designed for a lifetime. They sometimes fail, grow bitter, develop misunderstandings, or just fade away. It is important to recognize that and to realize we cannot hold on to every friend we have made or every family member we inherited. It is hard to let go

and to move on, but to hold on for longer than either or both of you want is not realistic. I contend that closure with a long- term contact that is not working should be done with good intentions and tactful disconnection. Recognize that the friendship has changed and that you both need to find new directions for your lives. Share that idea if you can. Then move forward by looking for new friendship ties. You can follow that procedure with relatives in the family as well, where contact has been difficult to maintain. Once action is taken, you will find yourself feeling a sense of relief and release. My experience is the other party will feel the same way also. So face the closure of friendship at the same time you are building new friends to replace the old ones that no longer have any meaning or are fading away.

****

Now let me move on to another vital issue in our social life: enjoying your leisure time through creative thought and planning. *Leisure-Time Options Need to be Chosen and Enjoyed:* Every senior I know needs time for sheer leisure and enjoyable activity. My experience is that they fall into three key categories: (1) entertainment; (2) finding and developing hobbies, sports, or crafts you enjoy; and (3) personal time for reading and reflection. Let me comment on each one:

Entertainment can be offered in stage performances. It can be at a private party gathering, and it can be even movies—either at a theater or at home on our televisions. Some of my best experiences have been as a participant at a sports event or at a major theme park. The point is, however, that we need a variety of entertaining experiences that enhance our lives and give us a feeling of pleasure and inspiration.

Find hobbies and crafts, sports events, or cruises that appeal to you and one that is available in your geographic area. My wife and I have friends who are fully involved in each of these areas of interest. For example, a friend of ours who retired started to learn woodcarving in a group devoted to woodwork, and he has now become so proficient at it he has won several ribbons in our state-fair competition. Many seniors love their golf games, tennis, or lawn bowling, and they never miss a scheduled event. Others we know love participating in the local symphony orchestra or nature painting or photography for exhibition. They love the time and effort it takes to master these skills. It provides new expression for their natural talent and interest. Seniors love it when they can find that very special interest that commands their full interest and attention.

Many older adults enjoy the quiet reflection while reading their favorite novels or magazines, or morning newspaper. More and more seniors enjoy computer skills and contact with the world at large. They may write their memoirs, find meaning in creating poetry, or take time to do extensive intercessory prayers for the needs and concerns of others. Some do nature walking, while others even find that building a garden near their home is a vivid way of renewing their spirit and getting close to God. Churches in many communities offer special programs for spiritual growth or retreats for personal reflection and spiritual understanding. Many Protestant churches, for example, have available "The Amass Walk," in which the participants spend a great deal of time in spiritual renewal and resetting their focus for their years ahead, often at a camp setting. These times for individual growth can mean a great deal for many senior adults who have time now to reflect on the essential purpose of their lives. But we all need to take the initiative to make these things happen in our daily activity and discover the joy that is in this new interest. Take advantage of these wonderful opportunities for pleasurable times with others or for personal growth for yourself. The choice of what you do is up to you, but make that choice now.

Let me now close this chapter on the value of developing our social skills, with an important statement on the critical importance of *staying involved in human services and the critical issues of the day.* My experience as a person who has been a leader for social change and a community activist all my life is that a vast majority of senior adults begin to retire from being involved in social change and health advocacy as they age. They sit back and say, "Let the younger people take the responsibility for building a better world because my time has come and gone." Now I can "rest and let the world go by." That attitude of social withdrawal from responsibility and involvement hurts them even more than the nation at large. They are retreating from part of what is vital for life: our passion and concern for human welfare, for building a better world, for serving people in real human need. The net result is that our nation loses their talent and leadership, but even more critical is that they are giving up on the benefits that come from being fully engaged in social service and action. Therefore, let me detail what I observe are the real-life benefits that seniors can experience when they give their full energy for important causes and social changes in American life:

1. *Seniors who become involved in worthy causes feel passion and excitement.* They may find new friendships on the Alzheimer's Walk or as a volunteer to raise funds for cancer research. Some find enjoyment in making toys for tots or building toys for the kids to use in a private or public classroom. In our retirement community, we

have several hundred volunteers serving on an emergency squad that responds to health crises and takes seniors who are in critical need to the closest medical hospital for immediate medical treatment. Another group of volunteers serves on a security patrol whose mission is to drive patrol vehicles twenty-four hours every day of the year all around our community to protect our residents from crime and vandalism. These volunteers feel important and valued because their time and efforts creates a better and safer community. They provide a necessary service to our community without charge. In the process, these volunteers develop social connections that last a lifetime. Our vital retirement community could not function as well without them. Everyone benefits, and the value of giving yourself to a worthy cause is endorsed again.

2. *Seniors need social acceptance and not social isolation, and being an active volunteer does that for them.* It is regrettable that there are number of seniors who retire to do-nothing and just take care of their own basic needs for money, food, and shelter. They often remain isolated into their homes, and sometimes, some of them even withdraw from their extended family connections. They do understand the tremendous value of being involved in social organizations and sport activities that give life purpose, meaning, and value to life.

I can speak as an active retiree when I say that we cannot function well or live healthy lives alone, without the love and active involvement with others. We need them like fish need to be in water. So resist your desire to withdraw from large social contact. Stay involved in whatever interest or activity you choose, but refuse to remain isolated. Our business is to love one another and to choose to be involved in building a better world for ourselves and our children who follow our living example. Being immersed in social services gives purpose and meaning to life. It keeps us vital and identified with the needs of others and the changing world all around us.

3. *Much of the Greatness of America is due to the Leadership of Older Americans Who Felt the Need to Be Change Agents:* The story of Sam Walton is one of many examples of successful leaders who saw a need and responded to it. He was a small town merchant (See his book: *Sam Walton: Made in America*) who felt a need for a better way to provide more goods, under one roof, at a better price than his competitors offered. He found a new means to package and sell merchandize for the public and now Wal-Mart is the largest company in the world with the greatest outreach compared to any other similar company anywhere on earth.

President Jimmy Carter could have retired and enjoyed his older years in Plains, Georgia, after he left office. Instead, he developed the Carter Center in Atlanta, Georgia (See the website: Carterweb@memory.edu) that has emphasized human rights and sought to alleviate human suffering around the whole world. It specializes in treating diseases that hit hardest on children in underdeveloped countries. The vaccination program has served thousands of children and saved countless lives. The center goes about doing spectacular things without fanfare or without seeking praise from public leaders.

The well-known entertainer, Danny Thomas, helped start the amazing healing center in the early 1960s called St. Jude's Children's Research Hospital in Memphis, Tennessee. It has the special mission of treatment of hard-to-diagnose diseases and treats children who come from all over the world for medical care. He began with a simple mission to serve children who could not find medical help elsewhere. These children were close to death or had no help for their problem. Thomas felt "no children should die in the dawn of life." He and the wonderful staff that followed have fulfilled that cause beautifully through medical innovation and a very specialized medical management program.

The central lesson here is that great things can happen when men and women have a vision for a better future and when they act to make that vision a reality. We simply need more people with that drive and talent to build a better future for us all.

Seniors everywhere would benefit and be blessed to be so well motivated. We hear from time to time about important innovations that some visionary senior has undertaken. That is so very commendable. The important point to emphasize, however, is the need to stay involved. Fight the temptation to withdraw, even with mild health limitations, and keep on helping others by making some contribution somewhere. Be a vital part of your community as long as you live . . . even into your nineties. Younger people really still look to their elders as a living example of how healthy seniors age well. They need mentors in their lives to follow. Be that model of social involvement, and they will benefit bountifully from your example, and you will be blessed as well.

Real-Life Stories of Social Outreach:

Wherever I have lived, I have known people who have devoted their life to building a better community. I recall the number of volunteers who worked in the Christian Medical Society in Sheboygan, Wisconsin, that offered a free medical clinic for the scores of low-income and disabled adults who could not afford regular medical services. Here were doctors, dentists, social workers, and counselors, working as a team, while serving real needs without compensation. They just showed up every week at the Salvation Army building to "care for those who could not care for themselves." The volunteers were quality professionals who recognized they had benefited from a good education and succeeded in their careers and now wanted to give back to others through warm quality care. I have always appreciated that about our American life, in which so many citizens reach out with a helping hand to others in need. It is as if we are all part of the human family of God, and we need to help each other when help is sorely needed.

Another example of simple helpfulness and human concern for others is the work that is being done by the Emergency Disaster Response Team that is staffed by our local church members in our Sun City Center community here in Florida. Team members have helped rebuild worn-out church buildings, recycled waste, repaired the roof a Vietnam veteran's house, and responded to crisis calls for help by a lonely widowed woman. They do this without fanfare while standing ready to meet a critical need with their well-equipped portable trailer whenever they called upon to serve. They say they are the hands and feet of the Lord, Jesus Christ. These are all senior volunteers who care about their church, community, and world. It is evidence of the best expression of the human spirit that motivates people to reach beyond themselves and to help people who are desperate for help from others.

It sets a high standard for the rest of us. Their model tells us that we cannot just care about ourselves, but that we should be part of a responsible community where we reach out to serve the needs of others. That spirit is not only a commendable part of the human spirit, but it reaches out with a helping hand to offer time and talent to others in the best traditions of our American life.

Supplemental Materials: (1) Suggestions for Developing Good Social Relationships, (2) The Loving Benefits from Owning and Enjoying a Pet, (3) The Values in Our Leisure Activity, and (4) You Are Responsible

Supplement 1, Chapter 5

SUGGESTIONS FOR DEVELOPING GOOD SOCIAL RELATIONSHIPS

- Be friendly and cheerful with others. Look on the brighter side of life in your contacts with others. Learn to *smile* and enjoy the *smile* back.

- Listen better and speak when others will listen also. Most of us are poor listeners. We often simply want to talk and be heard and not take time to hear and listen.

- Share thoughtful information and experiences in a colorful manner. You can be very boring to others without realizing you drive other away by your expressions.

- Maintain a calm manner, remembering that the way something is said may be more significant than what was said. The wrong tone or voice can turn people off.

- Keep an open mind and avoid defensiveness so you can relate to those you find take a position you cannot accept. We are to be commended when we can even be friends with people who live a lifestyle or hold political positions you find offensive or unacceptable.

- Maintain a balance between constructive criticism and praise with others. When talking to others, you can be honest and open about where you stand on key issues, but do it tactfully.

- Nevertheless, you can qualify your statements by being tactful and sensitive about their response when others disagree or are offended by you. Use praise when you can because it builds relationship even when differences exist. Develop the skill of offering sincere compliments to people you enjoy and appreciate.

It is amazing what one can get done when we give credit to others, even if we do not receive credit in return. Offer positive comments when in a work situation and learn the skills of regular encouragement. People are hungry for praise and approval today.

- Keep others informed in helpful ways so they appreciate new, important information. We all benefit when important news is shared, ideas are offered, and helpful suggestions are made on almost any problem that needs to be resolved. Be a positive force in a group setting.

- Avoid gossip, criticism of others, and passing on unfounded rumors. Display patience when others are passing out nasty comments about colleagues.

- Suggest to the speaker that it is not helpful to debase someone. It is better to find ways to be helpful for the troubled person in focus.

- Become good at finding praises and approval of co-workers, of family members, and of even leaders in the community. Look at their finer qualities and bring them to mind and comment on them. Be a positive force in a group setting.

- Remember: the mind and personality are like a refrigerator—until opened and used, it is worthless and its contents go unused. Realize that developing your social skills is one of the best goals you can continue to focus on all of your life.

Supplement 2, Chapter 5

THE LOVING BENEFITS FROM OWNING AND ENJOYING A PET

A senior friend told me recently about the many values she enjoys with her pet poodle. Her dog, Marci, is her constant companion. This little pet reflects her moods, her struggles, and even her accomplishments. This tiny creature seems to sense her every need and acts as her alter ego. The animal was chosen to be there for companionship, for intimacy, to hear outbursts of frustration, and even to celebrate when some new joyful moment comes in daily living. When my wife and I visit, Doris sits for our conversation, and Marci always sits on the same chair with her. Marci reflects and supports her every move, and this adult owner has come to depend on her endorsement. It has become a rich expression of love.

Pets provide a charming source of friendship, comfort, affection, and even entertainment. I enjoy, most of all, their unconditional acceptance of their caring owner. They are a companion to touch, to talk to, to nurture, and to simply enjoy. The pet owners themselves relish the amazing bond of human and animal connection. When one is not feeling well, the most attention you receive is usually from your favorite pet. The special task that benefits owner and pet best is usually the daily exercise (and potty) time when you take your pet to some nature park or walking area. Many grandmas tells me they cherish the way their loving companion jumps on the bed to awaken them or even enjoys working with them at the tasks that needs to be done around the home every day.

It is amazing, as well, how varied pet owners are in their selection of the pet they choose. Beside the most popular choice of dogs and cats, people choose birds like a canary, fish in an aquarium, rabbits, turtles, and even creepy creatures like snakes. It appears that pets are often chosen for casual companionship and amusement, not always for a deep emotional tie. One of the most useful choices for picking a pet is in the use of the seeing eye dogs for the blind and in the use of dogs, in particular, for surveillance by a large number of police departments across the country. I have even witnessed how effective animals are when used properly in a nursing home or even in a hospital setting. They bring excitement, comfort, and companionship that the residents often yearn to find.

There are downsides to pet ownership: the cost of purchase, the feeding, and caring for a dependant animal, and the loss of your companion when death occurs. It does restrict your plans, as well, when you want to travel from home and you need to leave your pet behind. Nevertheless, the benefits of ownership are overwhelming. Most owners report that their pet helps to reduce stressful moments, the singe adult feels less alone, and for most Americans it is absolutely clear that their pet has become a true member of their family. So you may want to join the majority of homeowners today and enlarge your world with a loving pet. It can enrich your life and activity as well as give you new joys. It can provide a different dimension for a rich retirement lifestyle.

Reference: Article by Nanci Hellmich, "A Little Puppy Love Can Enrich Life, Boost Health" in *USA TODAY* for September 3, 2014

Supplement 3, Chapter 5

THE VALUES IN OUR LEISURE-TIME ACTIVITY

We need to realize that being creative about leisure time produces amazing results. We have seen retirees develop skills in craft making and music they never knew they had before. It is opening a whole new world of positive experiences for each of them.

- Leisure-time activity could include a physical fitness program, joining a musical group for public presentations, learning a new craft skill, finding a new outlet to help others in need, or even reading or learning to enjoy the computer and its outlet to the world. Just being creative and following your passion helps make it all happen.

- Volunteering is one of the most popular outlets for seniors. It could be working in the local hospital as an aid in a ward. In our community, we have a large number of willing volunteers who serve on an emergency squad and make primary visits for referral when a health crisis appears.

- Leisure time may involve just enjoying new friendships with other retirees. My wife has a Birthday Club, for example, that meets monthly to celebrate the birthdays of any member who had a birthday that month.

- Certainly, we can take time for travel and sightseeing in our leisure years. Most of the healthy seniors we know take long trips to see their family members or take a cruise to see a new part of the world. They may even travel to other countries with a travel agency that helps them become acquainted with a world they have never known before.

- We have friends in our senior community who meet their entire family every year in a key location. They just enjoy each other, catch up on their news, and help make important decisions about their future lives in their own location.

- Many seniors engage in family reunions. Many seniors like to attend class reunions to meet old friends at their favorite college. Some seniors gather together around a special interest like their miniature railroad hobby or drag racing or a golf championship or to fly old antique airplanes. Whatever their interest, they want to share it with others and relive a key part of their past.

- In summary, leisure-time activity is a critical part of a healthy retirement. So do some introspective thinking and discover your keenest area of interest. Find a group or even an instructor to help you develop this new focus in your life. Be creative and find your passion so you can enjoy this new interest and activity.

Supplement 4, Chapter 5

YOU ARE RESPONSIBLE: A Senior Challenge

- You are responsible for what you say to others.

- You are responsible for what you do socially and feel emotionally.

- You are responsible for what you feel about yourself and other people.

- You are responsible for what you do with yourself and those you contact.

- You are responsible for what you eat and drink and how you act in social settings.

- You are not responsible for making anyone else happy or healthy.

- You are not responsible for becoming what someone else wants you to be.

- You are not responsible for how others react to your thoughts and feelings.

- You are not responsible for the prejudice and hatred that others exhibit.

- You are not responsible for the ignorance and lack of understanding in others.

- You are responsible for defending yourself when other people wish you harm.

- You are responsible for everything in your life you decide to do with others.

- You are responsible for a lack of faith, knowing a strong faith strengthens life.

- You are responsible when you fail to take leadership in a crisis when it is needed.

- You are responsible for standing up for strong American values.

- If you do not like your present lifestyle, you are responsible to change it.

- If you fail to act on weaknesses in your life, you are responsible for the results.

- If you do not like the way you are treated by others and fail to act, you will suffer.

- If you see someone in need and you ignore their concern, you will live to regret it.

- Failing to set goals and directions for your life could lead toward a troubled life.

Remember that a heavy responsibility is on your shoulders to think, plan, and act to build a life you will enjoy and one full of real accomplishments. You have just one life to lead, so decide carefully how you want to lead it. It takes responsible life choices to build the best life ahead; make a commitment now to build your life for your golden years.

"Managing our money well and living within our budget
is an important point of pride and satisfaction"

CHAPTER 6

CHOOSING TO CREATE A MONEY/ MATERIAL MANAGEMENT PLAN

A spending blueprint will protect (your) nest egg
. . . .the only way to get realistic picture of how
much you're like to spend in the future is to create
a retirement budget now . . . mulling every possible
expense could help you create a withdrawal strategy
that will protect your nest egg from the vagaries of life.

—Kiplinger's, *Retirement Report*,
August 2013

We have to begin building our financial security with a plan. Few seniors just muddle along and expect to be financially solvent. The reality is that every one of us needs a clear and specific means to meet our daily financial needs. Even the older adult who is living on a very limited income and has to cut costs needs a plan for surviving financial pressures. My preference is that this plan should be written down, along with achievable goals, to fulfill the dream of financial stability. It needs to be clear, precise, and understandable. The plan may need to change as we age in retirement, but if we review the plan every year and bring it up-to-date that should help resolve our concerns.

It would be helpful if you shared your financial planning with an experienced resource leader in the field. We like financial planners because they are specialists whose job is to help us develop a realistic direction for our financial future. You can often find a recommended adviser through your friends who have used one, but if that is not possible, you may need to turn to the yellow pages of your phonebook under the heading of "Financial Planning Consultants." Many seniors prefer to do business with a nationally known financial management firm, but some seniors prefer to do business with a local firm that has good word of mouth, or even Chamber of Commerce or Better Business Bureau recommendations. I would recommend that you interview them first with key questions you have written down in advance of your meeting. Ask not just about fees, but about how they can relate to the needs of the senior world and what success they have had in working with the senior population. Inquire about their ethical standards. Seniors tend to be more conservative and come with defined assets. So the financial adviser should know how to manage financial issues in the senior world and recommend financial decisions for people who are retired.

Certainly, the goals for your financial planning should include the following as a very minimum:

1. What is my intent or purpose in developing a financial plan?

2. What different areas of focus do I need in my financial plans?

3. Do I need a detailed net-worth statement that lists all my assets and my liabilities? How will I deal with any debt I have incurred, and where do I find the right loan agency to manage it?

4. Would it be helpful to compile a list of charities I prefer and the gifts I have given over the year past so my pattern of giving to others is clear? Does it need to change?

5. Is there a form to complete before any meeting with the planning firm? Would it be helpful to bring a supportive financial file record along? How often do we meet and make regular contact?

6. Are there questions to ask or convictions to share about their financial planning process?

7. What routines do we follow to manage our monthly financial plan with skill? Exactly what are all the sources of my annual income and expenses? Do I need to deal with both health and life insurance issues?

8. Do I have a concrete plan to financially support my extended family members? Is it a workable method or is there is better way to reduce my annual tax burden?

9. How can I develop a plan to cope with the financial demand of a medical emergency? Having an emergency fund available is essential.

10. Are all my legal papers in order so my financial assets can be easily transferred to my heirs with a minimum tax burden?

11. Is there a format or a printed booklet where I can keep regular records of my financial status, both my income sources and tax payments? I also need to keep a close record of my savings plan and its annual earnings.

Once these questions are answered and your adviser is clear about your goals and intentions, you can move on and begin the process together. My experience is that you need to take notes and to establish a clear filing system so you have a thorough record of what you have decided to do and exactly how you will put your plan into action.

The planning process itself needs to be the main focus, where you spend real time and effort with professional help and on your own or with your spouse. This period of financial management should include some of the following financial decisions that are critical to keeping you stay solvent in your retirement years:

1. Keeping topical files on all your unpaid and paid bill and receipts.

2. Maintaining records of your expenses and income. Make certain the information kept is confidential.

3. The use of a checkbook, credit cards, or computer payment system that give you an easy-to-understand payment plan for all your financial obligations each month. Most banks now have a computerized system to maintain your checking and savings account, along with a bill payment procedure that is very efficient.

4. A clear record of your tax obligations from all sources each month. Seek help from a CPA, an accountant, or a free tax preparation service to complete your annual tax

filing to the U.S. government and for your local state tax office. Most seniors are not capable of doing their own tax forms today, so assistance is needed to complete the filing correctly. Bring a summary of all your assets, liabilities, and insurance policies to the meeting.

5. Establish a payment plan for your income tax and local taxes so they are paid on time each month or at least every quarter. Keep complete records of all income tax deductions so they can reduce your tax obligations when you file your tax forms before April 15 each year. Keep a full accounting of all possible tax deductions, such as charitable giving and medical expenses that can help you reduce your tax obligations each year.

6. Understand the details of your current investment program. Learn to comprehend the financial marketplace and how you can record all your active investment transactions. Decide if you need a financial manager for your investment portfolio so your savings are handled efficiently, and you are comfortable with the risks involved.

7. Seek help, if needed, to modify your savings plan to meet changing conditions in your life and in the economy itself. Maintain an emergency fund to draw upon if you need a large draw of funds for a health crisis, the loss of a home, or for assistance for a close family member who has a personal concern that needs your financial support.

8. Include financial contributions for your local church and all other preferred charities, so that their needs are not neglected. A helpful method is to use an automatic plan that draws monthly on your savings or checking account and transfers that money to your local church office.

9. Borrow with great caution and seek solid financial advice
    when seeking a large amount of money. Choose carefully
    when you apply for a loan. Think through with great care
    when entering any new investment program.

10. Plan carefully for any new sources of income, even if a
    return to employment is needed, but make certain you are
    ready to take the risks involved. The marketplace does not
    hire a lot of senior adults, at least with high compensation
    for their time and ability. Develop a real understanding
    of the financial marketplace, save, and invest well, so you
    can have sufficient income to meet your basic needs in
    your retirement.

We should not continue without a real discussion about the
schemes and scams that are everywhere in the senior world
today. They are all around us, especially on the Internet,
and seniors are the most vulnerable of all age groups. Our
generations grew up trusting people with the expectation
that people were honest. That value is often not in evidence
today. A criminal who wants to steal money is now dressed
in a business suit, and he or she advertises a product through
the mail, in the paper, on the radio or television, or on a
computer site that seems very appealing to senior adults. A
tempting pitch is presented by malicious salespeople. Internet
sites even tell you that you have won a sweepstakes prize, or
you have a gift from a generous person who wants to reward
you because your name has been chosen in a special drawing.
Do not believe these false promises. They are generally just
intended to steal your money.

My wife and I have lost money on the time-shares we wanted
to sell, so I am not free from this vile salesmanship. Other
schemes involve the payment of a real estate or repair fee for

the sale of a home that never occurs or the cost of work by a contractor for work that is never completely done for the upkeep of a home or for home repairs when they are never done well or at all. Some of the recent ploys involve products such as screen work, attic insulation, or new plumbing that are usually totally unnecessary or overpriced.

One recent development is to offer you money from a sweepstakes you never entered. The crook who wants your money, however, is always creative about finding new ways to help you part from your cash reserves. So we all need to act with utter caution when we receive an unwanted phone solicitation or read it on the Internet. Watch also for that visit at your door for a product you do not need. This is a new day when seniors should heed warnings that are often posted by the attorney general of your state, suggesting major caution about buying products geared to the gullible senior citizen market. One key suggestion is never send money to anyone who says you have won a prize. If it sounds too good to be true, you can depend on the fact it truly is a *scam*. Don't become another victim.

****

Now I would like to focus on a critical area for senior living, and that is the creation of wills and legacies for our children and grandchildren or for the charities you may want to endow. First, you need to understand the concept that is now a common practice for estate attorneys: preparing *advance directives*. These are legal documents that express your preferences about your health care and the disposal of your assets when you are approaching the end of your life. There are three health care directives or instructions you will want your key family members or your asset administrator to know about when your physical care and declining health presents the possibilities of your imminent death. In addition, many younger adults include these documents in their financial planning even if death is not a possibility. Key documents give clear instructions about your plans to pass on your assets. They involve the following:

1. A legal will in which you identify the name of the person who will have power of attorney over your legal affairs if you are unable to make your own decisions due to your infirmities or death. You state simply your plan for disposing of your assets and paying your liabilities. It is usually prepared with legal counsel, and copies are provided for your doctor and the hospital where you will be treated, as well as your legally appointed administrator of your will. If you have assets in more than two states, you may want to develop a *revocable living trust*, which has more flexibility and less legal tangles than a legal will. The biggest advantage of this plan is that you avoid probate and that it does not require a special tax number. You have far more control over the settlement of your estate. As always, be sure you secure legal counsel before you make that decision.

2. The naming of a health care surrogate, or who becomes your representative who will make medical decisions for you if you are unable, due to your infirmity, to make them for yourself. This person is an individual you trust implicitly who will stand with you through the dying process and make sound decisions that reflect your preferences. That person should have access to all of your extended family members and to your full medical records. He or she can oversee the treatment procedure the medical team used to treat you in a life-threatening situation. That person

can honor and insist that your preferences be followed not to use extraordinary procedures to extend your life in a critical medical crisis when there are serious doubts about its success. He or she can also speak on your behalf to insist on an operation if it has a chance to save your life.

3. Make the decision about the donation of your body organs. You can sign a donation card that you keep on your person at all times, a card you share with your trusted family members. Nevertheless, you need a real person who may make the arrangements for the disposal of the body parts. You may choose to use a medical college for your organs for teaching or research purposes. Another option is to provide the needed body part (such as heart, lung, or liver) for people waiting for a donation in order to sustain their life. This is a very humane act in which you give new life to someone in your family or even to a stranger to help them live a longer, healthier life than they could have without the needed body part you donate.

4. Name a person who acts as your financial manager for disposing of everything related to your financial assets. He or she may be the same person as the executor of your will or a different individual, but the person or people named should be identified in your statement in your advance directives. This process takes keen skills because it can be very complicated and delicate if there are many survivors in your family. Even the process of giving away personal items, such as jewelry and clothing, needs to be managed with real finesse, or hard feelings can linger for years if the process is not handled tactfully. In fact, it would prevent a lot of hard feelings among your heirs if you would list your personal possessions that have high value and the individual you want to take ownership after you die and

put it in your will. They will be grateful for your good intentions and the fact they have been honored with the precious item you want them to enjoy.

When your estate is distributed, it often involves highly charged emotions and latent hostile feelings in an extended family. If the manager is a family member, he or she needs to have a high level of interpersonal skills and the ability to handle conflict. If there is no one in the extended family or friendship circle that has that finesse, a bank officer or an attorney might be able to be more objective and maintain more order and control in the distribution of all of the assets of the deceased.

5. Without written directives, personal wishes in this area are not always understood or implemented. In fact, if they are not written down, family members often get mixed signals about your real intentions. Your survivors are not clear, therefore, what you actually want. So I highly recommend that you consult with your doctor and attorney about your intentions in completing this final financial planning process. They will be able, therefore, to speak about your true preferences in setting up your will or the living-trust agreement. For helpful information about this process, contact your state agency for health care administration in your state to help locate and complete the right documents. In our case, it is located in Tallahassee, Florida, 32308, under the e-mail: FloridaHealthStat.com, ask for "Health Care Advance Directives." It is a free booklet and the appropriate forms are included.

Please note that your advance directives should include your legal will, in which you indicate how all your financial assets, including your life insurance, should be distributed. The document needs to follow your state law and be notarized. Upon your death, your will must be reviewed and distributed by your durable power of attorney to the rightful heirs, as listed in your legal document. The issue of whether or not key items need to be probated with your county clerk should be discussed in advance, and an attorney should be consulted if there is a question about the transfer of ownership to the rightful heirs.

Legal titling is a critical issue in the transfer of property. If you have prepared a living-trust document that does not have to be reported to the court, your assets can be distributed without having to report them to the court system. The assets are simply listed in a net-worth statement in the will so they can be distributed without complications to the beneficiaries involved. The problem that often complicates the settlement of an estate is the lack of proper titling or the lack of listing of all the assets in the will that are intended for distribution. This issue should be discussed and resolved before the impending death of a loved one.

For this reason, you need to prepare a net-worth statement every year that you attach to your will or trust, so the professionals your executor employs knows what is and is not to be reported for estate tax purposes. If your estate is of any significant size, my recommendation is that you employ a certified estate attorney to guide you through the process of estate planning rather than seeking to manage it yourself. Laws and proper procedures keep changing, so an attorney can usually help you avoid legal loopholes and plan your estate with more care and consideration.

Hopefully, every senior will include some charitable cause in their legal will. If you are concerned about building a better world and meeting the urgent needs of suffering mankind, you will find a cause you can support as your lasting legacy. In our family, we practice tithing, an ancient Judea–Christian discipline, in which you give, even in your will or trust, at least 10 percent of your assets for the work of Christian causes. It is not only an act of faith, but it sets a standard for your children and for your grandchildren to follow. In our case, we do it to strengthen worthy ministries that we want to support, but it is also an intentional choice to honor God and to obey the scriptural plea to share our financial resources with those in need. We will give the bulk of our assets to our family, but we intend also to serve others as well by tithing our estate.

In a well-laid plan, I also highly recommend that you complete an ethical will. It is not a legal requirement for settling your estate, but it is a vital piece of information you need to leave for your loved ones at your death. It is a thoughtful and thorough statement of your values, your statement of faith and beliefs, and your hopes and dreams for your loved ones. Some people will want to write about their faith journey to share where they have been and where they are today in their spiritual life. In addition, either way, it is clear it is NOT a legal will, but a straight declaration of your values and your hope that your legacy will continue to live on in those who follow you. You can also identify special mementos you want to leave with particular people and the reason they are so important to you. It is a deeply personal statement that comes from your heart, and it is intended to be your parting words for those you love and leave behind

Some topics that could be highlighted are the following: communicate your love for your family; share the wisdom that you have accumulated over the years; and transmit your wishes, dreams, and hopes for the generation that will follow you in the years to come. Sometimes, it could be left on a video recording, but generally, it is posted in a written statement. For key questions and information about this topic, you can go to the website: www.yourethicalwill.com. You might be surprised to learn how appreciative survivors have been to read and benefit from this last message by someone who was dearly loved. It is your gift of your lifetime and your final legacy.

Let me finally emphasize here the importance of keeping and maintaining good financial records. Sometimes there is resource information from your local bank or financial institution. In addition, you can access Internet sites to help you keep your financial records intact. (See: www. todaysseniors. com/pages/organizers.) Of course, we all need to maintain all tax records and income tax reports for the last five to seven years, according to Internal Revenue Service's regulations. My hope would be that you would keep a record each year of at least all your income sources, your expense and payment record, your record of charitable giving, as well as investments and savings reports. At any one time, all of us should be able to know approximately where we stand financially.

In fact, there are printed forms available in most banks and financial institutions for financial record keeping. My suggestion is that you find the form that best fits your needs and keep good records month after month, year after year. It is a real source of comfort to know your financial picture, so you can turn to that information when you are considering a new purchase or investment. Be cautious about making informed investment decisions and seek professional help. This kind of caution helps you to preserve a good credit rating among all the major financial institutions today, a very goal to achieve.

****

Now I would like to emphasize the value of being conscientious about clever ways to find, save, and spend money. Seniors are usually good at this task, but it might be helpful to bring together some of the best ideas that we can all use to our benefit. So let me share a random list of money saving, spending, and earning ideas that are time-tested:

1. Clip coupons to save money for the purchase of food, clothing, shoes, and everyday items. You can even find coupons now for travel trips, automobiles, and even the cost of medicines.

2. Prepare grocery lists before shopping and stay with those items. Make a comparison shopping tour of at least three grocery stores in your area for prices and quality of the goods you purchase. Decide where you get the best selection, price, and quality and stick with that store. Watch for special bargains at different websites and look for coupons there you can print.

3. It is surprising how many fine quality goods you can find at the local used clothing store or variety store location. Americans are donating even nearly new items because they are often overstocked at home. But be a very discriminating shopper who takes time for a purchase that will be used for a long time, like good clothing or furniture. Avoid impulsive buying, however, so take your time to make careful decisions.

4. Refuse to stay with just one nationally known pharmacy for your medications. You might benefit if you can locate a discount pharmacy. If you do comparison shopping, you will find a wide discrepancy between pharmaceutical

outlets. Some seniors may even want to check on the Internet for a Canadian pharmacy that offers a standard medication at a radically lower price, but do check on its reliability and safety of the product line before you buy and use them. In some cases, your health insurance carrier has a store where you can purchase your medication at a discount. The carrier may suggest you shop there to save considerable money each time you fill a prescription or buy an item.

5. Would you believe that you can also look around for the best medical service provider in your area? You will need to take time and thoughtful consideration to make the selection, but it is worth the exploration. Develop some standards you want met by the provider, the specialist you need to have available, and the attention to detail you feel is important. Your major requirement should be to find a medical provider who is personable, gives you time for the annual checkup, does a good job of financial management, and helps you maintain good medical records. Most of all, you need a doctor you can talk to and communicate with easily so you function well together as a team to decide how you can maintain maximum health as you age gracefully. The same procedure should be followed, as well, when you find your local dentist for your annual dental checkup and cleaning.

6. My wife and I have found we can save time and repair costs on the upkeep of our home and automobile by practicing preventive maintenance. We use a recommended handyman for routine repair work, and we make the stops at the auto repair shop that are recommended in our automobile handbook. We have also found that we can make timely upgrades on our household appliances

and furniture when the need for replacement is clear. The whole issue comes down to exercising better management of the maintenance of your home and property and the carefully planned storage and repair of all the equipment and personal items you use and need. Make it an issue not to store items that you no longer need. Each year, clean out goods that are not in use or even repairable or give them away. You will all feel better for that practice.

7. Every senior questions how many electronic devices are needed and will be used effectively. Most of us have lived through radical changes in the use of electronic devices in our lifetime, from the party phone to the Apple iPhone 5 cell phone. None of us had a laptop or an iPod when we were in school. Few have memories of ever using a CD for music or a Bluetooth connection in our car for listening to cell phone messages. But the reality is that these new devices are everywhere, and you need to be literate about them or you will soon get out of touch with your children or grandchildren. So slowly adopt what you feel comfortable to use and get training in its use, especially in the purchase and use of a computer. They can add much to the quality of your life, and it will enhance your connection with others and the world around. Start by becoming computer literate and learn to use your computer intelligently. It will open a whole new world you have never known before, if you are not there already.

8. Travel costs can be greatly reduced by purchasing automobiles that operate with gas-saving features. Local travel agencies can offer helpful suggestions for saving on airline costs and the expense of enjoying a new travel destination. You can access many excellent travel sites on your computer that can help you plan ahead for your next

vacation. One of the best cost-saving methods is to look for travel bargains in the newspaper, travel magazines, or on the Internet. Travel should be relaxing, enjoyable, and refreshing if it is to be a helpful part of your life. Most seniors benefit greatly from their travel experiences. Take your camera and take photos to preserve your memories.

9. In advance of hiring any professional service to perform work for you (i.e., attorney, financial adviser, dental care, inpatient hospitalization, or tax account, etc.), talk in detail about fee structures and services provided. Let them know in advance that you routinely look carefully at two or more providers before you contract for a new service. You will be surprised how much better the fee structure will be when the provider knows you are shopping around. By making careful inquiries, you will also learn more about the differences in the services provided, information you may not have had before you called for a service quote.

10. One important idea for good financial planning is to have an ongoing dialogue with your adult children and grandchildren about your financial planning process. You can decide how much detail you want to share, but they need some assurance that you have a plan and they are included in your thinking and your decision-making. In my clinical practice and in my own senior friendship circle, this issue often arises. As a counselor, I often found adult children were at odds why a certain will or gift was given by a deceased parent. Or there was a lot of tension between surviving siblings; some feeling they were treated differently by their deceased parents. You need to initiate better communication over how your assets are being offered and how they will be shared with your family members upon your demise. So either talk now or leave

clear instructions about your intent and your plan for passing on all your valuables.

11. One final issue that needs to be addressed by seniors is the choice of housing as they age and develop health problems. Many of the seniors who are in their seventies and even early eighties do develop dependency issues due to health changes. They start to limit their social activities, restrict their physical involvement, and spend more time at home. They are inclined to no longer care well for their home and property or even themselves or have the will to do so. They may need to move to an assisted living facility or a nursing home. That move needs to be decided in consultation with your doctor and family members. It requires careful planning and real negotiations about future costs and expenses with assisted living officials. Do that consultation when you see the clear value of relocation, and do it when you first feel the need to move. Most seniors wait too long to make the move they need for their overall health and well-being.

Here is where it would be helpful to seek professional help by consulting with a social worker who may specialize in senior health care planning. Then visit several centers for independent living and assisted living and learn their terms for occupancy, especially for lifetime care, and even the provision that they will sell your home if you move into their facility. This step involves serious financial planning and a huge social adjustment, so take each step carefully by making thoughtful decisions along the way. Make certain your family is supportive of your agreement and that the location meets your needs and you feel right about the choice. It is critical that your key family members become involved in this major decision so they can help you make all the necessary adjustments needed, especially about the move from your own home.

****

Material management and vital household care are important tasks for responsible care of your property.

1. The Problem of Poor Management of our Physical Assets: It is a common sight in our retirement communities to see how many garages are filled with used (and often unwanted) household items. Some of us have just recently seen a series of TV programs on A&E television channel on hoarding or the practice of obsessively accumulating a huge amount of unneeded physical goods that are simply stored in huge piles all over the household. It represents a serious mental disorder, but it is sometimes symbolic of the accumulation of "physical things" that haunt almost every senior family's life. We become attached to items we purchase, or they represent a precious memory, or we think we might use them someday. Whatever the cause, we are often overwhelmed with physical items that really need to be disposed of, given away, or sold at the best price we can find. We are victims as seniors of accumulating too many goods and appliances that no longer serve a useful function. We need to get the "mass of things" under proper control.

2. Our households are not always managed well either. They are often poorly kept and not maintained properly. Even for seniors with limited financial resources, they could do much to improve the environment where they live. Appliances are not kept in ready repair, walls of homes are dirty or damaged, furniture is often dated and unsightly,

and the yards are not maintained well. Storage facilities are usually overwhelmed and the home office is usually poorly organized or in disorder. Office files are not cared for well. Yes, we frequently do not carefully manage our homes. We get used to the neglect and disorder, and so we fail to take real initiatives to keep our household in good repair, and we fail to maintain our living space as an attractive and beautiful setting. In effect, we excuse ourselves because we want a "comfortable and a casual look." The reality is that we often do not value neatness, order, and the price in time and money we would have to pay for creating a lovely and attractive appearance for our home.

3. Therefore, let me suggest that we may want to reconsider our attitude and approach toward household management. We may begin to see the value of mimicking those seniors who do maintain an attractive home setting, even with limited income. If you would take time to evaluate their basic value system, you would find that there are common convictions that are usually shared by the conscientious homeowners whose homes are readily kept in idea order and are the envy of the neighborhood where they live. Here are some of their values:

(1) Every living area is a reflection of who we are as owners and occupants of this home. They are a reflection of how we manage and care for our physical appearance. They represent attention to detail, beauty, organization, and the efficient upkeep of the home. Household items receive regular maintenance so they serve our needs as they were intended to do when they were purchased.

(2) The occupants of these neat homes pay attention to style changes, to the upkeep of all appliances, to the replacement of worn-out furniture or lights, and place a priority on cleanliness and the overall appearance of the home, especially for visitors to see. They take real pride in maintaining a home that is not only functional, but it is a beautiful environment. They use color, wall decorations, good lighting, nice window treatments, and control clutter. They relish their home and are proud of it.

(3) The owners of these well-managed homes keep good records of their purchases and follow manufacturer's guidelines. They employ outside help if needed, so they may hire someone to maintain their yard or garden or paint their home or clean their garage. But they are clear what they want done and the quality they expect. They pay their bills on time, add services as needed, and get at least two or three bids for major repair before they hire the worker.

Another Issue of Material Management Is the Problem of Personal and Family Ownership of Our Property:

1. A related issue is the purchase, care, and disposal of personal and household items. It could be our personal automobile, a lawn mower, a set of cameras used for a hobby, or a complete wardrobe of clothes, shoes, and head gear—whatever it takes to live well and healthy, even our whole set of kitchen tools, cooking items, and dishes. The real issues related to all these items come down to when were they are purchased, how they are maintained, and where they are stored. People vary enormously in that regard, all the way from the perfectionist who keeps

everything in immaculate shape to the sloppy owner who seldom takes time to care or store possessions properly. Where do you fit? At least, have a plan for the cleaning, storing, and the timely replacement of the equipment you need for healthy living.

2. What is critically needed is a set of guidelines for all of us who own and use personal property. Let me be very bold, therefore, and suggest some Principles of Material Management that might be very helpful for seniors. They could even make their lives more content.

(1) We need to take more time to choose items that we purchase and use for our personal happiness and welfare. We need to do comparison shopping. In buying a car, for example, it would be wise to check with the annual auto issue of *Consumer Reports*. It recommends key models and identifies the weakness in others. It is usually very helpful in making an intelligent car purchase, and its new care price service is very beneficial for negotiating with the auto salesman.

(2) Keep your purchases in good maintenance and repair, so they will last. Our shoes, for example, are often neglected and not cared for well. Often, we could care more about of our clothing, not only in keeping them clean, but pressed and neatly stored and arranged carefully in our closets. Attention to detail helps when we find proper storage for the items we purchase. Certainly, we should know where every item is safely stored. In addition, we need to pay more attention to the safety factor in the use of our hazardous tools and in the care of the high trees in our yards. Fire prevention needs to get our real attention, and

the storage of emergency equipment needs our focus and interest.

(3) Finally, once-a-year inventory is needed on what items need repair or replacement. Sometimes, it simply means that certain stored items should be sold or given away and *not* replaced at all. Charity clothing drives may be the time to give away, with proper receipts for tax deduction, a large segment of unused clothing and even old appliances. Maybe a home garage sale would help clear out unneeded items and earn money in the process.

We all hang on to items also too long that have deep sentimental value. Here, one can make some exceptions, but treat that exception with limited use.

The final comment I want to make is about financial management issues. I want to emphasize the crucial importance of careful management of your assets and liabilities, your investment program, and your annual tax planning strategy. Even if your net worth is modest, it is vitally important for your welfare. So pay attention to your need to keep yourself on solid financial footing. For example, the simple decision about how you pay off your home mortgage needs to be done with care and consultation. Who helps you to make sound financial investments of whatever money you have available for growth and savings? What can you do to reduce your tax burden in legal and planned steps? Do you have an available emergency fund for health decline or an accident? These questions and others need to be answered, so you have a sound financial plan. that works well for you for your future happiness and well-being.

Real-Life Stories of Good Financial and Property Management:

In our retirement community in Florida, we have several computer consultants who work hard to meet a high demand for home visits to help residences repair, upgrade, or help make their home computer system work more efficiently. Many of these retirees use their computers to record financial data, life insurance information, and even personal health records. They copy key files, scan and send financial forms, and even engage in online seminars on topics that are related to their interests, such as new financial information from their investment company. They also use other new technology when they access an iPod or Kindle, handheld notebooks, or their newest cell phone. In senior centers, we are exposed to frequent free seminars or fairs on financial management issues as the information explosion has hit senior communities in a big way, and seniors are taking advantage of that exposure.

In addition, it is quite common for our elderly population to access the many financial planning firms in the area. They also make heavy use of attorneys to plan their advance directives to become effective when facing end-of-life issues. Funeral parlors often have seminars on the values of purchasing a funeral service plan in advance of death in which all the details of the funeral service, the disposal, and burial of the body are settled in a written document.

In terms of material management, it is not uncommon for seniors to do a carefully planned remodeling of their home and property after years of home occupancy. They upgrade their residence with new closets, new or remodeled kitchens, better furniture, improved lighting, and window treatment, along with more efficient heating and cooling systems. My wife and I have many friends that have done careful planning with quality home management firms to attractively remodel their home. It is an exciting experience to see the older household and then see what they have done to modernize it.

Supplemental Materials: (1) Steps in Financial Planning for Senior Living, (2) A Positive Approach to Estate Planning, (3) Personal Financial Record Keeping, and (4) Control over the Stuff It Takes to Live Today

Supplement 1, Chapter 6

STEPS IN FINANCIAL PLANNING FOR SENIOR LIVING

1. Come to Understand the Purpose and Intent of Financial Planning:

Financial planning is the process in which you set goals for your life through the proper management of all your financial resources. It entails all issues related to your current income, savings, investments, and estate plans. It also involves paying constant attention to issues related to your fixed and projected expenses. It includes all the decisions you need to make in regards to how you might offer financial help to family members or friends who are close to you. It certainly includes a decision each year about the extent of your charitable giving. Certainly, all these issues are critical to your future, so an objective qualified party would be helpful to you on an ongoing basis.

2. See the Value and Role of a Financial Planner.

In our contemporary world, financial decisions are complicated and often difficult.

Most seniors do not have the knowledge or the skills to manage their financial resources today. There are so many complications with tax laws constantly changing, the investment market in turmoil, and frequent uncertainties about dependable income. A real financial adviser will help (1) with the decisions about how money is spent, saved, and invested; (2) in tax planning and saving at all levels of income related to local, state, and federal tax obligations; (3) in setting up an annual budget and in living within those limits; (4) in learning to maximize your income from all sources; and (5) in doing advance planning of your will and your legacies.

3. Issues to Address in the Management of Your Financial Resources

Seniors especially need to be careful to avoid being a victim of financial fraud.

There are many people who offer a variety of scams on the Internet, and seniors seem to be their primary victim. In addition, seniors who become vulnerable due to declining health must choose carefully the person they want to take over their power of attorney for financial affairs. They need help to choose someone who is reliable, trustworthy, and wise and who can communicate well with everyone involved.

4. Seniors need to maintain good financial records, so they can benefit from advice in setting up a system that works for them. It may not be advisable to just talk to a close friend and follow his/her system. What is needed is to adopt the newest and most reliable bookkeeping and record keeping files available at a reasonable cost. There are sources on the Internet that can be located by a Google search under the title "Free Financial Records

for Seniors," but their reliability needs to be evaluated by your consultant.

Supplement 2, Chapter 6

FREQUENTLY ASKED QUESTIONS ABOUT GENERAL ESTATE PLANNING

1. What are the benefits of an estate plan?

An estate plan helps to provide for those you love who survive your death. You spent most of your life accumulating assets and various physical possessions. Now you need to plan carefully how they can be distributed to your family and friends. Your plan gives you the real assurance that your possessions will continue to help those you care about.

2. How can you prepare those who will receive your assets?

It is a shock and surprise to many recipients that you remembered them and often for more than they ever expected. When it comes to specific items, like jewelry or mementos, it is always so helpful if you could include a note about why these items were given to specific people. It is also helpful if you could explain why you divided your assets the way you did along with your hope about how they may be used.

3. How can you avoid probate of some of your assets?

In many cases, property can be transferred without the lengthy process of probate. To illustrate, IR As, insurance policies, and some other assets may be transferred through your legal will. If you are on the title of property with another person, like your spouse, that property will automatically shift to the other person. Making simple property transference is usually an important goal in estate planning. Basically, however, as we said before, the best plan is to create a living-trust document with the help of an attorney instead of a legal will. The property in the trust does not have to be probated.

4. The great value in establishing a living trust is that you serve as the initial trustee of your estate and select the successor trustee(s).

Your chosen successor will be able to take charge of your estate if you become ill or incapacitated as well. This role is important and creates a comfortable feeling that your ideas and goals for your estate will be honored and implemented as you have planned.

5. Your will or trust documents, statement of advance directives, and personal notes should be stored in a safe place.

Keep them safe, but let those close to you, including your attorney, know where the full list of your legal papers is located. In addition, they need to be updated annually, so that they reflect your personal preference and your picture of your changing assets.

6. How can a larger estate be transferred with a good result over years after our death?

It is important to know that distribution of an estate can be postponed to a later date and even age with your children or grandchildren. You can set up a target date and conditions for the transfer when you feel they are ready to take responsibility for their new assets. Spelling out specific conditions of the transfer of property is a prerogative of the giver of the asset.

7. You need to consider how you will contribute to charitable or Christian causes.

If you want to leave a legacy to help others outside your immediate family, you need to spell out your preference in a codicil to your will. Be specific and even tell how you hope the assets you leave will help the recipients. Think of your legacy and ask how best do you want your hard-earned valuables can enrich the world you leave behind.

Supplement 3, Chapter 6

PERSONAL PLAN FOR FINANCIAL RECORD KEEPING

Financial records are a vital part of life. These records form an organized way to maintain our total financial resources, to understand our financial progress, and to prepare for the payment of our financial obligations. Make sure key people know how to access these records in case of your disability or sudden death.

A number of record-keeping systems are available, even online, or you can design your own, but there does need to be a system about the storage so you can track your own information when needed. The following are some keys to good record keeping:

1. Keep all receipts and payment records to know how your assets are being spent.

2. Keep records especially that relate your tax payments.

3. Pay all bills by check or credit cards so that records can be easily recognized

4. Develop a budget so you set some parameters about where money will be spent.

5. Keep an account for financial emergencies so you can meet critical needs.

6. Purchase software on your computer for electronic record keeping and use it.

7. Keep a personal pad in your purse or wallet to keep a daily spending record.

8. Consult with your tax account as issues arise that have tax implications.

9. Compare life and health insurance companies, consider dental plan as well.

10. Adopt an automatic deduction plan for routine bills for utilities and electronics.

11. Hide a safe deposit box at home that is fireproof, waterproof and burglar safe.

12. Keep a list of the contents in your home file.

13. Develop a home filing system that is efficient, easily accessible, updated often

14. Keep a close relationship with the bank where you have accounts.

15. Consider a bill paying program through your bank. Ask for the training needed for an automatic deduction system.

Conclusion: Adoption of an efficient money management system is an essential key release from worry about your financial management.

Keep working at the task until you discover a method that works best for you.

Ask for advice from your attorney, bank official, financial consultant, or office supply manager.

Realize that when money is earned, saved, and spent well a great load of worry is lifted from our mind and thoughts.

Reference: OSU Extension-Franklin County, Ohio, on Record-keeping

Supplement 4, Chapter 6

CONTROL OVER ALL THE STUFF IT TAKES TO LIVE TODAY

If you could drive with me around our retirement community, you would be shocked over the way the "stuff" of daily living has taken over. When the garage doors are open, almost every house is packed to the gills. Many of my neighbors even keep one of their cars parked in their driveway because there is no room for the car. I would not even like to visit their attics because I suspect I would be shocked at the accumulation of items.

In a wonderful book called *101 Ways to Simplify Your Life* by Candy Paul, she says, "Life is much easier when your living space is clear of clutter. You are able to find what you need without scrubbing through piles of junk" (p. 53). She suggests we start with a simple closet or cupboard and go from there. I would offer the additional suggestions of developing a long-term plan for putting your whole house in order. It could include redefining where you store key items, what is essential to store and keep, and where it is best to store each piece of equipment or record. One difficult decision is what to do with the treasured items and historical documents that are a rich part of your past. Consider sharing them with your extended family, a historical society, or a special storage garage you rent or buy. Whatever you do, minimize space, organize and label items, and keep them in the best condition possible.

It is not helpful for daily living to walk over, around, and past useless items. It does not enhance the quality of life when you fill your attic to the brim with unused, wasteful equipment, records, boxes of miscellaneous items, and utensils. Some organization of the tools for living is critical for a healthy environment. Use an outside consultant or borrow interior design books from the library. Make your home a place you can take pride in because it is organized, pleasant to live in, and attractive to the visitor's eyes. Develop a commitment that you will no longer live with the "junk" of the past and the chaos that existed before you brought order and organization to your living and storage areas. You will never regret that move toward a simpler lifestyle.

Before you start, visit some model homes you admire. Check out the best furniture and appliance stores for the most up-to- date equipment. Examine home decorating books and current magazines. Ask your friends and family for input. Lay out a plan for short-term and then long-term remodeling. Prepare a budget and decide how much you can do yourself. Then start the long and exciting process of rebuilding your personal environment. Take your time and enjoy every step of the way. It can truly enrich and bring new job to you.

"Our computer helps us in the pursuit
of our growth and learning."

CHAPTER 7

A PURPOSEFUL LIFE FULL OF GROWTH AND LEARNING

You bring a future into your reality each time you make a choice, and as the future becomes your present, you must choose again . . . when you make (healthy) choices you come alive, your creativity follows, all that you do has meaning.

—Gary Zukor and Linda Francis,
The Mind of the Soul: Responsible Choice

It is exciting to be a senior adult with a strong sense of purpose and clear direction about your future. It provides real incentive to get up in the morning and to feel there is much to accomplish for the day ahead. It is my real-life experience that we need this goal setting in our retirement to give meaning and joy to life. That purpose could be a simple decision by a man who loves woodworking to build a wooden cradle for his newly born granddaughter. A woman might choose to join a craft club to do a set of needlepoint napkins for her daughter and son-in-law for Christmas. It can be a small hobby we are pursuing, but do it with real anticipation and fulfillment. The issue is always about what we want to be doing with our time and energy and whether or not it brings us rich satisfaction. Do you know why you get up and get going in the morning? My answer to that question is that we need to see each day of our life as an opportunity for enjoyment, for fellowship, for new discovery, and for real achievement. Daily life does not have to be boring or distasteful! It can take on real meaning when we find what brings us pleasure and rich satisfaction and then we do it! In my case, I find a real sense of accomplishment in volunteer work. I can afford to fully retire and to give my time and talent to worthy causes. I choose to take leadership in the field of mental health education and services that I know so well. It has been a rich experience for me over the years to take leadership in this field. In the profession, I have met so many very fine people, filled with great ability and skill. I have seen real emotional problems being resolved in troubled adults. I have found new information for myself and my family that has been helpful. It has been so meaningful, as well, to keep up with the changing nature of my professional area as a psychologist. My volunteer roles have kept me relevant, in service to others, and connected to the community I have served in for so long.

If you are also concerned about finding relevance and involvement in human services, you can do something similar as well. Just let the right people in your area of interest know you are available and ready to serve. Then learn about the needs and then volunteer to assist the group you join with their service to others. The key is to pick the area where you can best serve and be satisfied. Some of our friends are also using their natural talents in music, in artwork, and in the sports world. Go where you major interest leads you to go and offer the help needed. Then you will be satisfied.

Now I want to review in more depth the vital importance of having a life purpose for meaning and motivation. Let me summarize, for example, the several reasons why having a life purpose and life direction is so very valuable versus just floating along in life without giving thought to either idea.

1. Having purpose gives direction for what and how you use your available time. I am amazed at the large variety of activities seniors choose to do. I have a friend, for example, who has formed a miniature railroad club in his hometown, and he invites the few members to the basement of his home where he has devoted the entire space to building a large miniature railroad created to look like a small town in a wooded countryside. He and his friends spend nights and days working at this beautiful assembly, and they love every minute of it. It consumes and occupies much of their days, but for the members of this group, it is not work or a burden. It is sheer joy.

2. A thoughtful purpose can be choosing the route to learning new skills or to a new hobby or to continue an activity you have known for years. In the senior community, it is surprising to find many people who seek to learn to dance again and enjoy modern music. Some form dance clubs that keep them active and engaged. A strong commitment to golf, softball, swimming, volleyball, or bowling keeps many seniors very active and involved, as well. We have a biking club and a group of hikers who love active sports and the challenge of those activities. Whatever your interest, there are usually other seniors who like the same thing. Just choose to join in and make this activity the focus of your free time. The senior center staff in your community can help you find the right resource or at little or no cost to you, only your time and talent.

3. Many seniors have a burning drive to serve a special cause to help others in need. We have a regular walk-a-thon every year to raise funds for Alzheimer's research and services. For someone who has a close relative with dementia, this is a compelling cause. In addition, we see fund drives for cancer research, for diabetes, for arthritis, for heart health. You might be one of those who are swept up with the passion for a needed charitable cause. That focus becomes your compelling and valuable purpose. Then give your time and talent for that very worthy cause and enjoy the activity of this challenging mission.

4. We have witnessed how many seniors choose to spend much time traveling and sightseeing. We are recreational vehicle owners and are active in the RV Club in our senior community. We have friends who have traveled across the country, even the world. There are others who have a passion for cruises; others participate in Road Scholar programs (formerly Elderhostel), or boating with every kind of craft available. One couple recently told us they took their forty-foot motorized sailboat across the Atlantic and visited several European ports before they returned home to our East Coast. Traveling to see the world can be a strong driving purpose. A local travel agency might be the best resource for help to make that happen.

5. A life purpose can also include caring for someone near and dear to you. It is not uncommon in the senior world to find couples where one party is ill and the other party is the caregiver. In fact, as we age, this scenario becomes more and more a common practice. A neighbor who just visited us recently and shared that he has decided to care for his wife who is developing dementia. She cannot manage her time well anymore and does not know how

to put a meal together, so he fills in where she can no longer function. He was not really complaining to us as he explained his new mission. He just realized that this needs to be his life purpose for the uncertain future for them both. He realized that his love and devotion for his wife is that strong. She deserves his help when she needs it most.

6. Some deeply devoted Christians find their purpose is to serve God in their church nearly full-time or to volunteer for a short-term mission trip to help others somewhere in the world. There are several RV Clubs that travel to various locations in America where they repair and build new structures for local churches that need assistance. . (One is called the nomads). They spend weeks living in their RV while they work for free on the special needs that exist. Some seniors are called to serve in overseas mission stations in a variety of capacities: to do light construction, to provide teaching, to offer medical care, or to lead worship services and train natives in our Christian faith and values. Some seniors also work in offices, sort food and clothing to give away, or transport disabled people who want to participate in church activities. These core groups discover the values of being an instrument of God in their own local church community or in their world at large.

Another very significant focus for retirement living is to become engaged in *lifelong learning*. This means that we never stop the learning process because it is too valuable and important for the vitality of our life. Seniors need to place a special emphasis on the process of keeping up-to-date with the rapid changes around us, or they will surely be left behind. Some simply choose to not even try. We are acquainted with seniors who will *not* use a computer or cell phone. There are older adults who rarely read a book or even a popular magazine. They are content with watching television and reading a newspaper. They have bought into the old myth that you can't teach old dog new tricks. The exciting world of new learning is not for them.

Nevertheless, there is a growing body of retirees who love the pursuit of learning. Occasionally, you hear of a senior who wants to attend and finish college in their mid-eighties. Certainly, you know that most of our metropolitan areas today sponsor what is known as a senior college. It is usually a non-credit institution where seniors can learn together skills they find valuable or discover insights about topics they are hungry to study. Most of our medium to larger cities has book clubs, special health-focused seminars, challenging classes at the local library, and invitation-only training sessions for those who do volunteer work. Just examine the community schedule of almost any public library and Chamber of Commerce or Senior Center, and you will find some significant learning opportunities for the senior world. We are a generation that puts value on learning opportunities and that learning continues mostly in all our lifetimes.

One emphasis that I would like to make is for each of us to set some educational goals for personal achievement. I often recommend that we at least engage in reading a local paper or a popular magazine and be engaged in reading some book or attend regularly some seminar that excites our interest. I further suggest that you share your learning with someone else and engage in active discussion of the content. Some people I admire have the goal of reading several books a year, as well as regular Bible reading, and then they share the content with others and even within their own family.

It always seems more exciting when you can engage someone else in your study and learning experience. I have also encountered others who keep a growth journal or who are engaged in discovering more about their family history. In fact, some seniors love genealogy as a full-time course of study and engagement. They want to preserve the memories and the legacy of their extended family of origin. So whatever rings true in your mind and heart as a learning pursuit, follow it and reach for the stars. In amazing ways, people everywhere have found great meaning in learning new ideas and skills. It adds greatly to the power and joy of living.

Seniors also need to show continued interest and support in learning what your adult children or grandchildren are undertaking. It is obvious that they hunger for your help and encouragement, so offer it in many creative ways. One couple we know bought their granddaughter a new laptop for college and presented it on her birthday. Our son sends a report of the class grades our granddaughter receives each semester, so we can follow her academic choices and achievements. We can also offer praise for those adult children who take continuing education to keep up-to-date in their professional careers. Some grandparents even offer real financial help for tuition and college expenses for their grandchildren.

My final suggestion is that we take pride in mastering new technology when it directly affects our personal lives. A key illustration is the great benefit we have discovered in learning about and using a GPS or Global Positioning Service. It is a hand-operated mechanical tool you place in your automobile to help you locate where to drive to strange or unfamiliar locations. We have learned to program this GPS to the exact street and location where we want to go. It is an amazing tool we recommend for everyone. But we had to be open to learn and to be persistent until we mastered this technology. So the lesson is clear: discover what advantages selective technology brings you and master the ways to handle that new tool. Seniors everywhere will be advantaged if they open their minds to become familiar with the high-tech world of today, even if they select only the purchase and use of a new laptop. A key principle of our ongoing commitment to lifelong learning is to welcome new ideas and learn new skills that enhance the quality of our lives.

Before closing this chapter, I would like to make one more emphasis. That is that we need to commit ourselves to systematically learn *new ideas and innovations*. One tendency in the senior world is to close our minds to change and new ways to do old things. It is almost like we are afraid we cannot master a new task, or we will look dumb using some new tool for living. On the other hand, I believe that our adult children, especially, would be proud and pleased if we are open to change and new ideas. Specifically, it is an exciting experience to witness a young man or woman watch their senior mother drive a recreational vehicle, their father learn to enjoy drag racing, or both parents take a balloon ride. Our adult children are proud of us when we are open to new ideas and embrace them. It is a real experience of wonderful connection, for example, when seniors can connect with their kids or grandkids on Skype or Facebook. Our missionaries in faraway stations can now connect with each other across the world, like they are just talking in the other room.

To conclude, all of us need to see the wonderful values of learning new ideas and skills throughout our lives. The sheer amazement and wonder an older man in his nineties experienced when he learned to play an auto harp ought to be a more common experience. Seniors everywhere, at every age, would benefit greatly if they can make the choice to be committed to lifelong learning and accept new helpful innovations. Realize there is never a better time than now, in our retirement years, to simply enjoy the pleasure of finding new ideas and skills.

Your future is at stake here, so I would like to suggest that you compose your own set of *personal goals for retirement living*. It could relate to each of the chapters of this book and be a very thoughtful summary of where you want to go with your life. You could develop it, in consultation with others, or make it a very personal document for yourself. One of the newest developments in this area is the emergence of a new body of trained *life coaches*, whose primary role is to help others think carefully about their lives, values, and direction for the future. You might access them by doing a search on the Internet for the best source of referral. They are now available in most major cities and they follow ethical standards that are common to those of us working with personal lives and choices. In my experience, the use of a trained and certified coach can be very helpful. In addition, you can also seek help from close friends, family members, or a strong mentor in your life. Either way, it is best to seek advice from others rather than to plan alone. You need the input from the insight of respected professionals or people whose life and accomplishments you respect and admire.

It is also helpful to focus on the different areas of your life to set realistic goals for your evolving future ahead. Consider not only all of the key topics of this book, but areas that are personal and valuable in your life. Then plan to review each one at least once a year and modify your direction as needed. The benefit of this specific goal setting is that it becomes very concrete and, hopefully, it will motivate you to make some very significant steps of growth and positive changes in your life and in your relationships. It can be a vital tool, and I sincerely hope you use it. Consider this step a high priority in your personal planning for healthy living.

Real-Life Stories That Demonstrate This Value:

My wife and I discovered the rich value of having a clear purpose and plan for retirement. Once we decided to sell my clinical practice and retire, we had to decide where to live out our retirement. All the literature we read spoke about the importance of considering location, weather, price, and lifestyle when we were weighing our options. We did agree that we wanted a location away from our existing home in Sheboygan, Wisconsin. Our discussion leads us to lean toward a southern climate and a vacation setting, and we also wanted a relaxed, comfortable, and appealing environment for our new home.

We laid out a plan five years in advance of our relocation that involved visiting retirement centers in California, Arizona, Arkansas, Tennessee, North Carolina, and finally Florida. What we learned from the experience was to clarify our criteria for a new location that best fits our needs and goals. From numerous conversations about the topic, both together and with our extended family and many location representatives, we settled on six expectations that were important to us. They were good weather, numerous choices of senior activities, location near a large metropolitan community, superior medical facilities geared to the needs of aging seniors, many housing options, and appealing homes at attractive prices. After lengthy consideration, we chose Sun City Center, Florida (near Tampa), and we have not had any regret over these last eighteen years of residence. It is just another illustration that goal setting and a careful plan for implementing that goal works well. Finding and implementing retirement goals are critical skills that every senior needs to adopt. Workers in major business in America report that when they consult with their personnel office team about leaving employment to retire, the issue of goals and plans are always raised. Adult children and grandchildren ask repeatedly of pre-retirees about their plans, and they want specific answers. In workshops on retirement planning, the subject of goals and making clear choices is a major focus of attention.

It is very clear, as well, that goals and plans change as we age. We are more active, involved, energetic, and often sports-minded in the early years of our retirement. As we age, these issues change, largely due to our changing health picture and interest level. Therefore, it is even more important as our retirement unfolds that alert seniors reevaluate at least each year their goals and directions. It is often best to do that with a respected family member, a spiritual adviser, or even with your family doctor. Shift your options until you find the right plan to follow with confidence and clarity. In addition, it should touch on all the key areas I have addressed in this book. These are the critical areas for healthy retirement living.

Supplemental Materials: (1) What We Can Do to Find Our Basic Purpose in Life, (2) Living Examples of Seniors Who Achieved Real Goals, and (3) I Want to Make My Life Count

Supplement 1, Chapter 7

WHAT WE CAN DO TO FIND OUR
BASIC PURPOSE IN LIFE?

1. In his famous book, *The Purpose Drive Life*, Rick Warren says, "The purpose of your life is far greater than our own personal fulfillment, your peace of mind, or even your happiness . . . If you want to know why you were placed on this planet, you must begin with God. You were born by his purpose and for his purpose" (p. 17). He assumes that when we are not just focused on self-fulfillment, we can become a part of the building of a better world. In fact, he says that we must build our life on "eternal truths, not pop psychology, success motivation, or inspirational stories" (p. 20).

2. Having worked with hundreds of people in my professional career as a clergyman, a college professor, and finally as a clinical psychologist, I can report that seeking our life's purpose is often far from the mind of scores of people. They seem preoccupied with the business of maintaining a family, keeping a job, and retaining their health and well-being. They do not get involved with the basic questions of life: Why am I here? What can I do with my life? Where am I going? What can I do to make other people happy? Nevertheless, it always seemed to me that we do *need to take time* to ponder and answerer these critical questions over our lifetime. They center on our purpose for living.

3. Let me offer these key suggestions in your search for the basic purpose for your life on earth as follows:

   * Ponder how much education you need for a fulfilling career and financial status.

   * Think about marriage and family ties and what positive role you can contribute.

   * Consider the importance of succeeding in a career and finding happiness in life.

   * What can you do constructively with your leisure time so you experience a time of real pleasure in life?

   * Can you be a part of a religious community that challenges you to grow?

   * Are you committed enough to set some important goals you want to achieve?

4. Set aside times to consider what you want to achieve in life and how you can achieve some real goals in life. I recommend that you do the following:

   * Do a basic life review at the end of each year.

   * Consult with those closest to you about how they view your goals and achievements over your lifetime.

   * Consider what you can do to achieve your personal goals more effectively.

* Observe how other seniors set goals and achieve what they want for themselves and how they achieve themselves.

* Never give up your fondest dreams, but make them realistic and achievable.

Supplement 2, Chapter 7

LIVING EXAMPLES OF SENIORS WHO ACHIEVED REAL GOALS

1. Herb Jackson took up gardening to beautify his backyard for his daughter's wedding. From that day on, he was hooked with the joys of spending time making his living area attractive. He says that he had little time when he was working and raising the couple's four children to plant only a few flowers. With little gardening experience, he ventured out to learn on his own. He visited nurseries looking for ideas and asking questions. He was surprised at how much he enjoyed his new hobby. He found it was a natural for him and that he could create beautiful combinations of plants and flowers, even a sunken garden. In his retirement, he now devotes more time to building an acre of land into an object of beauty he is proud to share with others.

Reference: *Home and Gardens*, October 2005

2. Sharon R. Kaufman, a research anthropologist, interviewed sixty older adults in a research project on their lives and interests. One of her subjects was Alice, age eighty-one, who said her lifetime goal has been "an inner craving for understanding" of the world around her. She tells about Alice and her drive for answers as to why others fail. She was always occupied with the questions about why her parents divorced when she was three and the damage it did to her mother. The focus of her life was to discipline herself to become self-reliant and self-controlled. She also found that service for others became a life theme. That grew out of her deep search for spiritual understanding. Alice seemed most fulfilled when she was involved in helping others.

Supplement 3, Chapter 7

A Statement of Personal Belief

I WANT TO MAKE MY LIFE COUNT

I want to develop all the talents I have and use them for others.

I want to live life to the fullest and enjoy each day along the way.

I want to be kind and loving to others so they will know me by my love.

I want to smile, even to strangers, so I can put a sparkle into the lives of others.

I want to enjoy my friends and family and give them my deep interest and support.

I want to be active in a ministry to those in need so I keep my attention off myself.

I want to be a good marriage partner to my wife, a good father to all my children.

I want to set a high standard of faith and conduct that other will remember and follow.

I want to age well, to enjoy my leisure years, and to celebrate the life of other retirees.

I want to put God at the center of my world so I can be His willing servant day by day.

I want to engage in volunteer roles so I can serve others who can benefit from my life.

I want to organize my life and discipline my conduct so I can make every day count.

I want to be so adaptable that I can cope well with whatever difficulties come to me.

I want to have realistic goals that motivates me to high achievement even now.

I want to work to at overcoming deficits in social conduct, like remembering names.

I want to keep my emotional maturity and exhibit my strong sense of self-worth.

I want to continue to grow spiritually so I can be open to new insights from God.

I want to be happy, to be contented, and to enjoy the richness of life every day.

I want to leave a legacy behind that my family will treasure and always remember.

Let my credo in life be "Though our outward man is perishing, yet the inward man is being renewed day by day,"

1 Corinthians 4:16.

"Life is richer and more fulfilling when we
seek to develop a wellness lifestyle"

CHAPTER 8

BECOMING INTENTIONAL ABOUT CREATING A WELLNESS LIFESTYLE

> Wellness is a bridge that takes people into realms far beyond treatment or therapy---into a domain of self-responsibility and self-empowerment. If you are ill, the wellness approach works. (To help) you become an active participant in the healing process instead of a passive recipient.
>
> —Regina Sara Ryan and John W. Travis,
> *Wellness.*

This book is been focused on making responsible choices in our retirement living that reflect a wellness lifestyle. Our choices reflect and build on our desire to live a positive, healthy, and fulfilling life in our retirement years. What I observe, however, is that many seniors often make horrible choices, using very bad judgment about their lives. That is why I wrote this book, with the goal of providing a realistic checklist with concrete suggestions about how to live a healthy life as we move into the older years of our lives. Therefore, I am urging everyone reading these chapters to examine your pattern of choice making and to commit to do better about building a truly satisfying lifestyle you can enjoy, which your family and friends will be glad to witness and celebrate.

In that spirit, let us take time to examine the way seniors can live a wellness (or positive) lifestyle. First of all, let me suggest that you develop a *healthy routine for your daily life*, a pattern that is both satisfying and productive. That means that your sleep habits need to comply with the best medical recommendations: seven to eight hours of restful sleep in a good bed, with proper ventilation, set at a cool temperature. You eat a sizable breakfast of fruits and juices, or eggs and toast, and of coffee or tea that you can enjoy and appreciate. You engage in tasks during the day that are enjoyable, that involve contact with others, and that are not too stressful or conflict oriented. Your two other meals of lunch and supper can be modest combinations of salads, vegetables, and fruit, along with a meat and potato dish at either meal, with a light dessert only. At the end of the day, you enjoy some entertainment or contact with friends or family. Keeping active also is implicit in this schedule, so you can go to bed again ready for a good rest and enjoyable sleep.

Of course, we may have days when our routines are not very exciting, nor are they filled with much activity, but most days can be full of involvement with learning experiences, projects, volunteer roles, with other people you love, or just enjoying office work. It could also be work at your computer, doing volunteer phoning to connect with others, being active in a club or organizations, work at your craft or hobby or doing tasks that are needed such as shopping or visiting a sick neighbor. The key to it all is that you feel completely immersed in life, and each day is an experience of enjoyment in healthy living.

Another important part of the wellness lifestyle is a strong emphasis on *the simplification of life*. This step means that you make a conscious decision to slow down a hectic life, take time to do what is important to you, to get in control of the high stress in your life, and to find real joy and fulfillment in your activities and relationships. We are a stress-filled nation, always engaged in activities and schedules that press us too hard and keep us keyed up. Seniors can take on that mood and frenzied pace, or we as seniors can withdraw into ourselves and feel lonely and neglected by others. It seems we need to find the right balance between extremes in which we move at the right pace, find time for leisure, and feel acceptance and love by others, all at the same time.

The purpose of this commitment to the simplification in life is to manage our lives more deliberately, so we can enjoy our days with more zest and enthusiasm. All of us have pressures, stressful events, and even heavy demands that sometimes seem impossible to meet. Often the household responsibilities we assume, the difficulty of meeting a monthly budget, the disappointment with the failures of some close friend or relatives can all add to the tensions of life. What we need to do is to realize those are factors we usually cannot change, so we must learn to change what we can change and then learn to live with what we cannot change in ourselves or our circumstances.

Part of the process to achieve a happier life is to take each day in stride and not to magnify our problems out of proportion and beyond reality. It is learning to enjoy and appreciate the many privileges and benefits we have in America and not to take them for granted. We need to emphasize our rich blessings in life, count them one by one, and then live in the glow of the life we lead in this great country where we all live. In the process, never take on more than you can handle well.

Let me suggest some very specific things we can do to make a simpler life happen. Here is my list for your consideration and adoption:

1. *Organize your home and office* so you know where everything is and how to find what you are looking for. That means to place our clothes and shoes in orderly storage, arrange your food sources for easy location, and make certain your tools and household equipment are readily available. Records and office supplies need to be well organized and filed well. Maintenance tools should be kept in repair and operate well. When people visit, they should see an orderly and neatly used living space, with a beautiful appearance set in delicate balance. Clutter or a mess will be unacceptable and unwanted. We understand that organization and neatness create pride of possession, and with them, we can then better manage our lives. By the way, the same organization and neatness should apply for the care of your car and property as well. It is an extension of who you are so why not express pride in every personal vehicle or the lawn and outside property where we live?

2. You *schedule your activities* to arrive on time and set a time to leave. You plan your vacations with careful attention given to budget, transportation, and time away from your private life. You plan ahead to enjoy local entertainment and to find the kind of relaxed events you can afford and appreciate. Planning for your volunteer time or attention to helping others is an essential responsibility. The key to keeping this schedule implemented well is to keep a

pocket-sized schedule book and a posted calendar that bring clarity and efficiency to your weekly and monthly activities. Organizing your time commitments is a positive value, and it does reduce the stress of daily living.

3. Learn to *agree on job roles* for everyone in the household. The public media is often full of stories about rebellious teenagers who resist doing their fair share around the home. They ridicule them for being so obstinate and even lazy. We seldom hear, however, about the fight senior couples have over who does the work in the home that needs to be done. Agreement on this issue will greatly simplify life together and prevent tensions from arising. Take into consideration what interests you most and what skills you can offer. I am acquainted, for example, with some senior couples where the husband likes and does most of the meal preparation and the wife takes charge of all of their financial concerns and correspondence. Do whatever you do best to create a happy household of shared work and responsibilities.

4. It can be fun and enjoyable to develop *a sense of humor.* There are frequent reports of research findings that conclude enjoying humor has a strong, positive effect on our health, our sense of emotional well-being, and it helps build strong social relationships. When we laugh out loud, we feel better; we are even relieved of some of the stress of life, and certainly all of us can learn to be more content with our lives. Magazines like *Reader's Digest* and *Guideposts* frequently report humorous stories or tell jokes that provoke a smile for the reader. News reports or even television program reporters use humor as an enjoyable alternative to the somber stories that dominate the airwaves. Families benefit from telling funny stories

about some event or about themselves, along with the funny thing that happened to others. Yes, humor is a vital part of a wholesome life. It never grows out of style. It is always a benefit to life, so learn to use it often. Learn to appreciate it and even to add your own twist to the humorous stories that are shared in comfortable company.

5. *Engage in a hobby, activity, or sport that brings joy to your life.* We know a couple that relish every day that they play lawn bowling. This is a sport that is often a part of senior communities and that often involves a special uniform, a nice manicured lawn, and a set of rules that govern the way the game is played with a heavy ball that is tossed across the grass for a goal. I have no interest in the game, but for those who do, it is challenging, a wonderful contact with friends, and an easy time to compete.

It is clear that we all have our special preferences for the use of our free time. What is important is that we use that time for our personal fulfillment. So choose well, and even experiment and give a new activity a chance. Hopefully, it will be something you have long sought to do and now have time to do it. Like the senior who always wanted to play the piano for pleasure and now takes lessons to make that happen. He is never as happy as when he can entertain others on his piano.

6. Make it a practice to *do something regularly that brings pleasure and real happiness to others.* We always benefit when we are kind and loving in our relationship with other human beings. In fact, many of you may be familiar with the website RandomActsof Kindness.com. The purpose of the site is to encourage people to commit acts of kindness and thoughtfulness to others, usually without

any expectation of a reward for the action. It is built on the proposition that we will enjoy and appreciate doing many loving and caring things for one another all the time. When we act that way, it makes us feel good and worthwhile. We feel we have contributed to the happiness of someone in need or someone who finds enrichment because of our initiative. So being a loving person is not only morally correct and a righteous act of faith, but it makes for a better world. Therefore, learn to be creative and take steps needed to bring happiness and joy to someone you know or for a person who needs your help and acts of kindness.

7. *Do something innovative or creative.* One of the exciting experiences in life is to find a new pathway that no one has taken before, like the modern discovery and invention of the Internet and its enormous value or the simple discovery of an electronic wheelchair or golf cart for the disabled. These findings have benefited a large number of eager users. But the ordinary person may wonder is there anything left to uncover? The answer is a strong *yes* because the world of innovation knows no boundary. For example, a talented senior in our community just wrote an inspired poetic tribute to honor the heroes of 9/11 that has achieved much acclaim. We have artists that produce gorgeous artwork that glorifies the walls of our theaters, our churches and, our community centers. High achievers in our photo club have beautiful photography displayed in museums and exhibit centers all over the country. Someone conceived the idea to raise funds to support research and programs for Alzheimer's through a community walk, and now communities all over our country are sponsoring the walk-a-thon to raise money for this great cause. No, ideas and projects everywhere are still

to be discovered by ordinary people who want to create a better world. If you have a new way of doing things, pass it on or turn it into a small-business management team. Realize that new innovation is emerging all the time and it is there for you to learn about it and to enjoy the rich experience of discovery.

8. *Invest in offering frequent praise, approval, and appreciation.* It is an easy observation to discover how few people have learned the healthy habit of giving compliments and showing appreciation. I have often witnessed when some senior citizen who made a significant contribution to our community received little or no gratitude for the work done so well. What is the root cause of our reluctance to say, "Thank you" or "You have done well" or "I really appreciate your help with this task?" My own observation is that we have not learned the practice of showing deserved appreciation, or we take these gifts of time and talent for granted, or we are jealous that we lack the same skills ourselves. Whatever the cause, we need to learn the benefits of a habit to show praise and approval. It costs nothing, it takes such a short time, it can build relationships, and it can offer encouragement to those who give so much of themselves. So the next time you have a chance, start your new habit of including a regular act of appreciation for those who deserve it and who need your praise and gratitude. It will go a long way to help you become a better person, and it will give the senior who does good deeds the encouragement to go on and do even more good work.

9. Let me focus on an overlooked facet of human behavior: *pride in the way we present ourselves to others in our social attitude and personal appearance.* I have witnessed some

horrible examples of human interaction. Seniors, who should know better, have been offensive, cruel, obnoxious, and indifferent in their personal contact with other retirees. They are simply not considerate and not kind in their relationship with other people. Very often, it is due to their poor social skills, a troubled background, and self-centered attitude. Whatever the cause, it is harmful for everyone involved, and it is not the way to build a successful retirement lifestyle. We need to learn to be attentive and respectful to everyone we meet. It is a normal expectation that we control ourselves and show a friendly and hospitable attitude in our social contact.

In addition, I would strongly urge senior adults, especially men, to take better care of their personal appearance. Just because we are retired is not sufficient reason for us to be disheveled and unclean. We are old enough to learn to pay attention to our physical grooming and what we wear. People do partially judge us by how we present ourselves and that judgment can be positive if our appearance is pleasing to others. So take time to buy and wear attractive clothing, so you can dress comfortably, clean, and attractively. Develop a sense of pride in your personal grooming of your face, hair, hands, and shoes, as well as in your clothing. Can we reclaim the old value of a fine posture, a warm greeting to others, while dressed well and appropriately for the time and season of the year? Reserve your sloppy days for the privacy of your home and your leisure hours.

10. We need to *develop and maintain positive rituals and worshipful times when our faith is enriched*. Family devotions can be conducted when we are in our senior years. We can make it a point to decorate our home for the Christian

holidays of Easter and Christmas, as well as for other holidays. It is helpful, also, to have a library of Christian books and literature to read and to subscribe to Christian magazines and newsletters. We can display Christian symbols throughout our home so that everyone knows what we believe and what we represent. In addition, it is a good practice to host friends and family over the holidays and on special occasions, like birthdays and weddings. One other practice that my friends and I appreciate is the willingness of Christian retirees to open their home for church meetings, to reach out with a helping hand to their neighbors in need, and to offer encouragement and love by phone or the Internet when they are going through turmoil in their own personal lives. They can be sensitive and loving when it is really needed.

This concludes the section on the *simplification of life*. Hopefully, the ideas presented here have clarified how easy it is to live a simpler life. You need to understand also how this philosophy of life can contribute to the quality of your everyday experience in life. By adopting these easy habits, you can enjoy your world even more and start adding to the quality of the life you now lead. In her epic changing book, *Living The Simple Life*, Elaine St. James says: "I want to give you a glimpse of the tremendous freedom you'll experience when you start to eliminate some of the day-to-day complexities." She is saying that we all need to make personal, household, and lifestyle choices that can either simplify our lives or complicate them, and she is urging us to choose the simpler way of life.

Now we move on to the third component of a wellness lifestyle, and that is, *live with a positive mind-set day by day:* It is crucial for good mental health that we become a positive thinker, coupled with an attitude of hope and optimism. Negative thinking and a pessimistic attitude can take over and drive people away from seeking your friendship and contact. When you worry and let fear or failure take over your thought patterns, you lose every time! The gloom-and-doom approach to making decisions helps little and practically insures that you will make decisions that will fail or displease yourself. You need to change a basic attitude if you have given into pessimism. No matter how much you justify it in your mind, it does not work, and it will ultimately do you self-made harm.

With this assumption that a positive mind-set works better for all of us, let me delineate how it can change the lifestyle of the average senior adult. Let me explain how it benefits us all if we can make the critical shift toward a new, positive mind-set that can change the course of our lives.

1. Being positive and optimistic appears to open up more options for action on every issue you confront. If you are optimistic, it motivates you to try more possibilities for every weighty decision you need to make. One illustration is when you are seeking to buy a house or getting a car loan, the optimist will believe that by striving hard and finding alternative bids, he or she will discover the best loan at the best rate available. This hopeful senior acts on that assumption and closes a loan on favorable terms. The typical pessimist says that affordable loans are not available and so make no earnest attempt to find it.

The gloomy senior stays in the apartment where he or she lives. In addition, the pessimist is not sure you can trust the leaders today because there is not one out there that generates trust. So their lives are limited by negativism, and their mind is occupied by doubt. As a result, their gloomy perspective restricts their action and prevents the good results they need for a better future. They even fail to vote in a regional or national election because they believe their one vote will not make a difference, so why try.

2. Positive people are more enjoyable as friends and colleagues. It is far more satisfying to be with someone who is happy and outgoing than to spend time with a person who is bitter and cynical. Unfortunately, a negative mind-set can start with a belief system that others are selfish and unconcerned about your needs or are out to cheat you. When the cynic believes that about others, it colors everything that he or she does in relationships. It may be that they were conditioned that way from childhood or had some bitter disappointments in life. Whatever the cause, the results are the same. Our attitude colors our conduct, and we respond accordingly. Consequently, if we want to find friends, be loved by our extended family members, and enjoy our work world, we need to be positive, optimistic, and filled with hope. It goes a long way to building a happier lifestyle for everyone involved.

3. Let me emphasize here that a positive mind-set is built on a set of basic beliefs that support that attitude about life. A negative mind-set is also the product of a set of beliefs that produce and guides that attitude. It is helpful if we can compare these two belief systems so we can see clearly the assumptions they operate under each day. The following two columns show the contrasting assumptions of these two belief systems:

Negative Belief System	*Positive Belief System*
You cannot trust anyone anymore.	People are good at heart.
People are nice so they can use you.	Show trust and be trusted.
God does not care about my needs.	God loves me, and He cares.
Life is a struggle just for survival.	Life can be full of love and joy.
Happiness is there only for a few.	We can all find happiness.
The world is falling apart and in crisis.	Every age has issues to solve.
Sunday is my time for rest and leisure.	Sunday is time to worship.
I don't need close friends around.	My friends are my joy in life.
Optimists don't face harsh realities.	Optimists do face reality.

The conclusion from these starkly contrasting views about life is that your perspective makes a huge difference. So you need to examine your basic assumptions about the world around you and about the people in your life. Realize now that a positive attitude about life offers rich rewards that keep on producing a happier lifestyle. My advice is to work hard now to rid yourself of your negative mind-set and work at changing your outlook to reflect a spirit of hope and optimism, even in the face of a world that is too often full of gloom and doom. This may be a crucial shift of thinking and acting for some of you, but it is a critical change that can make a whole world of difference in the way your life is lived.

A final word about our wellness lifestyle is to *place an emphasis on environmental concerns:* That means that we demonstrate an awareness that we all need to take responsibility for building a better world by not abusing our environment and by taking steps to protect our fragile infrastructure. Our natural environment is under great strain because of many manmade abuses. We have wasted precious drinking water by our careless habits with our toilets, our showers, our pools, our lawn sprinkling, and our play areas, just to name a few. The environmentalists tell us that we have abused our natural resources of oil, forests, lake water, and the ocean itself. Everywhere we go, there are increasing signs that we need to protect our environment or we will suffer damage that may be irreversible. So it is critical that we take responsibility to protect the physical world around us, and do what is within our power to do right. Some of the best of the suggestions for taking personal initiative are listed as follows:

1. Save all garbage from our homes and see that it is disposed of carefully.

2. Separate our disposable items into metal, aluminum cans, and garbage when we dispose of them in a public facility.

3. Upgrade your toilets to low-flush, highly efficient toilet bowls.

4. Save on gas by buying and using more gas-efficient automobiles.

5. Buy easily disposable paper products that can keep our homes clean.

6. Dispose of outdated and used medicine in a community-sponsored dispenser that burns them in an approved incinerator.

7. Use solar cooling and heating for your home and roof when it is available in your area and when it is cost effective.

8. Be more sensitive to the danger of outdoor barbecue pits and open pit fires.

9. Refuse to order restaurant food that will go to waste. Order only the portions you can consume. Take leftovers home for consumption later.

10. Contribute to your favorite environmental organizations and support their cause. Become better informed about the issues they are seeking to address and correct. Search the Internet for critical new information. A very helpful site is articles.freeplant.net.

Concluding Remarks: My hope is that you have developed a better understanding of the wide-ranging area of high-level wellness. The fundamental concern at the heart of wellness is the quality of your daily lifestyle. The assumption is that every senior is challenged to achieve a fulfilling life (i.e., our golden years) in our retirement. We all know that this does not come easily nor does it occur by our neglect. It is a direct extension of our intentional choices to make retirement the best years of our lives. So whatever helps make that happen can be considered to be under the topic of developing a "wellness commitment" toward a healthy lifestyle.

One real concern in all the current geriatric literature is that seniors do not prepare well enough for this third and final stage of life. We slide into retirement and fail to examine and decide about all the issues that make for healthy aging and living in our older years. Consequently, we need to develop the habit of making responsible life choices. There are so many dilemmas about what choices to make. My hope is that this book has given you a fresh *checklist* for you to review to help you in those very settings. My philosophy is that all the areas in this book are subjects for a thorough review for your retirement planning. My intention is that this text acts as a key and helpful tool in that process. See it as your guide for your own retirement. Measure your situation against what is suggested for healthy living.

Let me conclude by sharing the four things my wife and I have done in our own checklist for making responsible life choices. Hopefully, you can make your own list and share it with friends and family. Here is where we are making our primary focus for our healthy retirement:

1. We put a heavy emphasis on a *health focus* by giving strong attention to preventing health problems and keeping the good life we now enjoy. That means we are reading, consulting, learning, and defining the best way we can live in our age group. If we find a new exercise we enjoy, we adopt it, but we at least seek to discipline ourselves by active movement all day, or we engage in some planned exercise (like walking, biking, tennis, golf, swimming, or using a treadmill) every day. We do take vitamin supplements that are approved by our doctor. When we locate a new highly recommended antioxidant, we check it out and use it. We do take regular flu inoculations each year, along with a routine health examination. We pay attention to dental cleaning. We do try to work at maintaining good mental and emotional health, starting by how we feel about ourselves, and learning to enjoy and appreciate others.

We maintain active participation in our community and are not sedentary seniors. We keep in contact with our eye clinic to check regularly on our vision and our eyeglass correction. I have learned to manage my hearing aids well, so my hearing loss is under control. Our marriage is strong and supportive, and we intend to keep it that way. Our friendships are rich and fulfilling, and our extended family connections are strong. We keep open to new ideas about health maintenance, such as taking testosterone supplement for me to preserve my energy and muscle tone as I age. We also join with other seniors in paying attention to the dangers of unintended falls. We keep our minds active by reading, playing table games, writing, and becoming proficient on the Internet because we do not want to succumb to dementia. What are you doing to maximize your health care in your stage in life? Isn't it time you made your list of your own plans for self-improvement and good health?

2. We seek to support a strong *faith focus* by giving much time and attention to our religious practices. That means we attend an adult education class at our local church (where I am the group leader), and we are in attendance at our regular Sunday worship services. We share two devotional resources as a couple prior to our bedtime. Both of us read the Bible regularly and discuss what we read. We have found that reading Christian books and literature is a wonderful outlet, as well.

We also keep up-to-date with the news in the world of religion where we find challenging articles for personal growth. Most of all, we pray at each meal and pray regularly for our own needs and the needs of others. When we can, we share our faith with others and help them find a commitment to Christ and a new church home. We are quite open and honest with our adult children and grandchildren about our faith in Christ, and we urge them to find a faith for themselves. Our experience is that living the Christian life is the most rewarding way for us to live. All other options have shortcomings and never supply the rich satisfactions we have found in our Christian lives. In addition, the strong value system that flows out of an active faith provides a critical alternative to living a secular, self-centered narrow lifestyle. It seems almost every day, we find our lives tested in some way, so this strong faith foundation helps us greatly to live a happy, hopeful lifestyle and to age well. In addition, the warmth and the loving support of our fellow church members make us strong and confident that we are coping well with the world around us.

3. We have made a real commitment to *social activitism*, so we have intentionally sought a large circle of wonderful friends. It takes real initiative, however, to make that happen. We go to social events, invite people to our home, respond to social invitations, and join social groups that provide a positive purpose, like our recreational vehicle club that travels to various destinations each month from our retirement community. In addition, we have found that there is a great value in being active in serving others through service organizations. In my wife's case, she is working with *hospice* and in doing visitation to disabled adults that need social support and prayer. In my case, I am fully invested in the work of a coalition for mental health and aging. We develop educational programs and support groups for seniors who want to focus on the many mental health issues of aging: depression, anxiety, marital conflict, loneliness, and declining physical and mental health. What are you doing for your own spiritual needs now and for your future? As we move closer to death,

these issues take on new meaning and become much more important. Why not address them *now*!

4. We have made a real decision to be active in our *mentoring role* for others. We have found that younger people, even our own children and grandchildren, need living models of healthy adult behavior. They need people to admire, to enjoy, and to model how to live well. So we are very conscious of this need to help a variety of age groups. That is why we often share with younger adults, as well as with our own family, the things we are doing and what is working and not working in our lives. It is very interesting how eager they seem to be in our conversations. They frequently want to know how we keep our health, how we handle our finances, how we maintain our values in a secular world, and even what we enjoy for fun and human-interest contact. We do want to leave our legacy with the people we have influenced and motivated to live a Christian life in a hard to manage world. What do you feel about your commitment to leaving a positive legacy for others who follow you?

5. We have decided firmly and realistically how to *manage our financial planning*. We have taken firm initiatives about the financial management of our resources. We do engage the help of a CPA to handle our financial reports to the Internal Revenue Service and an attorney to help us complete our advance directives to handle our final estate documents. We engage a financial planner to help us with setting our goals for our financial future and to manage the assets we now own and invest. We pay our bills on time, and we live well within our budget and keep good financial records. It is a nice feeling to realize your financial plan is working and under control. It is

obvious that many seniors have serious financial pressures and limited resources, but we maintain even those adults can manage their limited resources with more care by seeking the help of even volunteer financial counselors. You can sleep better at night knowing your financial plan is working. Have you found a financial plan that works for your peace of mind and welfare?

6. Often, I talk to seniors in trouble or speak to groups who want to learn how to live a fuller, richer life in retirement. I tell them that my favorite word for success in living is *resilience: learning to bounce back from hardship or a setback in life.* This means we can learn to change a threatening or troubling situation with a constructive and helpful course of action that offers a better life ahead. Resilient people are adaptable, flexible, creative, and good at problem solving. They do not let a personal crisis overwhelm them or destroy their peace and happiness. They cope well with life and move on without letting a bad relationship or situation harm or destroy their world. So when losses, trauma, stress, or change occurs in their life, they take it in stride and still find meaning and purpose in their daily life.

One vivid illustration of this principle of resilience is our recent trip to Boston to celebrate my fiftieth class reunion as a seminary graduate of Boston University School of Theology. For seniors of any age, this flight was highly stressful and demanded that we relate well to the intense demands of the travel world of today. We had real moments when we sought to locate an affordable hotel, which we found to be far below acceptable standards. Our transportation was complicated by the heavy traffic in that old city. Food and costs of entertainment were way beyond our budget. No one set our schedule, so my wife and I had to arrange our own. No face was familiar, so everyone we met was a new personal contact, so there were constant adjustments to a changed environment, and the experience required often-rapid adaptability, or we would be totally lost. The fact that we survived (and even enjoyed our experience) means we have learned some lessons about resilience that have served us well. The key seemed to be able to make quick and responsible choices that had to be made without warning. We as seniors are not often placed in that kind of setting, but sometimes, life has a way of forcing us into surprising developments that require us to make those same quick choices that can have long-term implications for our future. Developing our ability to be resilient helps greatly.

Many successful seniors use humor, a commitment to faith, and love as their primary tools to survive. It is quite telling, as well, that most of the survivors in the senior world I have known (even those over ninety years and beyond) seem to take this quality of *resilience* for granted. It appears to be built into their basic attitude toward life. They just understand they do not ruminate about their mistakes and failures; they turn to their faith and friendship or family connections for strength; and they seek the best counsel available to help them decide what to do. Developing an attitude of gratitude about what you do with your life is very helpful, as well. You do not get into the blame game where you stoke your anger or allow yourself to be full of resentment. What you do is to face the reality you must confront and then you *move on* to a fuller, richer life ahead. It is really a better way to live. What are you doing to learn to be a more resilient person in your life circumstance? Start today to find that wonderful human skill, and you can discover new joys in your daily life and relationships.

Let me finish this chapter by sharing the results of a classic, very meaningful study of 169 centenarians all residing in the United States who lived at least to the age of one hundred or longer. It was called the New England Centenarian Study, and it was in collaboration between Harvard Medical School and Beth Israel Deaconess Medical Center in the Boston area. Most of those successful seniors were found to share most of the key characteristics that helped them to live so long. The qualities that contributed to their longevity were identified as follows:

- Good longevity genes

- Emotional resilience or the ability to adapt well to change

- The ability to handle stressful events in their lives

- Intellectual activity or keeping the mind active and alert

- Maintaining a good sense of humor

- Strong religious beliefs that guided their life

- A close connection to other people and frequent activity

- An appreciation of the simple pleasures of life

- Finding a zest for life and the future

- Many played musical instruments

The conclusion of this study is that we all have much to learn about how to grow old gracefully. Nevertheless, there are lessons we can begin to comprehend. We need to commit ourselves to understanding the aging process itself and to become more skilled at aging well. My belief is that a critical part of that process is to start to *make responsible life choices* here and now today. That is a never-ending process, but by taking one step at a time, we can make it happen!

My prayer is that these retirement years ahead of you will be the happiest, most fulfilling years of the long life you will lead. May God guide you every step of the way. Celebrate and rejoice in your retirement now and in the years to come! Remember that better decision making will lead to better living for everyone and for the wonder years ahead. It is an essential habit to develop for healthy living.

A Real-Life Story of Wellness Living:

This is a story about several seniors we know and the exemplary lives they led over time. They seemed to have grasped intuitively what it is like to live well in today's world. First of all, there is Larry who is a full-time caregiver for his wife who has dementia and other related health problems. He cares for her constantly, twenty-four hours daily, seven days a week. He rarely hires a home health care worker because he believes that his life's mission is to serve his beloved. In fact, he shared with us that he had a distinct moment of insight when he felt and readily accepted the call. So he goes about his day with a positive, supportive, and healthful attitude in offering his daily care. He seldom does for himself because he feels so strongly drawn to this caregiving role. He doesn't complain either, since he believes these are still precious moments he and his wife can share together. Her health is so precarious that he could lose her any day, so he enjoys and appreciates the time they have left together. It is a new calling, and he has the respect of the neighborhood for the way he carries out his mission.

It is so inspiring to witness how ordinary people can rise to the challenge and do extraordinary things for others. I am a part of a retirement community where volunteers, who perform amazing services for others, operate effectively every day. Usually, however, it is the product of some visionary person who sees a need and responds to it. We have an organization that provides free rides for residents who have no vehicle for use. They take people to appointments, to meet their shopping needs, and even to a social gathering. Our small city has a heavily staffed emergency squad that is open twenty-four hours a day to transport people to the hospital when a health crisis arises. Many of our volunteers head up service clubs, veteran's organizations, and support groups that provide help to people with particular health needs. The point of this report is that these caring people represent one of the best qualities of our American life: We want to reach out and care for each other. That is not only a wonderful quality in our society, but it is another evidence of the wellness factor we call "showing compassion for others." It brings warmth and joy to countless people every day and it makes our lives richer for seeing it happen.

Supplements: (1) The Benefits of a Focus on Wellness in Our Lives, (2) Happiness is (A Senior Version), (3) Steps to Take to Incorporate a Wellness Lifestyle in Our Lives; and (4) Lifestyle Choices for the Senior Adult (A Checklist).

Supplement 1, Chapter 8

THE BENEFITS OF A FOCUS ON WELLNESS IN OUR LIVES

1. Remember that wellness means achieving our maximum potential for health and wholeness in our senior years.

It involves building strong and toned muscles, keeping ourselves emotionally well and content, and it entails developing strong faith and firm values. What we understand is that the result of that emphasis in life is that we gain more energy; we are usually more efficient with the management of our lives; we tend to have few physical complaints and illnesses, and generally, we live better and longer over time. Obviously, it is a real value, and it calls for our commitment to that lifestyle.

2. A key emphasis in wellness training is to establish a careful balance between body, mind, and spirit. That means we need to not only take serious care of our own health, but develop the skills to find peace of mind and a better relationship with others and with God. The result is that we feel that life is worthwhile and that we have purpose and meaning for our existence. It gives us a good feeling about what we do day by day with ourselves.

3. In each of the six dimensions of wellness, there are benefits that flow from the stress on developing a strong lifestyle. To be specific, here are the issues that make up an emphasis on wellness over our lifetime:

   *   Physical wellness produces a healthier body that gives a better appearance and a body that resists the impact of disease, bodily injury, and stress.

   *   Emotional wellness produces a better ability to cope with the demands of life and the changes we must all face. You learn how to manage, understand, and express your emotional feelings. You develop the ability to even handle a crisis with more intelligence and skill.

* Intellectual wellness helps you be more creative and stimulating so you become a more interesting personality. You learn to better expand your knowledge and understanding about the world around you.

* Spiritual wellness helps you explore the meaning of life and your purpose in it. You learn to appreciate that you are on a life journey, and you need to find our place in that pathway. You learn to draw strength and the ability to love yourself and others in your spiritual quest, as well as how to trust God and to serve Him.

* Social wellness emphasizes your contributions to the larger community around yourself. You become involved in helping others, not just relating to a few friends and family. You become involved in building a better environment and improving the conditions of life in our world.

* Occupational wellness means you carefully choose your career pathway and career preparation. You seek to use your natural talents and abilities for your own enhancement and joy in your career role. Then you exit your working world and move smoothly into the new life of healthy retirement living.

Supplement 2, Chapter 8

HAPPINESS IS (SENIOR VERSION)

1. Having a good night's sleep

2. Finding your car keys when you need them

3. Relishing a good cup of coffee and a roll

4. Enjoying the evening news on TV

5. Remembering people's names we have just met

6. Finding out you don't have to use that expensive medicine anymore

7. Discovering a talent you never knew you had

8. Having our partner scratch your back without you even asking

9. Sitting down with your grandchild to hear about her/his many accomplishments

10. Finding a friend from your past you have not seen for years

11. Sitting quietly in your favorite chair while watching the sun go down

12. Getting a check in the mail from a stock settlement you never heard about

13. Enjoying your very own surprise birthday party with friends and family

14. Getting a compliment from strangers about how young you look

15. Winning at cards with friends when everything seemed to go your way

16. Losing weight without really trying and being proud of your new look

17. Looking at the new world you can see after cataract surgery and being pleased

18. Having a very good night of sleep with no restless issues you have to resolve

19. Being told by people you trust that they admire how you have lived your life

20. Feeling a sense of personal satisfaction and contentment about your present lifestyle

WHY NOT ADD YOUR OWN LIST AND BE HAPPY YOU CAN ENJOY OTHER THINGS?

Supplement 3, Chapter 8

STEPS TO INCORPORATE WELLNESS IDEAS INTO OUR LIVES

1. Set clear-cut goals so you know what you want to accomplish in life. Most of the seniors we know have concrete goals. The ones we respect want to improve their health practices, do better with an exercise program, and expand their social world. All admit, however, that they have not developed a full plan for developing real wellness in their daily lives.

2. Wellness consultants suggest that we need to expand our understanding of a true wellness lifestyle, such as how to develop nutritional health, how to become involved in environmental concerns, or how to be better prepared for the next crisis that overwhelms the family. Other areas of interest are how to build our own capacity for sharing

humor, for developing our leisure-time activity, or how to appreciate music and the fine arts.

3. A wellness commitment means that we focus directly on the areas of our lives that need some radical reworking. Some people might need to improve their sleep habits, their weight control, or their social ties in their own neighborhood. So whatever the deficiency, view these deficits as a focus for new growth and for real change in our lifestyles.

4. If you are new to the wellness concept, some serious research is in store for you. Do a search on Google if you are computer savvy. Check the local library or look for a subscription to the *Wellness Letter*, published by the University of California (WellnessLetter.com), or check at our local university for seminars on the topic. You may find a section that may trigger a major interest you may want to pursue for study and involvement.

5. One of the major obstacles seniors face is their resistance to *change*. They are used to doing things a certain way and they hate to be pushed to do differently. It is important, however, to realize that the key elements of wellness living are a real benefit to the quality of your life. So be open to take the steps needed to make the changes that a new lifestyle will require. You will never regret that you decided to move forward and onward into a better future.

One concept that is basic to a wellness lifestyle is the focus on finding models of healthy living that inspire you and motivate you to move forward into healthy living. Let me suggest you read positive biographies of inspiring people whose lives reflect wisdom and a high quality of life. Find people in your own contacts that you admire and respect and learn from them about how to live your own life. Look for outstanding examples in the news and discuss what they can teach you. Talk to people who have achieved much about how they were motivated and how they learned to accomplish what they did.

CONSIDER HOW WELLNESS COMMITMENT CAN CHANGE THE COURSE OF YOUR LIFE

Supplement 4, Chapter 8

LIFETYLE CHOICES FOR THE SENIOR ADULT TODAY

The following is a list of items that need to be addressed either in pre- or post-retirement if you are expecting to get the most out of your retirement experiences. Check your own preferences and use this checklist as a guide in your planning. Add your own items to this list.

Keys for Decision Making	To Be Done	Completed	Not Interested
Where will we live in retirement			
How will we finance our retirement			
How will we maintain our health			
How will we relate to our family			
What will we do in estate planning			
How will we expand our friendships			
How do we plan to simplify our life			
How are we going to give up bad habits			
What will do about travel plans			
How will we enrich our marriage			
How do we plan to use community resources			
How do we plan to handle stress effectively			
How can we develop our skills and talents			
How can we set and keep spiritual goals			
How can we do long-term planning			

"It is sometimes difficult to deal with our family
history and the memory of deceased loved ones"

CHAPTER 9

COPING WITH LIFE WHEN PROBLEMS OVERWHELM US

Even in terrible circumstances, you can experience
great happiness, despite your problems and losses, and
sometimes even because of them. No matter what
your situation is, you can get good care and live as
fully as possible. In other words, you can become a
Healthy Survivor.

—Wendy Schlessel Harpham,
Happiness In A Storm

There are many senior adults who have had their dreams of
a happy and healthy retirement deeply shattered because of
various circumstances. They struggle daily just to maintain
themselves and keep going. They may develop physical
problems that become lifelong and seriously limiting.
Many older adults become drawn into long-standing family
conflicts or deeply troubling emotional turmoil of their own
making. Then there are those seniors who have never resolved
their spiritual doubts or have become bitter against God
and the church at large because of some disappointing life
circumstances. In addition, we have seniors who have never

developed their social skills and have lived lonely, isolated lives for most of their lifetime. Add to this list those seniors who have badly managed their financial affairs and are always in some financial crisis and work to survive.

This chapter seeks to address these issues: (1) what are the key causes for failure to thrive in our retirement years; (2) describe the depth of the struggles they face every day to find a healthy life for themselves; and finally (3) what real strategies do they need to find some real happiness and significance in their lives despite their limitations and struggles to survive. Some of these ideas have been mentioned before, but they are offered here for special emphasis.

Key Issues that Cause Seniors to Not Thrive:

1. Inherited Problems of the Past: It is more common than most of us realize that many seniors live with issues out of their control. We are talking about a physiological propensity for a weak heart, diseased lungs, mental illness, limited vision or hearing, or even the absence of a body part, like a functional leg or arm or an internal organ. This is often a life sentence that requires major adjustments and limited movement. These issues are often thrust upon adults without their choosing. They are often also the product also of a dysfunctional family life history and a larger family network that offers little help or support.

2. Major traumatic events can limit movement, career choices, or even the ability to marry and have children. Some seniors have had a serious accident that has left a permanent scar. Sometimes, it comes over the loss of a career, the breakup of a long marriage, or the early loss of

a life partner in death. Whatever the cause, it is a serious blow to their life and future plans. They feel wounded and restricted in their ability to enjoy life and relationships.

3. Sometimes, seniors have simply made horrible choices with seriously harmful consequences. It is not hard to understand the consequences of choosing the wrong career and then living with that choice for a lifetime. The problems of finding a marriage partner that only causes havoc is real to many adults, and the results of that choice are often devastating. In addition, one could only imagine the long-term end results of making bad financial investments and having to live with those results, even of being in bankruptcy. Talk to attorneys who work with those clients, and they will tell you harrowing stories. It is saddening to talk to new residents in our retirement community who moved to Florida too quickly after retirement only to discover they want to live close to their adult children. They wasted time and a large amount of money to reverse a poor choice that would have devastated their lives.

4. Many older adults have never developed wholesome, healthy, and positive attitudes about how to live out their lifetime. They started as youth with a pessimistic, critical, hostile, and bitter attitude, and that basic approach toward the world around them has never changed. They are often loners who are always on the edge of society and never happy with the world around them. Their basic perspective is one of hostility and discontentment. Unfortunately, that life pattern never leaves them, and they suffer dearly with negativity. Talk to a person like that, and you come away feeling down and discouraged yourself.

5. One major issue in retirement is that of loneliness and isolation. Many of the widowed women in our community can tell you how it feels. When you lose a life partner in your older years, your social life suddenly changes. You are not invited to couple activities anymore. You go home to an empty place. You have to plan for social events to attend alone. When you go out for social events, you function by yourself and you come home with no one there to share your experiences. For the partially disabled senior, it is even worse because there is no real companion to help you move around or to assist you to move in and out of a locations. The one who suffers the most are those older adults who have limited social skills. Their world is a series of lonely days with few contacts with other adults at any time. That is one reason for the rise of suicides in the senior world today. Loneliness is a real factor in their daily lives.

6. A real issue that impacts the senior world especially is that of unmerited suffering. So many seniors struggle with declining health, with the loss of family members, and with limited mobility. In an excellent book by M. Esther Lovejoy entitled *The Sweet Side Of Suffering*, she says: "We have all seen the bitterness and anger that suffering can produce. We have known those who have never recovered from the onslaught of its pain and heartache" (p. 14). It is part of the reality of aging or one of the prices people pay for neglect or poor choices. Either way, it is a heavy burden for many senior adults and one that they live with for the rest of their natural lives. It is a reality, however, that must be faced and dealt with through a creative approach to problem solving. There are many healthy adults who have had large losses in physical health and relationships who still find joy and meaning in daily life.

7. Finally, there is a whole segment of the senior world that has never achieved the American dream. They have struggled all their lives just to meet their basic financial needs. They are behind in their bills and are hounded by bill collectors. Many of these people have moved from job to job or are part of the homeless society that moves from place to place. They may have little or no family support and share few friends. Sociologists describe them as being a part of the disenfranchised segment of our total population. They are an enigma for the county social service department staff in most states because it is hard to know what to do with them. They often defy solutions and what help is often offered proves to be fruitless.

Many Seniors Struggle to Cope with Their Life Situation Every Day:

1. They need to resolve some long-standing issues that have plagued them for years. Just one issue will illustrate the point. For some seniors, the topic of not being able to forgive an offense against their integrity by a family member or friend is a difficult problem. It may be over some debt that is never paid, some decision to move away from family contact and to live in a faraway place, or marriage to a person that does not fit into the family network at all. Whatever the cause, many seniors live with anger and resentment against someone who they consider has offended them deeply. Unfortunately, they carry the burden of hurt and hard feelings, and they never go away. They need to lift that heavy burden, learn to forgive, and move on to a fuller, richer life. None of us need to remain victims of injustice. We can find a life free of hurt and rejection. We can learn to love and enjoy life again.

2. Many seniors live with an untreated mental or emotional disorder and never seek treatment for their condition. It could be depression that hits the hardest with older adults. Sometimes, it can be high-level anxiety or a worry habit that never goes away. There are many senior adults with bipolar disorder that causes them to gravitate from depression to anxiety sometimes during a single day of life. In addition, a significant segment of seniors have serious marital problems and divorce seems the only alternative. Whatever the issue, it is very important that these older adults take initiative to seek the help they need, and stop staying in denial with the belief the problems they are experiencing will gradually go away on their own. This wishful thinking is a myth that needs to be confronted and corrected.

3. The daily task of coping with physical limitations is very difficult. Talk to someone who lives in a wheelchair every day and ask them how they handle the task. They will tell you that it is a struggle that goes on and on. They will explain that getting someone to help you move into the chair easily is a challenge. It takes just to be the wheelchair user. Or consider the blind adult who needs either a human aide or a guide dog to move anywhere, and you see the difficulty of living with a physical loss. Just coping with the basic issues of preparing for the day, eating, or traveling is a major task that needs planning and assistance. Don't forget, as well, the senior adult who has lost his or her hearing and now lives in a soundless world. Some victims struggle to enjoy life when they cannot hear a human voice or a bird sing. New technology, however, offers hope for the people with hearing loss and for other physical issues

4. Consider the struggle of living with memory problems or even full-scale dementia. The increase in the frequency of this development is probably due to our bulging population of older seniors, but it still a scary trend. Talk with people who cannot remember their children's names or who miss critical appointments, and you get some feel for their dilemma. Their caregivers will tell you that these demented adults live limited lives; They do not remember the past clearly, are troubled by what they experience each day, suffer over making decisions about daily living issues, and show concern about thoughts over their future. They are living half-lives with limited awareness about their losses. They become dependent on others to make the decisions that they can no longer make for themselves.

5. Some seniors still have not developed sufficient self-esteem and a true self-confidence in their own abilities and their possibility of building a better future. They go through life meekly seeking acceptance and approval from others because they have not found it in themselves. They are often filled with fear of being rejected, being left behind, or being ignored. It is such a tragic loss for them when they constantly feel unacceptable by so many essential people in their world. Most of the time, it is only in the mind of the sensitive senior, but their social withdrawal makes it almost certain that they will be left behind. They never achieve the goals they want so desperately. What they need to do is to find a new life for themselves and rebuild their world. It can happen if we are persistent and if we open our world to new friendships and ties.

6. So many senior adults are worrying constantly. It may be about their health, their adult children, their financial standing, and their acceptance by others, even the

appearance of their home or living area. It seems certain that most of that is wasted time because it is repetitive thinking, uncreative problem solving, and even a route to a depressed mood. For most worriers, it is a lifestyle that they live with all the time. If they have no worry for a day, they create one. They have not learned to let go and to just live with the changes in their world. They have not found the keys to enjoy life and to live with a positive, wholesome attitude about their future, but they need to try to learn to live again.

It is so appropriate to ask these troubled adults why not go for expert help by seeing a doctor, a personal counselor, or a financial consultant. Take their professional advice and then decide to make the essential step to *move on* or *let go* so they can move forward with their lives. To hang on to worn-out worries is only self-defeating. It rarely solves anything, and it certainly is harmful for wholesome living. They need to develop a healthier approach to problem solving and move along into a brighter and happier future. Of course, address the worry, and then stop lingering on it until it takes over your life and relationships.

7. One of the most difficult concerns for seniors is the issue of accepting losses in life. It could be the loss of a friend who died in an accident or the loss of an adult child or the loss of health or even a favorite location where they once lived. Losses come to us all, and we have to take them in stride, face the reality, and move on with our lives. But there are older adults who become fixated on their losses and cannot get past the loss. They constantly review the circumstance, they think about the issue all the time, and their life is handicapped by this fixation. They cannot let go and let God guide them into a new and brighter future.

8. Many seniors still have religious doubts and struggles over the reality of death and a future life. Seniors in general become more devout as they age, but there are countless older men and women who stay on the sidelines and never attend a church or synagogue. They are filled with doubts, questions, and real uncertainty, and they do not take time and effort to visit a spiritual counselor or religious leader or participate in a worship experience. They stay on the sidelines and keep their feelings to themselves. Most of these seniors are tied into themselves and rarely get involved in church-sponsored activity either. Some of them may pray at home or in private, or even read the Bible or a devotional book, but they have chosen to live their lives outside the network of a supportive and loving religious community. It is certain, however, that they can find meaning and richer lives within the framework of the family of God. That community will accept them and incorporate them into a loving community if they only reach out for a helping hand.

My obvious conclusion is that there are a host of seniors who are living very limited and unhappy lives. They have not discovered the joy and fulfillment or the sheer happiness that should come with healthy aging. They need to commit themselves to overcome their limitations and move forward to develop a wholesome and satisfying life for themselves. So I now move on to outline what they can do to achieve a richer, freer, and fulfilling life ahead by making responsible life choices in their daily lives.

There are strategies we can choose to adopt to achieve a healthy lifetime in our senior years, despite the limitations that exist in our lives. Here is how . . .

* Bring humor and lightness back into our lives. We are in danger of taking life too seriously. We go around with grim faces and bent shoulders, carrying the burden of the world on our backs. It is as if we were responsible for the health and happiness of everyone we see and meet. No, we are not responsible to solve the world's problems, just to care well for ourselves, and to help others when we can offer aid. So take it easy, learn to laugh often, read humorous stories, go to funny movies, learn to tell a joke, and learn to tell one on yourself. It will bring joy and comfort to your life. Laughter lightens up your daily routine.

* Develop the highly valued quality of resilience or the ability to adapt well to whatever life brings into your world. Psychologists now emphasize the important of a quality called *hardiness* or the ability to be in control and command of your life. That means we take charge of a problem and then persist until we solve it by our perseverance and creatively. We can refuse to give up, give in, and simply yield to forces that are hurting us or blocking our pathway to a better life. Those who are *hardy and determined* will take the challenge and find a solution to the dilemmas that needs to be faced. Stand up to the monsters in our lives and win the battle of wits by our force of will and the hand of God.

* Be a positive thinker, coupled with a strong commitment to optimism. Negative thinking does more harm than one can imagine. It actually freezes us and keeps us from acting to find successful solutions to a problem. But the real optimist and positive personality looks for healthy alternatives to a difficult dilemma. So it is imperative that we think, speak, and act in a positive

manner so that we get the best results from our action. Robert A. Schuller in his wonderful book *Possibility Living talks* about the enormous benefits that come to those who are not defeated, who are determined with faith, and the best of intentions to find a real answer to difficult problems. Answers do come, however, when positive approaches are selected to solve any issue.

* Learning how to cope with the stress of life is essential for a wholesome life. All of us have pressures, unexpected events, and difficult relationships that occur in our lives. We need to learn to manage them and not to allow them to overwhelm us and keep us in constant tension. One of the best methods is to do some concrete thinking, and then plan about to take charge of a particular problem that is adding to the conflicts in your life. By writing it down, analyzing it, thinking in new ways optional solutions, and even consulting with a trusted friend, partner or counselor can be a helpful process. The point is that you need to have a plan for coping with the stress and conflicts you face. Face them directly and find a way to deal with them. You will be better off when you plan and take concrete steps to cope with every conflict or problem before you, one by one. Think success and think of positive action, and you will find a way.

* Find living examples or models of healthy living. Learn how they handle their lives and learn to copy the best methods they have used. Let me even suggest that you find a mentor to follow or someone who has learned well in the school of life and has mastered problems well. Some of you might find it even helpful to read biographies of famous people who have made

a remarkable success of daily living. Of course, the Bible and other religious texts are full of models of healthy and creative living, like the lives of Moses and Paul. Whatever you do, look around you to find real wholesome stories of contented adults and ask yourself what those stories can teach you about living a wholesome and healthy life. There is nothing like seeing success in living to get us motivated.

*   Keep your mind and memory alert and active. What we see is that many seniors become lethargic and indifferent about reading, learning, and being open to new ideas and issues. What happens is that their brain responds to that in deference, and it becomes dull and unresponsive to new thoughts and to our changing times. We simply cannot afford to let our mind slip into a condition of passivity. It will respond by changing to an ineffective instrument of learning and retention of important memories and new insight. It will even become a poor tool for effective problem solving. In fact, it will become open to the early stage of memory loss and even of dementia. We simply cannot afford to lose the valuable resource of an effective mind, so do everything possible to keep your mind alert and open to new ideas, to good memories, to happenings in the world around you. A healthy mind is a terrible thing to waste, so do not let it happen to you. Focus on building good brain health every day.

*   Learn about the value of volunteering your time for some worthy cause. It is important that we help to build a better world around us by being part of the force that helps to serve others in need. Volunteers report constantly about what a joy it is to be engaged

in helping worthy causes. It gets you out of your own focus on meeting your own needs, and it helps you identify with the needs and struggles of others around you. It provides a valuable service that would not be available without your help and the help of others. You could be involved in your local church, your community center, a service organization, or a health care agency, or even offering assistance at your local hospital. Just open your heart and mind and you will find the area that fits you most, then go and offer your time and talent. You will benefit and others will be blessed by your presence.

* Be open to change and new perspectives on the problems you are facing. It is my clinical experience that resistance to changing ideas, lifetime habits, and sound values can become a major obstacle for seniors. Seek to find ways to look at your problem area with a totally new perspective or attitude. A solution may arise before you know it. I have witnessed seniors who have found a solution to their health concerns, family conflicts, financial pressures, or even found new directions for their lives by attending a retreat, finding a spiritual renewal, talking to a treasured friend, or even during a health crisis. We must get over our rigidity, our inflexibility, our stubbornness and see issues that need solution in a new, fresh attitude. It could mean that we join a new group of seniors, start to date if we are single, move to a warmer climate, or let someone competent manage your financial resources. Just take the initiative to make the changes you need to bring happiness into your life and stop resisting change any longer.

* Vary your daily routines to provide a variety to your daily life. Seniors especially get themselves tied into doing the same thing, seeing the same people, keeping predictable contacts always in their weekly schedule. But there is real value in changing that pattern and in trying a new way to carry out your day or your week of activity. Variety can be the spice of life and, in this case, it can add real richness to your world. Stop being so predictable and do the unexpected and the creative thing to give your life a new lift and bring excitement to your daily routine. You will discover the fun and pleasure that a new experience can offer.

* Find some spiritual practices that add richness to your life. Not only do we need to learn and follow the best in religious values and teachings, but we do need to become active in a vital spiritual community. It is clear that we cannot live alone, without the support and comfort of other adults. We need those sincere believers in our life, and we need to gather together to worship with them. They can be there when a crisis comes, or when we just need comfort or friendship. In addition, you need to find inspiration and guidance for a life of prayer, meditation, and biblical study. Reading the best of Christian literature is a good practice. Attend classes around the topic of your chosen faith. Whatever you do, make the spirit of God a vital part of your life. You will learn that divine guidance is a special gift you will come to appreciate and trust in your daily life at work or at play. If you are to choose well, make this act of commitment an essential part of your active schedule.

Let me close this chapter with a real-life model of healthy aging: I refer to the life and ministry of Joni Erickson Tada, who has been nearly a lifelong quadriplegic. She broke her neck and became paralyzed when she dove off a pool platform as a young adult outside a swimming area in Chesapeake Bay in 1967. She went through two years of rehabilitation in which she experienced anger, depression, suicidal thoughts, and even religious doubts. Finally, she emerged as the mature, motivated, loving, and faithful personality she has been thereafter. She started to get public notice with a beautiful painting she produced by holding her paintbrush in her teeth, and her completed artwork was highlighted and sold everywhere.

She continued to become an outstanding spokesperson for her newly renewed Christian faith. She wrote her bestselling autobiography, *Joni*, and, thereafter, published some forty books, recorded several musical albums, and starred in an autobiographical movie. She even faced the new threat of death with the emergence of breast cancer, but her strong will and good medical care succeeded to beat that danger as well. Her biggest passion has been her intentional organization for the disabled called "Joni and Her Friends." One of its major projects is a wheelchair ministry in which she raises funds to buy, transport, and donate wheelchairs to crippled adults around the world who cannot afford to buy one. She continues to bring inspiration to people everywhere in her five-minute radio program that is broadcast on over one thousand stations all over the world. She is now married to a loving and caring man who helps her in her outreach to others. Her life is a living proof for everyone who feels defeated by their limitations and cannot move on that one can find a positive future ahead despite severe limitations. For the most discouraged or troubled, follow the example of Joni and discover ways to express your best in life, even with severe physical, emotional, social, or financial limitations.

Let me say that the reason I have included her story in this book is because of her outstanding ability to overcome enormous obstacles. She is saying to us all that you need *not* let the limitations of your life defeat you, stop you from giving vent to your natural talents, or block you from caring for and serving others. So even if you are handicapped yourself, there *is still a good life* ahead for you and a special expression of your abilities just waiting to be tapped.

We are living in a world today where there are still new challenges and opportunities for the disabled, the rejected, and the rejected minority. Take steps to move forward and find a pathway for a positive expression of your life despite the problems and limitations you must endure. Life situations can open up for you, so go find a useful life full of joy and happiness. Decide to live up to your best human potential and make it happen as you move forward with confidence. Seek the advice of professional consultants, find the support of others, and discover the strength and insight that comes from a mature Christian faith in God. Handicaps and limitations no longer need to keep you down and defeat you any longer.

Some Added Real-Life Stories:

Some of you may be acquainted with the work of Alcohol Anonymous, a support group for the alcoholic. If you could slip in as an observer, you would be amazed to hear the stories from people who have been hopelessly lost and have discovered how to live again. They tell how they slowly slipped into heavy drinking, often as a method of coping with a troubled life. They offer details about the heavy cost in money, lost jobs, a failed marriage, and loss of self-respect that alcohol brought them. Nevertheless, they will relate how their life turned around, and they were able to control their drinking and then stop entirely. Their face starts to light up when they describe the wonder and the excitement of living alcohol-free! Their message is real and clear: there is hope for every problem in life, just find the avenue and pursue it faithfully, with the help of other and the guidance of God.

We have in Tampa an amazing organization called Metropolitan Ministries. It is home to scores of paid staff and hundreds of volunteers. Its sole aim is to minister to those who are down-and-out in our downtown area. The staff meets with them, assesses their needs, and then develops a *care plan* to help them move out of poverty into a life of dignity and self-sufficiency. The agency will house, feed, train, and assist the applicant in finding employment. It is an amazing place, but it only mimics other self-helping agencies all across America. The wonder of our great country is that we are a compassionate people with a warm heart and a willingness to help others in real need. No senior in serious need of real assistance should end up empty. Agencies, both government and private ones, are everywhere, so take initiative and seek the help you need. There is a solution for a troubled life, just find the right assistance and be persistent until you are back on your feet. God is not finished with you yet, so seek His guidance, and your future can be bright and hopeful.

Supplemental Materials: (1) Pathways to Health and Wholeness, (2) All about Attitude, (3) Finding Value in Holding unto Hope, and (4) Promise Yourself

Supplement 1, Chapter 9

PATHWAYS TO HEALTH AND WHOLENESS

As long as suffering has existed, people have sought ways to make sense of it. Here are some thoughts to support you as you struggle for answers when hardship comes:

1. Keep feeling hopeful as you continue asking for answers. Just as your body hurts in order to heal, so must your spirit. If you run from the pain now, you will have to face it later, when it may surface in even more destructive and hurtful ways.

2. Reach out to people for support. That alone won't give you answers, but it will bring comfort and strengthen you in your search. Reach out to people, also, for their stories. Find out how others have tried to make sense of suffering, through art, film, and even poetry, or the Bible.

3. Accept the world as imperfect. Natural disasters, accidents, illness, and human acts of free will are expressions of an imperfect world and imperfect people. They are beyond our control. Even when our actions bring on suffering, these actions are the results of our limitations that we are not able to correct as yet. Stop blaming others because it solves no problems.

4. Realize you are not always alone. You share the experience of suffering with others. It is part of being human. If you live fully, if you love deeply, you open yourself up to deep hurt. So live with the reality and seek to find help and support from your faith in God, who is always there to offer you strength and comfort.

5. If you have a religious tradition, examine what it says about suffering. The question of suffering has been a fundamental concern of religions for all of human history. There is much wisdom to be found in these explorations. Do remember, however, tragic events soften shatter your belief system, leaving you doubting your spiritual beliefs. You may need to rebuild your spiritual structure by finding new spiritual answers by talking to someone to give meaning in your life.

6. Work through resentments, blame, anger, and hostility. Learn to let them go and not to rule your life. It is natural to feel these negative emotions toward anyone you see as causing or contributing to the tragedies you face. But face these emotions, even acknowledge them and then release them so you can move forward with your life to a positive and affirmative attitude about living.

7. Stay open to growth and transformation. Suffering in itself may seem meaningless, but you can find meaning in your response to it. Let yourself grow from these experiences with losses. Become more compassionate; open yourself up to others in their wounds and hurts. Work to improve the world. Embrace healing and embrace life.

Though you may never solve the question of suffering, you can accept it as a part of life. Refuse to let those realizations stop you from living passionately and hopefully. Move on to cherish life every day, despite the hazards of suffering that blot your vision.

Supplement 2, Chapter 9

ALL ABOUT OUR OUTLOOK

We all have one, whether we want it or not. And each of us has the responsibility for creating our own and spreading it around. Someone else's can certainly affect us, as ours can affect others. It is called *outlook*, and it governs us much of what we think and say and so. It sets the tone for our day. Yes, it even sets the tone for our lives.

A positive, uplifting, thankful spirit makes our lives better, as well as those whose lives we touch. It's reflected in our expression, walk, talk, and sure enough, in every word we speak or write. It can even be detected over the telephone or in the cards and notes we send.

These attitudes are a product of what life has been dealing with us over the years. But the problem comes when we choose to dwell on the negatives or the unpleasant adventures and let them control our lives today. Having lived long enough to be called senior adults, it goes without saying that we have all endured the good with the bad, the bitter with the sweet. Sometime, the thorns are so sharp that we suffer for too many years, focused on the pain of the past. It is a choice we make for ourselves.

Who do we think we are that we should have escaped the normal pain and suffering associated with life in this sin-sick, imperfect world? No one gets off without heartache or two or three, or even more. It is time to put it all in perspective and get on with life, making the rest of our days the good ones.

We must learn to be thankful for the pleasant experiences and let go of the rest. Just think of all you have not had to go through, and your own story will not seem so bad after all. Surely, there are situations that could have been yours, but you were spared. Pick up the pieces and reset our attitude button. That is how to enrich your days and years and affect others in a positive way.

You can and will become the complete person you were meant to be, one who is fun and uplifting to be around, rather than someone who drags others down to their negative level. We all like to be with those who will give us a lift, share a word of encouragement, make us laugh, and give us an all-around good feeling. Just one word of caution: Make sure your positive attitude is real, not one conjured up as part of an act. It will not work; people will see through this phoniness.

Most of all, pray for an outlook of gratitude. Remember all of your blessings, and you will be better prepared to cope with the troubles that come your way.

Your attitude reflects your real self, so exhibit a wholesome perspective, and people everywhere will be blessed by your fresh perspective on life.

Reference: A Positive Commentary by Eileen Schipper of Sun City Center, Florida

Supplement 3, Chapter 9

FINDING VALUE IN HOLDING UNTO HOPE

Hope looks for the good in people instead of harping on the worst.

Hope opens doors when despair closes them.

Hope discovers what can be done instead of grumbling about what cannot.

Hope draws its power from a deep trust in God and the basic goodness of human nature.

Hope "lights a candle" instead of "cursing the darkness." Hope regards problems, small or large, as opportunities for all of us.

Hope cherishes no illusions, nor does it yield to cynicism. Hope sets big goals and is not frustrated by repeated difficulties or setbacks.

Hope pushes ahead when it would be easy to quit.

Hope puts up with modest gains, realizing that "the longest journey starts with one step."

Hope accepts misunderstandings as the price for serving the greater good of others.

Hope is a good loser because it has the divine assurance of final victory.

"In the world you have tribulation, but be of good cheer; I have conquered the world, "John 16:33.

Reference: Fr. James Keller, MM, Founder of the Christopher's, A Roman Catholic Spiritual Life ministry

Supplement 4, Chapter 9

PROMISE YOURSELF

* To wear a cheerful countenance at all times and give every living creature you meet a smile;

* To give so much time to the improvement of yourself that you have no time to criticize others;

* To be too large for worry, too noble for anger, too strong for fear, and too happy to permit the presence of trouble in yourself.

—Christian Larson

"We are celebrating over the way we are building
a Healthy Lifestyle for the whole family!"

CHAPTER 10

MAKING RESPONSIBLE LIFE CHOICES FOR SENIOR LIVING

Over time, the capacity to rise above adversity by developing skills (in human relationships) expands and ripens into lasting strengths or aspects of the survivors self . . . that I call resiliencies.

—Steven J. Wolin and Sybil Wolin,
The Resilient Self

Let me summarize and emphasize the message I want to leave with you, my dear readers. First of all, I hope that I am clear about our common need to be more deliberate and intentional about making the responsible life choices we need to make about living out our lives every day. I have tried to be specific about the values of choosing to be committed to healthy aging. In addition, most of the human development writers today strongly support the goal of achieving a *wellness way of life*, especially during our senior years. So I would like to offer some critical comments about the kind of essential choices that will make that happen. It could be a real summary of new lifelong goals that you may want to adopt for yourself and share with your loved ones. So here goes . . .

It is best to begin by explaining the value of choosing a commitment to a *wellness lifestyle*. It means that we want to live up to our best human potential to develop all our talents and abilities in the living out of our life. This concept implies that we become more self-aware of who we are, what we are doing with our lives, and what we need to achieve to gain full health and happiness. There is no end-point, however, when we can feel we have arrived. We are always in a state of constant growth and development. Nevertheless, when we experience feelings and thoughts of wellness, we can feel a sense of peace, joy, and personal contentment. It is a wonderful way to live. Most writers who speak about a wellness way of life devote their efforts to help us achieve that lofty state of mind and body. They offer suggestions, sell products, highlight attitudes, and concentrate on relationships in an effort to help us work at that lofty goal for ourselves.

1. People who write about *wellness* make a sincere effort to help us understand self-responsibility and even self-empowerment. (See: *Wellness Letter* by the University of California, Berkeley). This emphasis is on taking charge of our lives and to rid ourselves of bad habits and behavior. It means replacing those regrettable qualities with a higher quality of life. It also assumes that we want to live lives of high achievement, not just fill space on earth. So setting ourselves on the pathway of living our best and achieving our finest is the worthy goal of a *wellness lifestyle*.

2. One insight is important toward understanding this lifestyle. You can be working on healthy aging even if you have some physical or emotional limitations that have developed naturally over the course of time. It is not true that just those who are vigorous, energetic, healthy, and achievement-oriented are on the road to *wellness*. You can

be older, infirm, disabled, or socially limited and even emotionally unstable and still be working at achieving your best goals for healthy living. Age and time do inflict damage to us we often cannot avoid, but we can still work at living out the best life we can find for ourselves. The essential commitment is to achieve our very best, with the help of God, in every aspect of our daily lives. Hopefully, we will come to the end of our life and feel very good that we have fulfilled our purpose on earth and have made a positive contribution toward the building of a healthy family, enjoyable relationships, and a better world for all to enjoy.

3. Now let me emphasize the vital importance of choosing lifelong learning, even though I have highlighted it as a key goal before. The seniors I know by name who have engaged in new learning have all experienced the excitement, the awe of new discovery, and even the thrill of mastering a new idea or craft. One of the best avenues of new learning for seniors is *travel* not only in the United States, but also all over the world. My wife and I have discovered that type of learning through our many ventures with the Road Scholar travel ventures, or the former Elderhostel program. The program offers the experience of learning, visiting, and discovering new places and things that can be eye opening and entirely satisfying. Many friends tell us also that they have been very pleased with the river cruises down the Rhine or the Danube Rivers in Europe. Other seniors report they have had surprising discoveries in China, in Russia, and in some of the African nations. Travel presents some challenges in getting to new locations in terms of airline schedules, travel restrictions, money exchanges, and the management of baggage, but the experience overall is usually worth all the down side

of travel. Incidentally, for those who want or need less expensive outings, senior centers often offer day trips to exotic places and exciting sports activity geared to the senior world.

Most senior communities offer seminars, support groups, study sessions, and even major conferences with an intentional focus on some area of particular interest. (Of special interest is the International Conferences on Positive Aging sponsored by Fielding University.) Libraries, museums, non-profit organizations, and even commercial companies aimed at the senior market also offer educational ventures for senior living. So the opportunities available are endless if you just look around your community or nearby city. It simply requires your commitment to growth and learning and your willingness to take time to become engaged in new ventures.

In towns and cities all over America, groups are organized to offer craft classes in hand skills like needlework, jewelry making, or creating lovely works of art. There are woodworking shops for building household furniture and wooden toys for school age children. The most popular new offering is for a club for popular photography or for learning computer skills. Other ventures focus on maintaining our physical health through classes of yoga, Tai Chi, or ballroom dancing. The list goes on, and the number of seniors who now participate keeps growing. We have learned that senior living is more exciting, more rewarding, and more fulfilling when we are engaged in some new activity that helps us grow, develop our creativity, or keeps us in better health and well-being.

4. One of the most challenging frontiers for seniors today is to choose to face and adapt to the *world of change* all around us. Failing to do this has serious impact on our lives, and unless we adjust to this new world, we will be left behind with serious consequences. For some older adults, they react by shutting out the cry for change by simply saying "no" to learning computer skills, traveling to new locations, or adopting the latest cell phone available. It is troublesome to have to give up our old ways of living and to adopt new ways of experiencing our new world, but it is necessary for our survival and for our health and happiness.

5. So let me describe some of the necessary changes we need to make to live in the world of today. The first I would mention is to fully embrace the new world of technology today! It is an exciting and sometimes a difficult world to understand. It involves much new learning, careful management of your recent purchases of a laptop, a notebook, or cell phone, and the ability to keep up-to-date with the constant innovations in computer hardware and software. If the jump into regular computer use is too difficult, there are simpler computers or tablets (i.e., first street's WOW computers or touch screen tablets) and easily operated cell phones (i.e., jitterbugtouch2) and even easy to use new amplified phones to purchase for people who have a vision or hearing loss (i.e., Captioning Telephone), all of which are advertised in the *AARP Magazine* each month.

* The marketplace is fully saturated with almost every device conceivable for senior living, such as a medical-alert system to use in case of a medical emergency (greatcoat/medical alert), an A ARP driver safety course to help you refresh you driving skills and save you money on car insurance (aarp.org/driving30), and electronically operated stair lifts for seniors who need help going up and down a stairway in their home (bruno.com). Many of us have accepted the challenge to become computer literate and to master the use of the cell phone for our daily contacts. The point is that we are living in a technologically focused world, and it is time that we adopted that worldview for ourselves and started to take advantage of all the new resources available to enrich our daily living.

* Another change that is already here is the emergence of tensions in the extended family over the way our adult children and our grandchildren live today. They have adopted different values (some have no interest in a vital personal faith or the ministry of our local churches). Many have values that are not based on the same principles that we were taught when we were young (they cohabit before marriage and divorce quite freely when disagreements cannot be reconciled). Our grandchildren, especially, may take new job assignments that move them far away from the family circle, so they are seldom in attendance at holiday time or for family gatherings. In addition, some family members do not have the same memories, family ties, or real commitment to maintaining a strong larger family connection. Seniors are faced with a real dilemma: how to live well with this new and rapidly changing viewpoint about the value of maintaining extended family ties.

* My suggestion is that you accept the existence of these new issues and that you discuss and confront these issues head on with your loved ones. Come to some consensus about how all of you live with this new world of values and

relationships. Talk to them and agree on some standards to follow to keep your ties alive and well. Find a pathway that is comfortable for everyone, even if your values collide. Find that middle ground where you can cope well together. Deal with the distance between your locations and learn to find solutions you can all accept. Sometimes it is long and difficult to reconcile, but keep at it until you find solutions. Healthy contact and a loving commitment to each other can go a long way to build ties that last and are truly meaningful.

* One of the most difficult changes to accept is the revolutionary nature of our modern health care system. We are not only living longer as older adults, but we face far more problems to manage our health as we age longer in life. For example, we visit the doctor more often, pay dearly for health insurance, and daily consume medication. If a major health problem emerges, we have to make many arrangements for leaving our household in the care of someone else, for paying for the new costs incurred, and for scheduling the time away at the hospital. Then there is the new reality of facing surgery, recovering from that treatment, and finding a way to participate in rehabilitation exercises and care. It is a much more complex system than the days when the family doctor came to your home for his routine examination and some surgery was even performed simply in his own office. Even the task of transporting the sick and dependent family member to frequent medical appointments, getting that person to the hospital, and then bringing the recovering adult home for an extended care is in itself a big demand today for most senior citizens. We have no option but to accept this new reality and to learn to cope with it. It is usually an advantage if seniors can consult with each other in the neighborhood and in our friendship circle how we have managed well to live with this practice of medicine and counseling services today.

6. Let me emphasize the complex nature of choosing to face the constant demand that comes from our changing world. I did not even dwell on other difficult issues in today's world, like our changing environment and its new demands, our changing legal system and its new requirements that can raise havoc with our lives, and the new money marketplace that requires new strategy for investment of our funds to survive and even thrive in a financial world where smart management is the key to success. It is obvious, therefore, that we need to become more comfortable with *change* and to learn to adapt to it! The alternative is to withdraw from life and become cynical about the new world we live in with all of its new challenges to senior living.

* There are really many new advantages our new world offers us all, so we need to stop our constant reflection on the past, or our hold to our "old ways," and learn to embrace modern times and wholesome ways. It is the best way to live today, and it certainly will pave the way for a more positive means to live a wellness lifestyle for us all. So enjoy this new world and enjoy the benefits of a new way to live, while at the same time hanging on to the basic values you hold dear that never change with the times. In this regard, I like, especially, the collective comments of Gordon MacDonald in his wonderful book, *A Resilient Life*, in which he outlines the nature of resilient people. His contention is that we never give up and that aimlessness in life is a waste. He states that resilient people are quick to forgive, they maintain a life of gratitude, they

resolve the past, and they have a clear direction of their future. He urges us to learn to be full of confidence and to have a generous heart and to develop Christian character. To quote: "Resilient people are committed to finishing strong. They believe that quitting is not an option . . . they are convinced that resilience is a daily pursuit . . . they have the faces of champions." That is exactly the direction we need to take over the course of our lives so that we enjoy the full richness that life can bring to us all.

7. My last reflection focuses on the critical importance of making the choice to commit to the value of *organization and having a sense of direction* for our life in the senior world. Take any course on household management, and you will find three goals are clear: (1) Be certain what you want to accomplish; (2) Find a method that works for you and one you can master; and (3) Carry out your plan and then evaluate how well you have achieved your goals. Apply those principles to the simple task of building an office in your home or apartment and keeping your personal and financial records complete and up-to-date. Certainly, most seniors know instinctively that they need a well-organized office that is efficiently operated. They usually have an accumulation of records of all kinds: financial, social, family history, religious, and community events, etc. It seems incumbent on all those adults that they preserve those records with some ordered and careful design. The call is for a plan and to execute a plan that will make you proud of its appearance, organization, and efficiency.

* Every senior adult who values organization and order needs to hear the call to begin the process of an efficient household management system. They need to feel that their household furniture and appliances are well planned and working as designed. Their whole living space in their private home or apartment should reflect careful planning and orderly attention to detail. Their living space needs to designed, as well, to offer an attractive and pleasant appearance. They need to feel they have a home where they can be proud to entertain others and a place where they can invite houseguests and family members overnight.

When you visit senior residences, however, you discover that some live with much disorder. You ask yourself, why is that so typical of senior living? The answer seems to be is that we seniors let down on keeping order and organization as high values. I empathize with those who want to be less driven and disciplined about their life in their own home, but I would suggest that we find some balance with the call for order and organization. Do more than you want or feel you need to do, but less than those whose career depends on a household with a beautiful appearance and costly furnishings. Come to terms with the need for some careful management of your daily living space and your physical possessions. It becomes a matter of finding a lifestyle that fits your personal preference and values. Hopefully, you will discover a direction to take that will bring you real peace and personal satisfaction.

Now let me suggest a concrete plan for healthy senior living in our complex world:

1. *Develop the Quality of Self-Discipline for Healthy Living.*

   • There is a tendency for too many seniors to neglect, avoid, and be too casual about basic responsibilities. We reason that we are retired now, and we resist having to be on time, take new roles, or just do what the work world requires. It appears that we are reacting to being ordered around or to meeting someone's agenda or expectations.

- My contention is that we need to get over our rebellion against schedule keeping or suggestionsfrom key leadership in our retirement community.. There is much value in retaining the discipline we needed to exercise in the work world. We need to take pride in keeping a calendar, arriving at meetings on time, taking volunteer work roles, paying bills on time, having strong standards about the care and upkeep of your personal property, and being attentive about social engagements.

- Get over your resistance to being disciplined about your role as a marriage companion, a caring parent or grandparent, or a volunteer for your church or community activity. Value these roles carefully and do whatever is necessary to be a responsible adult in your role with any of these areas. It is important for those who know you and interact with you have trust that you are a person of your word, and you will do what you say you will do. They can depend that will do what you say you will do.

- Here is a vivid illustration: Ed has just finished being the key leader of the board of directors for our senior community. He moved into our retirement community, but he felt deeply that he had a responsibility to help guide the direction we take as a body of retired adults. He had some ideas that would work for our betterment, and he wanted the chance to test them out. He stuck with it for fifteen years and brought a level of administration that few leaders before him had ever shown. Now that term limits have forced him to leave his role, he is only now going to fully retire to enjoy his leisure time. The lesson learned here is that he is a man who is disciplined about his work roles, and he is willing to take a role and do it well when he sees a need he can fulfill. His self-discipline helped him do well what needed to be done, even in his retirement years.

- Just remember that to exercise self-discipline about your personal life, you need to do the following: (1) Be clear about the task that needs to be done. (2) Take the responsibility personally and do it well. (3) Refuse to complain or do you work poorly. And (4) Give your tasks your very best and you do it with a positive, cheerful attitude. So the next time you agree to take care of your lawn, to paint the house, or to fix the car, you offer your best skill and your positive attitude toward the completion of the task. When you do something, you do it right. That needs to be the perception of others who watch you give your best to the task ahead.

2. *Accepting the Reality of Change and Living with It in Our Senior World:* Every year, there are significant changes in the world where we live. If you are retired, you notice these harsh realities. Your adult children and grandchildren are achieving new goals and directions for their lives. Sometimes new, even threatening health issues emerge in your own life or in the lives of your dear friends. The financial markets are in a constant state of flux, and sometimes, it is not to your advantage. The shifting values in our world, like the acceptance of co-habitation

by young adults before marriage, are often disturbing and very upsetting.

We have choices about how we react to our changing world. One approach might be described as the cynical, bitter, or resistant perspective. There are a lot of older adults who fall into this category. They resent the lifestyles they see around them, and they have nothing but harsh criticism of these new practices. This perspective only alienates them from the young adults they resent. This deadlock creates a conflict over values that seem to never get resolved.

What senior adults need to do is to face boldly the reality of our changing world and embrace it, not fight it or continue to resent it. We need to accept these changes, even if we do not approve of them. We need to come to terms with them and agree to not become bitter, cynical, extremely critical, or resentful in the process. Let me illustrate:

One major change is the world of technology. Our adult children and grandchildren fully embrace that world and live with their new tools every day. They fully embrace their laptop computer, their cell phone, their iPad, and their headphones for listening to their rock music. We can choose to criticize this new commitment to technology or at least be tolerant of this shift in communication and embrace some of these new skills ourselves.

- Recognize that many of the changes we are experiencing are good and positive additions to our world. Many of those positive changes are in the fields of medicine and engineering, for example. We are able to live longer and experience a higher quality of life due of modern medical innovation. The engineering world has helped us improve the quality of our homes, our highways, our major manufacturing units. We have a better quality of life now because of new innovation, so stop your insistence about being so critical our contemporary world.

- Finally, start to become aware of the many changes in our modern world we have accepted and enjoy them. Start with the increased quality of our automobiles and how comfortable they are to own and drive. Appreciate the improved operation of our modern appliances and approve and endorse these nice developments. Our modern world is certainly a better environment than we have known it when we were children. So embrace this new world and refuse to get cynical about the modern world where we all live.

3. *Review the Choices below by Using Your Natural Talent and Creative Ability:* Each of us is gifted with certain talents and skills that are unique to our life. We watch seniors who can play musical instruments and who use that ability by joining a band or orchestra. Some of us have skills to write or speak with eloquence. Many seniors are wonderful parents or grandparents for their extended family and are sincerely loved for the role they play in their extended family connections. So it is important to recognize your gifts and talents and to be determined to use these God-given skills and insights to build a strong family connection and to contribute to a building a better world where we live. Unfortunately, we observe many seniors who hide their talents, deny they exist, or fail to use them for the betterment of the world around them. Their shyness or denial harms their effectiveness and deprives the world of their contributions. Our hope is that these words here will encourage anyone who has been in denial

of their God-given talent and ability to use the time and attention they can devote to an important task in their life. If you have a chance to serve, use your natural skills and your time as a real volunteer to help meet real human needs and to volunteer to serve a very worthy cause.

It is a thrill to be in the audience when an orchestra of senior volunteers is using their musical talents to provide beautiful music. I have witnessed the work of volunteers in our local church's project called congregational care. It is through this medium over forty senior volunteers call on the shut-ins, the hospital patients, and the assisted living members of our congregation. Those who are called upon are full of praise for this kind gift of caring. It is an evidence of the true Christian community in action, and it is a wonder to witness.

We have watched senior volunteers help lead in worship services, serve well on the *administrative board*, or even teach young children in a local church. It is very pleasing to see seniors take the lead in our retirement community by serving with real skill on the various committees in our civil government. One of the best evidences of self-giving of time and talent is the way seniors pay attention to the health and support we experience as we age. We have a very large body of volunteers serving for our local churches and our service organizations that reach out with a helping hand. We take time to help one another, and that is a vivid example of what every community needs to do for themselves. The point of emphasis is that using our time and talent in a loving community builds a better world for everyone concerned, every day.

4. *Discover the Rich Value of Initiating and Cultivating Cross-Culture and Interracial Contacts*:

We have a strong tendency if our senior world to stay with our same racial and even economic class. This habit is to our own determent because there is so much we can learn about other cultures if we open our mind to unbiased contacts. There are national organizations, like the National Council of Christians and Jews or the Interracial Organization, in most major cities, but these structures are usually beyond the access of most senior populations. We need to take the initiative on the local level to make it happen.

The reason it is such a good cause is due to the fact that satisfying personal contact is inevitably the best way to confront our bias and prejudices. So we have to approach the issue with an open mind and a willingness to see rich values in other cultures. One of the best ways to begin is to attend a festival or a celebration of some event that is important in another cultural group. Another way is through an introduction by a friend or family member. Sometimes the contact occurs when you join mutual interest group like a photography club or a noon service organization. These contacts give you the rich opening you need to begin the personal contact and friendship.

Many people I have known who have succeeded in broadening their world tell me how interesting it is to meet and enjoy people from other backgrounds and racial identities. They often have different interests in life; their family ties are expressed in a new and fresh ways of contact; and their perspective about life is often at variance from your own. A vivid illustration of this lifestyle is the kind of music they enjoy, the main food they consume, and the way they manage and decorate their household. It is simply a different world for them, but what you learn is there is *no* set way to express your home and family life. In fact, right here, variety is the spice of life. They are enjoying things you might not appreciate, but it is not essential that everyone become an exact imitator of your values and pattern of living.

Let me summarize the rich values that can come when we reach other to others who are different from us, but whose life is just as rich and meaningful as is our own. Here is my list:

1. Racial and cultural exchanges can offer us knew and interesting experiences with people who have a different perspective and way of living. Sometimes even their language and dress vary from our own.

2. When rich friendships emerge from the contacts, it is often very eye opening. A friend of mine once said of his black companion, "He is a wonderful man with a deep faith I can admire and emulate."

3. We discover on contact that our bias and prejudice we held so strongly has little or no basis in fact. We learn that even though they do some things differently, we have the same values, hopes, and dreams.

4. It is an eye-opener to hear about how these minorities view our "white world." They will tell you in all honesty that they had a negative and critical perception of our white culture that they had to overcome. So prejudices and deep doubt about other racial and cultures work both ways.

5. One of the best things we can learn is how to become socially comfortable in the homes or the full family

gatherings of another racial or culture group. It is exciting, stimulating, and satisfying. So take the next steps to make this experience how to you. It could provide you with rich new relationships you never experience before. It could open your social life to a whole new world.

5. *Find and Plan for Enriching Travel Experiences that Enlarge Your World*

- One of the most exciting experiences for senior adults is to travel, both short and long distances. It is a wonderful variation in our daily routine. We have had travel experience all over the world, so let me pass along some impression and some travel tips that may help you in your planning.

- Some impressions of short-distant travel: There is a great deal of refreshment awaiting you just to travel within a hundred-mile radius. Contact your local travel agencies, and you may be very surprised at the variety of options available to you and your loved ones. You may think you know everything to be known, but you will be amazed at the variety of options, from historical places, state parks, amusement parks, nature walks, and local farm operation or wineries. Most of the time, you will be assisted by a local guide, with plenty of written material. You can see it all in a day-trip with friends or family and enjoy your travel time.

- Planning and impressions of long-distant travel experiences: It is vital that you take time to decide where you want to go, when you want to leave, and the length of your stay. Usually anything under fifteen days seems a waste to us because of the time it takes to travel and return home and the time consumed to get oriented to your new location. Once you are there, be sure you have your lodging set up, your meal plan confirmed, and your itinerary set up. We always recommend that you work through a recommended travel agent who can plan details for you and provide helpful materials, as well, that will assist you in your whole experience.

One of the best ways to travel long distance is to do it jointly with another couple or friend. Try also to include variations from the planned schedule to respond to your special interests, like a trip to a horse farm, a winery, a waterfall, or a historical spot that is *not* on your prepared schedule. In addition, keep a travel diary in which you record your fond memories of real highlights you fully enjoyed. In addition, it is valuable to do some research about the area you plan to visit and some "must-see" spots you need to plan in advance. Just go then and enjoy every day, but make sure you protect yourself from medical emergencies. Seniors are often prone to fall in strange places or catch the local flu if they are not careful to avoid becoming victimized by the unexpected.

- Including travel time in your yearly schedule is important for many reasons: (1) You need time to get away from your daily routine to give you a fresh perspective and outlook; (2) You will discover the wonder of the natural world and experience several inspirational moments if you allow yourself to be carefully observant; and (3) Your world will enlarge and grow when you meet new people, new cultures, new lifestyles, and find new products you have never seen before. We found it valuable, as well, to buy at least one small item to symbolize our visit to that new location, and we display it or hang it on our wall.

GO TR AVEL AND ENJOY THE WONDER OF OUR
WORLD. YOU NEED THE CHALLENGE AND THE
CHANGE! PLAN IT THIS YEAR.

6. *Find the Life-Changing Experience of Making a Firm Faith
   Commitment:*

- One of the most consistent observations I have made
  about the clients I served for eighteen years as a clinical
  psychologist was the emptiness of their lives. A vast
  majority of them were afflicted with depression, anxiety,
  or persistent worry because they had no internal resource
  to give them strength and confidence. When I suggested
  at a tactful moment that a faith-oriented life might give
  them hope and happiness, they were often surprised and
  shocked. They simply did not see the connection between
  a faith-centered life vs. a troubled-centered existence. Once
  they made the connection, they were frequently asking
  how they could find a faith-focused life for themselves.

It is critical that you examine in depth the reasons why a firm
faith commitment can help to transform your life. You need to
start with what the Bible defines as "sin." That simply means
that our human nature tends to lead us to a selfish-centered
focus and to omit the needs of the world at large where we
live. Sinful living means we center only on ourselves, no one
else. On the other hand, the Christian perspective is to not
only serve the will of God, but to show real compassion and
love for the needs of our fellowman.

- Trust me when I tell you that there is an abundance of
  study and research that indicates that a faith-centered life
  is the best way to live out your daily life. I can share with
  you many case histories or refer you to volumes of articles
  on faith-centered living or simply tell you here that it is

a vital part of a healthy life, mentally, physically, socially and emotionally. We need to find a spiritual center to be whole because it is the best pathway to help guide our lives toward a life of peace and joy. We are not whole just living alone as a secular person caring only for our own needs and wants. We must learn to become a strong believer and to join a community of believers who care about each other. If you take that initiative, your life will assume new meaning and new purpose. So make that reality a part of your future plans, and you will find a contentment and happiness you have never known before.

- If you are not convinced, read the Bible, attend a Bible believing church, read Christian books and literature, and seek the counsel of a truly committed believer and follower of Christ. Be open-minded and make a sincere inquiry. If you are a Christian already, then come alive with your Christian faith and witness it to all who are seekers or are lost to the secular world. The bottom line is that we need a firm foundation for our life so we can have a strong foundation of belief and values to guide us through each day of our lives. If you make this decision, I can assure you the faith I am sharing will never fail you, and it will guide you will have the best life ahead you can find in this world. You will also prepare yourself for a wonderful eternity. So don't hesitate. Take the steps now to address your need for a faith-centered life or renew the faith you carry with you every day of your life.

7. *Take Some Risks over Your Lifetime: Playing Safe Is Not Always Best:*

- The well-respected book by David Viscott on risking make the very strong point that "there is simply no way you can grow without taking chances." He argues that risks need to be calculated and that they require courage to take action, but they are essential for our growth and health. He does say, however, that people avoid risking all the time . . . to their determent.

- Let me illustrate with a real-life example. Harry is a farm boy from Wisconsin who had great natural talent as a potential engineer. He would have achieved much had he gone on to college and graduate school, but he let fear and worry overwhelm him, and he never left the farm. He is still there milking cows and planting corn and that is where he will retire with his wife and family, but he can never quiet that deep desire to do more in life with his keen mind and insight. He knows now he simply avoided the risk that he would not be able to complete a college degree and achieve in a new field of endeavor.

He gave into his fear and he regrets it.

- Risk-taking applies to countless areas of our life. You take a risk when you marry a still, fully unknown personality, so some seniors have never married because it is too challenging with an uncertain future. Adults with low self-esteem are afraid to speak up, to stand strong for a very controversial position, and to take tempting leadership roles. They simply avoid the risks. Then there are the older adults who have lived with regret for years because they never took the real chance to start a promising business in their small town. They stayed with their hourly pay position at the local factory. New and risky chances come our way, in different forms, all the time, and we need some time to say *yes* to that risking moment.

- Of course, we must avoid being foolish, hasty, blind, or reckless, but there are prudent risks that are a natural part of new decisions. So weigh the issues carefully, but find the courage, the determination, and the strength to take a chance. You will find some threatening moments and even criticism from someone, but risks do not come easily. There are always hazards and tense moments, but all of the hardship is worth the effort. Risk-taking can have its rewards. You will find a new confidence level emerging within yourself, and the pride of winning at a risk is there for you to enjoy. So stop always playing it safe and move ahead into planned risk-taking.

- For many senior adults, risking is often centered on major health care decisions. Shall I agree to a major operation, with always the possibility that I could die in surgery? Risks come in the form of taking a big loan on a major investment, buying a home, taking a cross-country trip, or going on a lengthy world travel venture to China or India. Just because we are retired does not mean that risking goes away; it just takes other forms. So the next time a major risk comes your way, be prepared to evaluate it carefully, and when you are convinced it is worth the risk, take that chance and do it boldly! It is one great quality of life we need to develop for ourselves. It is a wonderful part of a healthy senior living.

****

* Let me conclude with this insightful comment about healthy aging: It is from a book entitled *My Time* by Abigail Trafford. In it, she says because we are living longer, healthier lives we have a "who knew stage in the life cycle, which we haven't had before." It can even be

called our time or my time, not just our retirement years. She maintains that our new longevity and health span should be a big bonus for us all and that we need to choose to make the most of it. We need to realize that the golden years are for you to enjoy your life as never before. Simply recognize that these extra years are for you to fully relish every day. Become the person *now* you always wanted to be. Each new year offers you the time to achieve your best living potential. Relish the days, enjoy your friendships, embrace your family ties, find new experience, and enjoy places to see and celebrate your maturing faith. Make responsible life choices. These are key ideas that never die.

Here are wise words to ponder from an article by Stuart Sorensen entitled "Taking Responsibility for Your Own Life." "Many people think about their lives as something that just happens to them, instead of something that they can control themselves. They just drift through life reacting to the actions of others, instead of taking steps on their behalf . . . If you don't take steps to get what you want, other people will take steps to get what they want, and that isn't always going to be in your best interests. You owe it to yourself and to those around you to take control of your life. Otherwise life just gets harder for everyone." I often say that I am in charge of what I think, feel, say, and do, but it is God who guides me with those thoughts and feelings. Now let God guide you to make responsible life choices, so you find your senior years the best years of your life. Make the golden years happen and enjoy your world as never before. Create the happy and healthy life you always wanted. Choose to find the life you can build for yourself and enjoy it fully as you move along into your unfolding future. May God help you to make this happen, now and forevermore! Remember, as well, what Helen Keller wisely said: "I am only one, but still I am one. I cannot do everything, but still I can do something. I will not refuse to do the something I can do."

In closing, I love the spirit and the quotes from an interracial body of retirees in an article in the A ARP Magazine for July-August 2005 by Sarah Mahoney called "10 Secrets of a Good Life." A ARP asked a few veterans of the world of stressful living, all over age 85, what are their secrets for staying young, both mentally and physically. I cannot quote their lengthy comments, but I can inspire you with their opening words:

Pauline says: "Just deal the cards, okay?"

Ernest says: "I keep laughing."

Agnes says: "I don't feel my age, I just feel happy."

Bob says: "I am passionate about my work."

Lilly and Marie say: "Keep your friends close by."

George says: "I try to make the world a better place."

Thais says: "I've got the music in me."

Grace says: "I don't worry about anything and I pray about everything."

Clarence says: "I exercise every single day."

Brownie says: "Humor comes naturally."

My feeling is that retirement has given my new freedom to finally be the person I want to be. My hope and prayer is that your golden years will bring the happiness and joy you have wanted all your life. You know, as I do, that we have to help make it happen!

Your Friend and Happy Retiree,

Ken Barringer, Ph.D.

United Methodist Minister and Retired Clinical Psychologist

Sun City Center, Florida, 33573

P.S. I welcome comments, questions, and ideas for future publications. I am already thinking about a follow-up book to be entitled *Success Stories of Seniors Who Have Made Responsible Life Choices*. For suggestions and comment, send a note on the internet. Address me at: <u>kdbmailbox@aol.com</u>

Supplemental Materials: (1) A Positive Perspective on Retirement, (2) Plan the Steps to Making Responsible Life Choices, (3) A Planning Guide for Maintaining a Healthy Lifestyle, and (4) Lifelong Holistic Health Focus Diagram

Supplement 1, Chapter 10

A POSITIVE PERSPECTIVE ON RETIREMENT

Each day . . . in retirement we can.

Be thankful for another day of life

Turn to our creator and offer a prayer of gratitude

Greet the new day with hope and expectation

Each day . . . in retirement we can . . .

Be in awe over the simplest beauty all around us, in land, sky, and sea

Think of the wonder of human birth, the beauty of a newborn child

Stand in amazement at the interrelationship of all of life

Each day . . . in retirement we can . . .

Banish pessimism when we recognize the new medical miracles we enjoy

Share pride in our hospitals, caring places for the elderly, even hospice

Even wonder over the amazing new medicines for our aging bodies

Each day . . . in retirement we can . . .

Agree to share pride with others for being part of our great country, America

Read about the great heroes that have made our nation the envy of all

Never take for granted the freedoms and liberty we all enjoy

Each day . . . in retirement we can . . .

Depend upon our social security (and pensions) that make our life secure

Realize that we are in demand if we choose to be employed again

Many agencies are available for us to meet some special needs

Each day . . . in retirement we can . . .

Turn to family and friends as means of love and support when we need them

Depend upon the compassionate love and guidance of God in our lives

Become active in the Christian community, the family of God

Each day . . . in retirement we can . . .

Reach out to help someone who needs our concern, our help, and our love

Volunteer for any of the many worthy causes available in our community

Stop focusing on our own needs and reach out to others

THE REWARDS OF LIVING LIFE THIS WAY IS TO ENJOY LIFE TO ITS FULLEST. IT'S LIGHTING THE CANDLE TO BRIGHTEN THE DARKNESS. THIS IS THE BETTER WAY: TO LIVE A FULL AND ACTIVE RETIREMENT.

Supplement 2, Chapter 10

PLAN THE STEPS NOW TO MAKING RESPONSIBLE LIFE CHOICES

1. Develop a concrete plan to maintain the best physical fitness you can for your age and your level of physical health. Work with a fitness consultant, if necessary, but put your plan into action.

2. Plan now to achieve the best level of emotional well-being you can achieve. Rid yourself of all negative emotions and maintain a consistent positive mental attitude every day.

3. Discover the rich resources of maintaining an active Christian faith by developing private devotional practices and actively participate, and even volunteer, in a local Christian church.

4. Learn the value of developing a close bond with your extended family and the wonderful benefit in developing and maintaining close personal friends.

5. Create a financial plan that really works for you and a plan that will keep you financially solvent throughout your retirement years. In addition, focus on maintaining your home and property at your highest level of good management.

6. Realize the value of having a purpose for living in your retirement, even as simple as enjoying a hobby, engaging in a sport activity, or volunteering for a worthy project in your community.

7. Find out more about living a wellness lifestyle in which you bash in the *joy of living* and discover ways you can find inner peace and happiness in daily retirement living.

8. Find out that you can accept the changes we all have to live with daily and discover the real strength that comes when we learn to be resilient by bouncing back when problems overwhelm us and seek to knock us down.

9. Finally, realize that we pay heavily in troublesome consequences when we fail to choose wisely. So make it your life plan to make responsible life choices in your retirement years.

10. Every day we make choices in a whole variety of area of life. Please pray that you will take time and pay careful attention to the process of making good ones. Then enjoy the rewards of your wise decision-making. This is what a healthy retirement lifestyle is all about. Relish these wonder years!

Supplement 3, Chapter 10

HERE IS A PLANNING GUIDE FOR MAINTAINING A HEALTHY LIFESTYLE

The Goal Ahead: Make a decision to make responsible life choices in your senior living experience. Now decide how you will make this happen in each of the key areas discussed in this book. Use the guide for clearly defining and planning what you will do for your future life and happiness.

1. TO IMPROVE AND MAINTAIN MY PHYSICAL HEALTH, I WILL DO THESE THINGS.

2. **TO MAINTAIN MY EMOTIONAL WELL-BEING, I WILL DO THESE THINGS.**

3. **TO KEEP MY SPIRITUAL HEALTH AT A MA XIMUM, I WILL DO THESE THINGS.**

4. **TO INSURE I W ILL BUILD MY SOCIAL WORLD, I WILL DO THESE THINGS.**

5. **TO PLAN WELL FOR MY FINANCIAL FUTURE, I WILL DO THESE THINGS.**

6. **TO CREATE A PLAN FOR MATERIAL MANAGEMENT, I WILL DO THESE THINGS.**

7. **TO DEVELOP PURPOSE AND DIRECTION FOR MY LIFE, I WILL DO THESE THINGS.**

Note: Some added suggestions: Set a date you want to achieve your goal for certain areas. Talk about your plans with a person or people close to you and get their input. Be forgiving if you do not achieve all of your goals on your schedule. Keep at the task of building a healthy retirement all your life. Enjoy the adventure as it unfolds. Make it a fruitful journey.

Supplement 4, Chapter 10

LIFELONG HOLISTIC HEALTH FOCUS

All forces in balance make for the best defense against the impact of stress and change

The Concept: All Forces Need to Work Together for a Healthy Balance to make the Best Defense Against the Impact of Stress and Change in our Lives

Key Issues for a Life-Long Holistic Health Focus:

1. Physical Health needs to be maintained by good and consistent health practices over time.

2. Developing Emotional Stability as a goal through the development of positive thinking and healthy self-worth.

3. Healthy Social Interaction is Essential, Coupled with a Real Concern for the Needs of Others.

4. Be Committed to Ongoing Moral and Spiritual Values, Supported by a Vital Personal Faith

5. Enjoy the Creative Use of Your Leisure Time, along with an Appreciation and Support of the Fine Arts

6. Be Committed to Productive Work Habits Through the Effective Use of Time Management Principles

7. Develop and Retain Your Mental Skills Through a Conscious Focus on Building a Healthy Mind

Note: You Can Develop These Qualities in Your Life by Seeking Better Self-Management That Makes for the Best Defense Against the Impact of Stress and Change Over Time.

HELPFUL
REFERENCES FOR
FURTHER READING

Develop A Habit of Healthy Reading;
Then Share What You Have Read!
Consider Joining A Group to
Discuss Healthy Aging Issues.

KEY RESOURCES FOR HELP IN CHOOSING TO AGE WELL IN RETIREMENT:

1. *Some of the Best Internet Sites*

- An Exciting Guide for Maintaining Good Health Care Over Your Lifetime
  www.lifelonghealth.com

- Resources on Mental Health through the National Institute on Mental Health
  www.cmha.us.edu/NIMH.htm

- Report of the Surgeon General on Mental Health
  www.surgeongeneral.gov/library/mentalhealth

- Resources on Creative Aging Ideas
  resources.rea.org/aging.php

- Open Directory – Health: Aging
  dmoz.org/Health/Aging

- An Excellent General Guide for Healthy Retirement
  DirectoryRetirement.com

- An Essential Faith-Focused Site with Constant Inspiration
  focusonthefamily.com/faith/faith in life

- Healthy Tips on Aging Issues from the National Institute on Health
  NIH SeniorHealth.gov

2. *Some of the Biggest Advocacy Groups for Seniors in America*

- The America Association of Retired Persons or aarp.org

- State Agencies on Elder Affairs

- State Councils on Aging, which represents Professionals in the Field

- National Department of Veteran Affairs

- U.S. Department of Health and Human Services

3. *Some Recommended Magazine Sources for Seniors*

- Modern Seniors Living Magazines
  Alfa.org/magazine and worldmag.com

- A Medically Oriented Information Source
  Webmd.com

- A Monthly Bulletin of Helpful Information for Senior Living
  A ARP Bulletin: Real Possibilities

- A Magazine with Focus on Coping with Anxiety and Depression
  Esperzana Magazine or hopetocope.com

- A Magazine for Purchase of Tested Goods and Services
  consumerreports.org

- Helpful Suggestions for Money Management
  Cnnmoney.com/customerservice (Money Magazine)
  KiplingerRetirement.com (Retirement Report)

- A News Magazine with Christian Content and
  Perspective
  customerservice@worldmag.com

- Widely Read Devotional Magazines
  todayintheword@moody.edu
  UpperRoom.org
  guideposts.org

- For Leisure-Time Events and Activities
  vantagetravel.com
  oattravel.com
  roadscholar.org
  vikingcruises.com

4. *Some Excellent Pamphlets and Booklets on Healthy Retirement*

- Series of Program Booklets from Aid Association for
  Lutherans entitled:
  "What I wish someone had told me about
  retirement . . ."
  "How to stay healthy the rest of your life"
  "How to swing into retirement without stumbling"
  "65 mistakes to avoid in retirement"
  For Contact Address: A AL, 4321 Ballard Road,
  Appleton, WI 54919

- Publications of the National Institute on Aging
  Information Center
  "Making Your Website senior Friendly"
  "Can We Prevent Aging"

"Understanding Risk: What Do Those Headlines
Really Mean?
Regular e-mail alerts at: www.nia.nih.gov/
HealthInformation

- A ARP.ORG Publication for Senior Living Called
  Life Answers
  Prepare to Care: A Planning Guide for Families
  Taking Charge of our Health
  Medicare and Other Health Insurance as Your Retire
  Grand parenting: The Joys and Challenges

5. *Excellent Books with an Emphasis on Healthy Aging Ideas*

- Lifelong Guide to Your Health and Well-being
  Andrew Weil, *Healthy Aging*
  New York: Anchor Press, 2007

- A Natural Way to Achieve Your Brain's Maximum
  Potential
  Daniel Amen, *Magnificent Mind At Any Age*
  New York: Three Rivers Press, 2008

- The Newest Book by a Popular Entrepreneur on
  Healthy Aging
  Martha Stewart, *Living the Good Life: A Practical Guide*
  New York: Clarkson Potter, 2013

- An Excellent Guide to Building Long-Term
  HealthAnthony A. Goodman, *Lifelong Health:
  Achieving Optimum Well-being*
  New York: Teaching Company, 2010

- A Guidepost to a Happier Life from a Landmark
  Harvard University: Study on Adult Development:

George E. Vaillant, *Aging Well*
Boston: Little, Brown and Company, 2002

- Surprising Results of a Major Study on Aging
  John W. Rowe and Robert L. Kahn, *Successful Aging*
  New York: Dell Publishing Company, 1998

- New Study by Road Scholar Staffer on Achieving
  Healthy Retirement Status
  Peter Spiers, *Master Class: Living Longer, Stronger,
  And Happier*
  New York: Center Street, 2012

- A New York Times Bestseller and Practical Guide for
  Better Living
  Phillip C. McGraw, *Life Strategies*
  New York: Hyperion, 1999

- An Excellent Guide from a Highly Rated Hospital Chain
  Edward T. Creagan, Editor, *Mayo Clinic On Healthy
  Aging*
  Rochester, Minnesota: Mayo Clinic Health
  Information, 2001

- The Famous Humorist and TV Star Gives a Light
  Hearted View about Aging Issues
  Art Linkletter, *Old Age Is Not for Sissies*
  New York: Viking Press, 1998

- An Essential Compilation of Helpful Information on
  Healthy Aging
  Judy Lindberg McFarland, *Aging Without Growing Old*
  Palos Verdes, CA: Western Front Lta, 1997

- An Exciting Book with an Emphasis on Keys to Achieving Happiness
  Shawn Anchor, *The Happiness Advantage*
  New York: Crown Business, 2010

- A Classic Bestseller about How to Stay as Youthful as You Can
  Isadore Rosefield, *Live Now Age Later: Proven Ways to Slow the Clock*
  New York: Grand Central Publishing, 1999

- A Key Resource for a Variety of Resources for Senior Living
  Charlie Crist, *Consumer Resource Guide*
  Department of Elder Affairs, State of Florida, 2010

- A Helpful Resource for Vital Information about Mental Health Issues
  Kenneth C. Haugh, *When And How To Use Mental Health Resources*
  St. Louis, Missouri: Stephen Ministries, 2000

- A Helpful Guide to Living Simply in the Complex World of Today
  Elaine St. James, *Living The Simple Life*
  New York: Hyperion, 1996

- Guidance in the Development of Maturity in our Spiritual Life
  Jane Marie Thibault, *A Deepening Love Affair: The Gift of God in Later Life*
  Nashville, Tennessee: Upper Room Books, 1993

- Very Helpful Suggestions about How We Can Develop Resilience

Steven J Wolin and Sybil Wolin, *The Resilienet Self*
New York, Villard Books, 1993

- Suggestions about How We Can Help our Families
  Develop Their Spiritual   Lives
  Betty Shannon Cloyd, *Parents and Grandparents As Spiritual Guides*
  Nashville, Tennessee: Upper Room Books, 2000

- Navigating Your Way Through Difficult Times and Events
  Elizabeth Harper Neeld, *Tough Transitions*
  New York: Warner Books, 2005

- A Key Aid in Handling Crisis in Physical Health and Well-being
  Wendy Schlessel Harpham, *Happiness In A Storm*
  New York: W.W. Norton and Company, 2005

6. *Book Listing Referred in Book Chapters*

- Chapter 1: Making Healthy Choices
  Barry Neil Kaufman, *Happiness Is A Choice*
  New York: Fawcett Columbine, 1991

- Chapter 2: Keys to Maximum Health
  Edward T. Creagan, Editor, *Mayo Clinic On Healthly Aging*
  Rochester, Minnesota: Mayo Clinic, 2001

- Chapter 3: Developing Our Emotional Health
  Daniel Coleman, *Emotional Intelligence*
  New York: Bantam Books, 1995

- Added Text: Robert Schuller, *It If 's Going To Be It's Up To Me*
New York: Harper Paperbacks, 1997

- Chapter 4: Building a Spiritual Life
Walt Larimore, *10 Essentials Of Happy, Healthy People*
Grand Rapids, Michigan: Zondervan, 2003

- Referred Text: Billy Graham, *Nearing Home*
New York: Thomas Nelson, 2011

- Chapter 5: Acquiring Good Social Skills and Leisure Activity
Meika Loe, *Aging Our Way*
Oxford, New York: Oxford University Press, 2011
Referred Text: Sam Watson, *Made In America*
New York: Doubleday, 1992

- Chapter 6: Choosing a Money/Material Management Plan
Kiplinger's Retirement Report, August 2013
Candy Paull, 101 WAYS TO SIMPLY YOUR LIFE
Franklin, Tennessee, Spirit Press, 2006

- Chapter 7: Choosing a Purposeful Life Full of Growth and Learning
Gary Zukor and Linda Francis, *The Mind of The Soul*
New York: Free Press, 2003

- Chapter 8: Becoming Intentional About Creating a Wellness Lifestyle
Regina Sara Ryan and John W. Travis, *Wellness*
Berkeley, California: Ten Speed Press, 1991

- Referred Text: Elaine St. James, *Living the Simple Life*
  New York: Hyperion, 1996

- Chapter 9: Coping with Life When Problems
  Overwhelm Us
  M. Esther Lovejoy, *The Sweet Side of Suffering*
  Grand Rapids, Michigan: Discovery House, 2013
  Alexa Fleckenstein and Roanne Weisman, *Healthy to 100*
  Deerfield Beach, Florida: Heath Communications,
  Inc. 2006

- Referred Text: Joni ErIckson Tada, *Joni*
  Grand Rapids, Michigan: Zondervan Books, 1996

- Chapter 10: Making Responsible Life Choices for
  Senior Living
  Steven J. Wolin and Sybil Wolin, *The Resilient Self*
  New York: Villard Books, 1993

- Referred Text: Abigail Trafford, *My Time*
  New York: Basic Books, 2004

- Referred Text: David Viscott, *Risking*
  New York: Pocket Books, 1977

- Referred Text: Gordon MacDonald, *A Resilient Life*
  New York: Nelson Books, 2004

7. *Key News Letters that Focus on Healthy Aging Issues*

- Life-Saving Information on the Use of Healthy Nutrition
  Nutrition Action Healthletter www.orders.cspinet.org

- A Key Informational Guide for Resources and
  Training Options in the Field of Geriatrics

Human Values in Aging Newsletter (*aarpnewes@ news.aarp.org*)

- Key Health Information from Harvard Medical School on Healthy Living (*healthbeat@mail.health.harvard.edu*)

- The Best Free Newsletters to Help Resolve Health Challenges Health Guide (helpguide.org/life/healthy)

- An Excellent Free Guides for Health and Wholeness Beliefnet beliefnet.com/healthandhealing

- A Major Health Service Hospital Provides Key Information *johnhopkins@e.johnhopkinsdheallthalerts.com*

- Another Major Health Network Sends Free Alerts *berkeleywellnessalerts@berkeleywellnesssalerts.com*

- Information for Persons Coping with a Mental Health Issues psychcentral.com

- Helpful Information from Mount Sinai Hospital for Healthy Aging Customer *Service@Focusonhealthyaging.info*

- An excellent guide for financial planning for senior living Kiplinger's-usa.com

- Strategies to Boost Your Financial Investments Fidelity.com or tiaa-cref.org

- A Helpful Resource for Better Nutrition, Diet, and Food Safety
  circo2.com\

- A Key Resource from UCLA Division of Geriatrics HEATLHY/Years: Helping older adults lead happier, healthier lives

8. *Recommended Organizations to Consult About Healthy Aging Issues*

- National Coalition on Mental Health and Aging
  Contact: Deborah DiGilio, Office of Aging, APA, 750 First St. NE
  Washington, D.C. (202) 336 6135

- Mental Health America: A Major Source of Key Information
  Info@mentalhealthamerica.net

- A Search Source for Key Information on Senior Living
  Info@searchlist.com

- A Major National Council on Aging has an emphasis on Healthy Aging
  NCOA.org

- Best Source for Information on Healthy Aging Ideas
  Info@healthyaging.net

- The Respected American Association of Retired Persons
  Info@aarp.og
  A ARP Bulletin

Note: For the Serious Student in the field, look under the following topics

Healthy Aging, Applied Gerontology, Caregiving, Geriatrics, Senior Living, Health and Wellness, Aging Issues, Guides to Adult Living, and Products and Services for Senior Care

For current information, check for the geriatric departments of most major universities or senior living centers in large communities.

Ideas For Establishing a Senior Focus Group on Healthy Aging Issues

It has always seemed to me that seniors in America would benefit highly if they would gather together in serious study and exploration about all the issues related to making responsible life choices about senior living today. We can learn so much together and add enormously what we have learned individually. We can share, question, probe, and find answers to key issues in our lives. In that vein, I would like to make these suggestions about starting a group study project for senior citizens who want to share and support each other in their ongoing search for healthy aging clues and resources. So here goes . . .

1. Choose a core group of leaders who would gather a list of prospective members and then take responsibility to handle all the necessary organizational tasks of a well-functioning group: decide on an attractive name and symbol, define your purpose, decide on location, time, publicity, group leadership, gather resource information, and decide about the role of your discussion facilitators. Set your meeting times and start your group, then evaluate after the first month of activity.

Change your model to meet the needs of the group always. Consult with professional leaders in the field of continuing education for ideas about keeping your group interesting, active, and relevant. Keep the focus on the topics a reflection of the interests of the group membership. Bring in outside resource leaders on certain occasions to provide new and up-to-date information the group needs of a new topic for discussion. Become familiar about how to use appealing videos, recorded interviews, TV broadcasts, and Internet contacts. Sometimes you might even use key contacts with resource leaders on Skype. Evaluate your progress at least once a year. Keep your discussion relevant and challenging.

2. Share with others in your community what you are focusing on and bring in the best talent you can find to give you key information you need to know. Always work with full cooperation of your local community agency on aging. Invite their full cooperation for your activity and their active endorsement. Enlist the support of your local churches, your senior-centered organizations, and the local governing body.

3. Keep your group friendly, inquisitive, focused, and loyal. Sometimes, a mixed group of men and women work; sometimes, a single-sex groups works just as well. Be open to providing the group to a wide age span of seniors. Do some research into the issue about how to maintain good group dynamics. Some groups I know, for example, have died because of the domination of a few members and the silence and acquiescence of most members. Keep enlisting new people to join, but hang on to the older and loyal members.

4. It may be helpful if you focus on each of the topics of this book, so you can look at them in depth. Start with my checklist and go from there. Review again the supplemental information at the end of each chapter. Place real value on personal stories and troublesome questions by participants.

5. Sometimes publishing a newsletter about your activities to a very large audience of elders can be a fine service for the community. It will help you get a name for yourself, besides offering helpful information for everyone. Offering literature and free films can attract the public at large.

6. Make certain the discussion leader is acquainted with the key concepts that build for the success of small study groups. He or she will need to protect the group from any member being too domineering, withdrawn, or critical of everything done. Troublesome members can destroy a small study group. They need to be approached and kindly asked to fit in or leave. Keep the group a healthy, positive, and supportive body of seekers who can grow and learn together, while supporting their desire for healthy aging ideas. Be sure all the group members help to set your agenda.

7. Finally, learn to enjoy the study, build new friendships, seek the solutions to problems presented, and offer the chance to grow and develop as a healthy senior adult. Real fulfillment in older adults living should be a real goal that is shared by all. It should be the best time of your whole life and you need to share that joy and satisfaction with each other. In addition, be there to offer personal support when a group member is in some difficulty and needs your interest and active involvement. Learn to be a body

of caring, loving, interested, and exciting people to know. Discover how to be the envy of the community.

SUGGESTIONS FOR AN EMPHASIS ON SELF-STUDY ON HEALTHY AGING:

There is a growing body of retirees who love the pursuit of learning. Occasionally, you hear of a senior who wants to wait and finish college while living in their mid-eighties. Certainly, you know that most of our large metropolitan areas today sponsor what is known as a senior college, a non-credit institution where seniors can learn together skills together they find valuable or discover insights about topics they are hungry to examine.

One of the most interesting senior learning experiences is through the Road Scholar Program, connected with Elderhostel, Inc. in Boston, Massachusetts (*www.roadscholar. org*). They provide an unmatched series of learning experience that may include cruises, bus line trips, or sailing ventures all over the world. It usually consists of three elements: the educational component, the field trips to exotic places, and the fine fellowship with other engaging seniors. We have gone on twenty such ventures, and everyone has been an exciting experience in learning. The unique thing about this service is that the ventures are scheduled all over the world, as well as in every state in America. You can pick a topic that interests you, a time of the year when you are free to participate, and the time frame that fits your availability. My wife and I have found that the richest value has also been the chance to meet some outstanding and interesting seniors from all over the world.

One emphasis that I would like to make is for each of us to set some specific educational goals for ourselves. It is essential if we expect to keep growing and expanding our world of understanding about achieving healthy senior living. We found that it also keeps us feeling younger and in touch with the world around us. It is too easy to suddenly get "out of touch" with the changing world we live in today. The simple task of learning new ideas or keeping up-to-date in a field we love can help us connect with the world around us. So keep relevant, and do your part to reach out to others who are seeking to learn. Help them grow by giving them regular support and ideas that will challenge their minds and spirit. Most of all do it for that most important person—do it for *you*!

THIS ENDS MY COMMENTARY AND BEGINS YOUR NEW VENTURE INTO THE EXCITING WORLD OF AGING WELL. GOD'S SPEED! NOW THE NEXT STEPS YOU TAKE FOR YOURSELF. DON'T WAIT. CHOOSE TO PLAN FOR A BETTER TOMORROW AND LEARN TO ENJOY HEALTHY AGING EVERYDAY!

Information about the author:

Kenneth D. Barringer, PhD. is not only a retired clinical psychologist, but he is also an ordained United Methodist minister, living in a highly respected retirement community of Sun City Center, Florida, 33573. He has an amazing background of being engaged in several interesting job roles: as an employee in his father's livestock business in Iowa, now a farm owner of a working Iowa farm, a former Navy Medical Corps serviceman, a local pastor for years in three states, a college professor in two locations, and a licensed clinical psychologist in Iowa and Wisconsin. He is now an active volunteer in his retirement community in his local church and in the mental health field in Florida.

He has published chapters in two books on adult education, and he was a contributor to a major family-focused magazine. He has published articles on issues related to senior living. He has headed an effective coalition on mental health and aging in his retirement community for years. His intention for writing this book is to help seniors everywhere find concrete ideas about how they can make responsible life choices for healthy senior living. His concern is that seniors are not well equipped to cope well with the important task of aging well, so he speaks to community groups and teaches at a senior college. His hope is that every senior who seeks it with good intentions and positive choice making will *enjoy and relish their golden years as never before.* His dream is that healthy seniors all over will catch the vision of exploring the fascinating world of *healthy aging and wellness living together and Enjoy Every Day of their Retirement.*